Robert Briscoe

Robert Briscoe

Sinn Féin Revolutionary, Fianna Fáil Nationalist and Revisionist Zionist

Kevin McCarthy

PETER LANG

Oxford • Bern • Berlin • Bruxelles • Frankfurt am Main • New York • Wien

Bibliographic information published by Die Deutsche Nationalbibliothek.
Die Deutsche Nationalbibliothek lists this publication in the Deutsche National-
bibliografie; detailed bibliographic data is available on the Internet at
http://dnb.d-nb.de.

A catalogue record for this book is available from the British Library.

Library of Congress Control Number: 2015952199

Cover image: Photograph of Robert Briscoe and Dwight D. Eisenhower, courtesy of the
family archive of Robert Briscoe Jr, used with permission.

ISBN 978-3-0343-1841-9 (print)
ISBN 978-3-0353-0781-8 (eBook)

© Peter Lang AG, International Academic Publishers, Bern 2016
Hochfeldstrasse 32, CH-3012 Bern, Switzerland
info@peterlang.com, www.peterlang.com, www.peterlang.net

This publication has been peer reviewed.

Printed in Germany

Joe Briscoe passed from this life on 30 September 2015 on the Gregorian calendar or the year 5776 on the Hebrew calendar. He was a patriotic Irishman who served for fifty years in the Forsa Cosanta Aitiuil (Local Defence Force), and also a loyal and loving son, who understood better than anyone else the extent of his father's pre-war attempt to rescue a remnant of European Jewry from the Nazi Shoah.

Chuid eile i síocháin
בשלום משכבו על ינוח

Contents

Acknowledgements

My appreciation of the many wonderful archivists in the National Library of Ireland, the National Archives of Ireland, the Irish Military Archives and the National Archives of the United Kingdom at Kew cannot be overstated. I wish to include a special mention for Amira Stern, the head archivist at the Jabotinsky Institute in Tel Aviv. She facilitated my many demands with patience and courtesy, and guided me through the complex documentation that passed between Briscoe and Ze'ev Jabotinsky, the head of the New Zionist Organisation.

Having expressed my gratitude towards the scholarly community, I must state in the strongest possible terms that my research into Briscoe's complex political metanarrative would never have progressed beyond the briefest of surveys, if it had not been for the extraordinary generosity of Mr Ben Briscoe and his lovely wife Carol. Ben granted me full and unrestricted access to a private family archive, which contained several hundred documents pertaining to his father's Jewish immigration initiative in the 1930s and 1940s. In the meantime, his wife Carol, who does Trojan work in the wonderful but woefully under-resourced Jewish Museum in Dublin, guided me through its partially un-catalogued archives until I discovered several documents which proved beyond doubt that Briscoe had risen to the very highest echelons of the NZO. This gave me the background information I needed to justify a trip to Israel. I would therefore like to take this opportunity to express my deepest appreciation to Ben and Carol Briscoe.

It is clear that I received support and help from many individuals during my research; however, it is also clear that I would never have embarked on such a demanding endeavour without the love and encouragement of my family – my two sons Billy and Peter, who have my deepest love and respect, as well as my partner Dr Freda Mishan. She held my hand when it was needed; she consoled me when it was needed; she bullied me when it was needed; but most of all she loved me when I needed it most.

Tribute to Honorable Briscoe

'Bob' Briscoe a fighting Irish Jew
Stalwart son of Erin-Brave and true.
Capt. 'Bob' to all his men
Who fought in the hills, dale and Glen.
To help free Ireland from her chains
Gave all his money, time and brains.
For this patriotism which he gave vent.
Was rewarded with a seat in the Irish Parliament.
After succeeding what he set out to do.
And is now giving his life to free the Jew.
Making speeches here and there
Building up friendships everywhere.
To awaken spirit as Jews of old.
Asking for warriors brave and bold.
Trying with all his might and mein
To return to the Jews their Palestine.
So in the future they can dwell
All loyal son of Israel,
Go ye forth far and wide,
Increase the ever spreading tide
Inculcated with an intense desire
To emerge from the filth and muck an mire.
For centuries, Jews have been in flight.
Shoulder to shoulder and man to man
This wide bridge we will now span
All ye sons of Israel together band
spread the news throughout the land
For this is the language they all understand.
Under the sterling leadership of Bob Briscoe

Forever onward forward we will go.
Untill we attain that land-all our own.
Our final sanctuary and our home.
On 'Bob's' leadership we can rely.
We will follow to Do or Die.
Our future happiness will then be seen.
In that country and our HOMELAND PALESTINE.

From the Briscoe Files, Jabotinsky Institute, Tel Aviv
(Hereafter BFJITA). 0/253.

Introduction

This biography makes the case that Robert Briscoe, the Irish state's only Jewish TD for nearly four decades (1927–1965), was one of the most important Irish politicians of the twentieth century, as well as being one of the most undervalued and under-researched. To support this argument, the book will primarily focus on Briscoe's political evolution from a youthful Sinn Féin activist in the Irish War of Independence, to a senior Fianna Fáil representative in the early 1950s. This chronological methodology will illustrate how Briscoe evolved from a Sinn Féin revolutionary to become a member of Michael Collins's personal staff and an IRA gun-runner in Weimar Berlin, before becoming a founding member of Fianna Fáil (Soldiers of Destiny) and valued political confidant of Èamon de Valera. If this were not impressive enough, the next stage of the book examines how Briscoe through tragic circumstance in the 1930s became an active member of the New Zionist Organisation (Revisionists) and senior aide to Ze'ev Jabotinsky, the organization's charismatic leader, in a desperate attempt to save a remnant of Europe's Jews from Hitler's murderous onslaught.[1]

However, despite his immense contribution to revolutionary Ireland, and perhaps in part because of his association with radical Zionism, his patriotism and loyalty was oftentimes questioned by compatriots in an

---

1   The Revisionists were a militant Zionist faction led by Vladimir [Ze'ev] Jabotinsky who had split from the conservative World Zionist Organisation led by the Anglophile Chaim Weizmann. The organization advocated an immediate mass Jewish emigration to Palestine and rejected the WZO's conciliatory approach to the issue with Britain. For further reading see: Yaacov N. Goldstein, 'Labor and Likud: Roots of their Ideological-Political Struggle for Hegemony over Zionism, 1925–35', *Israel: The First One Hundred Years: Politics and Society since 1948: Problems of Collective Identity* (Routledge, London, 2002), pp. 80–92. Jan Zoulpna, 'Revisionist Zionism: Image, Reality and the Quest for Historical Narrative', *Middle Eastern Studies*, Vol. 44, No. 1 (January 2008), pp. 3–27.

overwhelmingly Catholic nationalist parliament.[2] The foundation for this mistrust was the dominant Catholic dogma of the era, which depicted Jews as deicidists, and imparted in its obedient flock a suspicion that Jews were the progenitors of an atheistic Bolshevism intent on global domination. Consequently, throughout his long career as a nationalist politician, Briscoe was treated with suspicion and contempt by a considerable number of his peers. This was confirmed in the release in October 2014 of pension records by the Irish Military Archives. Briscoe's statement was made at the height of his Zionist evolution in October 1937, and showed that a number of Briscoe's colleagues in War of Independence Sinn Féin had attempted to delegitimize his contribution to the formation of an independent Irish state. Briscoe's sworn deposition made it clear that he had been subjected to:

> Accusations, insinuations and unfair suggestions made about services given freely, readily, and without hope of a reward and at very great personal risk. I am quite aware that many would like to prove I made no contribution to the national cause.[3]

Therefore, I was somewhat taken aback at the reaction from friends and colleagues when I first flagged my intent to write a political biography of Briscoe. I received a number of puzzled looks, which seemed to suggest that I had taken on a project that, at best, would only appeal to a small demographic interested in Jewish Ireland. Their comments ranged from the mundane (asking who would be interested in reading about the life of someone who was essentially a backbench politician) to the slightly provocative (asking whether it was a good career move, given the global anti-Israel ethos of the minute, to be writing about anyone or anything with a Jewish element or content).

After a period of reflection, I could to a degree understand their queries and reservations; they were based on the available public information

---

2   Ronit Lentin, '"Ever and always alien": From Jewish Refugees to Swastikas on the Museum Wall', in Ronit Lentin and Robbie McVeigh (eds), *Ireland, Racism and Globalisation* (Metro Éireann Publications, Dublin, 2006), pp. 117–120.
3   Irish Military Archives, Military Service Pension Collection (Hereafter IMA MSPC) 34 Ref 297. 11 October 1937.

on Briscoe or, as I put it to my somewhat sceptical friends, the accessible documentation that has been the foundation of 'the Briscoe myth'. This myth was grounded in existing accounts of Briscoe's pre-war endeavours, which were singularly lacking in either insight or appreciation of his global significance as a senior member of the Revisionists and close confidant of Jabotinsky's.

These accounts oftentimes focused on Briscoe's infamous Berlin clash with the rabidly anti-Semitic Charles Bewley in 1921 or his largely unsuccessful Jewish immigration endeavour in the 1930s, which were more often than not written from the perspective of an Irish policy position. This is not, however, surprising; such scholars were working with a limited amount of archival material, which in the main consisted of the severely limited Robert Briscoe Files in the National Library of Ireland, which contained tantalizing hints of his immigration endeavour and Zionist activities. Their analysis was oftentimes reinforced by an over reliance on Briscoe's ghosted and overly romanticized 1958 memoir, *For the Life of Me*, which was, as is typical of the genre, exaggerated for commercial purposes. Consequently an historical narrowness has defined the existing Briscoe historiography, which has only begun to change in recent years, when access to a wealth of new archival material began to challenge the existing narrative.

For example, although Dermot Keogh in *Jews in Twentieth-Century Ireland: Antisemitism, Refugees and the Holocaust* gives a reasonably comprehensive account of Briscoe's position in a nascent Irish political culture and immigration efforts on behalf of German Jews, he only once briefly mentions Briscoe's involvement with the Revisionists and Jabotinsky.[4] This is replicated in the other major study on the subject, Cormac Ó Gráda's *Jewish Ireland in the Age of Joyce*, which is equally remiss when it comes to Briscoe's Zionist engagement. When Briscoe is mentioned, the emphasis is on his role as a Jewish member of the Fianna Fáil nationalist project, or his

---

4   Dermot Keogh, *Jews in Twentieth-Century Ireland: Refugees, Antisemitism and the Holocaust* (Cork University Press, Cork, 1998), pp. 88–114.

problematic involvement in the 1926 IRA campaign against moneylending.[5] This is also true of a wider Zionist historiography, where Briscoe's role, although acknowledged, is oftentimes confined to a superficial examination of his part in the 1939 Revisionist American political mission.[6] There is no mention that Briscoe also headed revisionist political missions to Poland and South Africa, or that he also became a senior member of the Nessuit (Revisionist Executive Council), and was involved in formulating policy at the height of the Holocaust.

However, as previously mentioned, the availability of new archival material which had been either unavailable or hard to access, due to isolated location, has enabled new insights into Briscoe's complex and multi-faceted narrative. Recent publications have shown that he had a far more substantive role in the contentious Irish immigration discourse of the era, including a previously unknown and heart-breaking participation in the aftermath Kristallnacht (night of the broken glass). This was the horrendous nationwide German pogrom of November 1938, which finally proved, if further proof was needed, that Hitler was intent on at the very least expelling Jews from National Socialist Germany. His involvement centred on an episode which saw members of the Dublin Jewish community try unsuccessfully to secure visas for more than 130 Jewish children who were fleeing Berlin in the aftermath of Kristallnacht.[7] This singular event became a core

5   Cormac Ó Gráda, *Jewish Ireland in the Age of Joyce: A Socioeconomic History* (Princeton University Press, Princeton, NJ, 2006).

6   For further reading see: Chanoch Howard Rosenblum, 'The New Zionist Organisation's American Campaign, 1936–1939', *Studies in Zionism*, Vol. 12, No. 2 (1991), pp. 180–185. Monty Noam Penkower, 'Vladimir (Ze'ev) Jabotinsky, Hillel Kook-Peter Bergson, and the Campaign for a Jewish Army', *Modern Judaism*, Vol. 31, No. 3 (October 2011), pp. 338–342. Shmuel Katz, *Lone Wolf a Biography of Vladimir (Ze'ev) Jabotinsky* (Barricade Books, New York, 1996), pp. 1597–1622. Rafael Medoff, *Baksheesh Diplomacy: Secret Negotiations Between American Jewish Leaders and Arab Officials on the Eve of World War II* (Lexington Books, Lanham MD, 2001), pp. 133–154.

7   Kevin McCarthy, 'An Introduction to Robert Briscoe's Extraordinary Immigration Initiative, 1933–1938', in Gisela Holfter (ed.), *The Irish Context of Kristallnacht: Refugees and Helpers* (Wissenschaftlicher Verlag Trier, Trier, 2014), pp. 80–90.

precept of Briscoe's pre-war Zionist awakening; within a month, he had accepted Jabotinsky's invitation to lead a Revisionist political mission to Poland, designed to facilitate a mass emigration of its Jewish population to the Palestine Mandate. This was yet another unsuccessful endeavour that would have tragic consequences for Poland's three and a half million Jews, as well as being deeply distressing on a personal level. In turn, research into Briscoe's evolving Zionist engagement revealed the extent of his political and personal relationship with Éamon de Valera's. This alone was worthy of an independent study.[8]

To recover the full complexity of Briscoe's multifaceted political reality, it was necessary to reassemble a disarticulated personal archive which was geographically dispersed. This documentation included an extensive Irish-Jewish immigration archive, still the private property of his son Ben, who also became a Fianna Fáil TD after inheriting his father's seat in the 1965 General Election. This was the single most important step in the writing of this biography. When Ben and his gracious wife Carol became aware of my intent to write about Ben's father, they invited me to their lovely home in Kildare. After establishing my bona fides, Ben revealed that he still possessed a cache of material not donated to the NLI Briscoe archive. This consisted exclusively of documentation pertaining to Briscoe's immigration efforts in the 1930s and 1940s; it made for heartbreaking reading, although from a scholarly perspective it was like discovering a previously mythical El Dorado.

This cache confirmed my belief that Briscoe's significance to both a confrontational and exclusionary pre-war Irish political discourse and a global Zionist rescue effort has been grossly underestimated. On that basis, I broadened my research to include the partially uncatalogued archives in Dublin's Jewish Museum; the National Archive of Ireland; the Irish Military Archive; the Jabotinsky Institute in Tel Aviv, and the National Archive (GB). These were supplemented by an extensive examination of 40 years of Dail Éireann (Irish Parliament) Debates, and the Hansard (UK Parliament) record. Only when these disparate documents were holistically

---

8   Kevin McCarthy, 'Éamon de Valera's Relationship with Robert Briscoe: A Reappraisal', *Irish Studies in International Affairs*, Vol. 25 (November 2014), pp. 165–187.

examined did the full extent of Briscoe's importance to Fianna Fáil and the NZO's global rescue attempt emerge.

Once this methodological template was established it immediately brought to mind Jacques Derrida's passionate essay 'Archive Fever'. In a wide ranging treatise tracing the concept of the archive back to ancient Greece, Derrida argued that a safe, secure and inclusive repository is an essential component of archival integrity that acts as both guardian and shelter for valuable material, thus legitimating reality, rather than an oftentimes constructed memory:

> The archontic power, which also gathers the functions of unification, of identification, of classification, must be paired with what we will call the power of *consignation*. By consignation, we do not only mean, in the ordinary sense of the word, the act of assigning residence or of entrusting so as to put into reserve … in a place and on a substrate, but here the act of *con*signing through *gathering together signs*. It is not only the traditional *consignatio*, that is, the written proof, but what all *consignatio* begins by presupposing. *Consignation* aims to coordinate a single corpus, in a system of synchrony in which all the elements articulate the unity of an ideal configuration. In an archive, there should not be any absolute dissociation, any heterogeneity or secret which could separate (*secernere*), or partition, in an absolute manner. The archontic principle of the archive is also a principle of consignation, that is, of gathering together.[9]

This was certainly the case as far as Briscoe's complex and multi-layered political reality was concerned, and although Derrida's essay is highly theoretical, it is evident that he prioritized over all else the necessity of a secure repository to house a complete and unrestricted archive. This is, of course, an essential prerequisite if the historian is successfully to impose a documentary or self-sufficient research model on a project. Only then can the researcher objectively make truth claims based on evidence, rather than supposition. Otherwise conclusions based on constructed and/or incomplete narratives become the norm, and are thereafter perpetuated through reproduction.

---

9   Jacques Derrida and Eric Prenowitz, 'Archive Fever: A Freudian Impression', *Diacritics*, Vol. 25, No. 2 (Summer 1995), p. 10.

CHAPTER I

1894–1914
Prelude: A Jewish Formation in Nationalist Dublin

Leopold Bloom, Ireland's most famous Jew, was 'born' on 18 May 1866 at 52 Upper Clanbrassil Street, Dublin. His birth spawned a literary phenomenon that elevated his creator James Joyce to the pinnacle of world literature as he recounted Bloom's eponymous stroll through the streets of Dublin on Thursday 16 June 1904.[1] However, if 1866 was the fictional birth year of Bloom, it was the actual year of arrival in Dublin of Abraham Briscoe, a Lithuanian Jewish immigrant who would become the patriarch of a large Irish-Jewish family. In the fullness of time, the arrival of this unheralded Jewish immigrant would through the birth of his son Robert (Bob), have a far greater practical impact on Irish society then the literary musings of Joyce's fictional Irish Jew as he assumed a prominent and oftentimes controversial position in the developing Catholic nationalist discourse of an independent Irish state.[2]

Like many recent Jewish immigrants to Ireland, Abraham's origins were in 'a cluster of small towns and villages in northwestern Lithuania', and his arrival in Dublin had seen the city's Jewish community increase from a couple of hundred in the 1850s, to more than 2,000 by the turn of the

1   For the uninitiated, the best available introduction to Joyce and Bloom is the following seminal work: Neil R. Davision, *James Joyce, Ulysses, and the Construction of Jewish Identity: Culture, Biography, and 'the Jew' in Modernist Europe* (Cambridge University Press, Cambridge, 1998).

2   Kevin McCarthy, 'Exploring the Zionist Evolution of Robert Briscoe: History and Memory' (unpublished PhD thesis, University College Cork, 2013), pp. 30–35.

century.[3] Although Lithuania was by no means the most anti-Semitic region
of the Russian Empire, the Briscoes had faced many of the same issues Jews
had endured for centuries in Tsarist Russia.[4] Abraham's arrival in Dublin
liberated him from the fear of a 25 year conscription into the Russian army,
this was an imposition all Jewish males had to endure, and had became a
major factor in male emigration patterns.[5] He had embarked on this youthful adventure with the full blessing of his father, a small businessman, who
thought an enterprising young man could avail of the economic opportunities that the then second city of the British Empire must surely offer.[6]
Moreover, the timing of Abraham's arrival in Dublin was perfect; the fact
that he was at the forefront of the first wave of Jewish immigration into
Ireland was fortuitous as it enabled him to settle quickly and develop a
business footprint before any substantive anti-Semitic ethos manifested.[7]

This was an important advantage; the new arrivals were ethnically,
socially and culturally different to the established English-speaking Jewish
community that had had a presence in Dublin for centuries.[8] Abraham was
fortunate; he preceded the rapid influx of a Slavic speaking eastern European
cohort that embarrassed the English speaking Jewish community, a situation that immediately created intra-communal tensions.[9] Abraham was
also blessed with the farsighted vision of assimilation unlike many of his
contemporaries, and had enthusiastically embraced his new Irish identity
by quickly mastering a basic English which enabled him to secure a job as a

3   Cormac Ó Gráda, 'Dublin Jewish Demography a Century Ago', *The Economic and
     Social Review*, Vol. 37, No. 2 (Summer/Autumn 2006), pp. 123–147: 131.
4   William Korey, *Russian Antisemitism, Pamyat, and the Demonology of Zionism*
     (Routledge, Abingdon, 2013), pp. 65–80.
5   Cormac Ó Gráda, 'Lost in Little Jerusalem: Leopold Bloom and Irish Jewry', *Journal
     of Modern Literature*, Vol. 27, No. 4 (2004), pp. 17–26: 18–19.
6   Robert Briscoe and Alden Hatch, *For the Life of Me* (Little Brown & Co, Boston
     and Toronto, 1958), pp. 1–10.
7   McCarthy, 'Exploring the Zionist Evolution of Robert Briscoe'. pp. 30–40.
8   Katherine Butler, 'Centenary of a Synagogue: Adelaide Road 1892–1992', *Dublin
     Historical Record*, Vol. 47, No. 1 (Spring 1994), pp. 46–55: 46.
9   Cormac Ó Gráda, 'Settling In: Dublin's Jewish Immigrants of a Century Ago', *Field
     Day Review*, Vol. 1 (2005), pp. 86–100: 87–88.

travelling brush salesman.[10] This was the first stage of a successful business career, which was reinforced by a contented and rapidly expanding family life, Abraham had met Ida, a member of the Yodaiken family, on one of his earliest business trips to Frankfurt in Germany and brought her back to Dublin after they got married.[11] Robert (Bob) Emmet Briscoe was born on 25 September 1894, he was the third child of Abraham and Ida's happy union, and had been preceded by Rachel and Arthur, before being followed in quick succession by Herbert David, Wolfe Tone, Judith and Henrietta.

By the time Bob was born, Abraham, through a combination of hard work and economic acumen, had firstly become an equal partner then sole owner of a successful import-export company called Lawlor Briscoe.[12] This enabled the growing family to move into the upstairs apartment of his workshop on Lower Ormond Quay, which was adjacent to Dublin's famed Liffey River.[13] This address was somewhat unusual as it was nearly three kilometres from the warren of streets and alleyways between Clanbrassil Street and the South Circular Road that was the heartbeat of a vibrant emerging Jewish Dublin; an area that would soon acquire the sobriquet of Little Jerusalem.[14] This dense demographic concentration was a clear indication that the majority Ireland's new Jews had not left the ghetto mentality of Lithuania behind.[15]

Perhaps the establishment of a Jewish enclave was a subconscious acknowledgement that safety in a homogeneously Christian city could only be assured by sticking together. This belief was not without substance as fin-de-siècle Dublin was not without problems for its new Jewish residents.[16]

10 Briscoe and Hatch, *For the Life of Me*, p. 10.
11 Anne Lapedus Brest, 'The Yodakiens: Migrations and Re-Migrations of a Jewish Family', *Jewish Affairs* (Chanukah 2008), p. 25.
12 McCarthy, 'The Zionist Evolution of Robert Briscoe', pp. 37–39.
13 Briscoe and Hatch, *For the Life of Me*, pp. 12–14.
14 Ray Rivlin, *Jewish Ireland: A Social History* (The History Press, Dublin, 2011), p. 9.
15 Erwin R. Steinberg, 'Reading the Vision of Rudy Reading', *James Joyce Quarterly*, Vol. 36, No. 4 (Summer 1999), pp. 954–962: 958.
16 Ira Bruce Nadel, *Joyce and the Jews: Culture and Texts* (Macmillan, London, 1989), p. 58.

There was a real resistance by nationalist elements to Jews entering the mainstream of Irish society; for example, in 1906 *Sinn Féin* the official paper of Sinn Féin the republican political party founded by Arthur Griffith, featured a number of viciously anti-Semitic articles by one of Ireland's literary giants, Oliver St John Gogarty.

> Sludge in Ireland is snudge. He has no money because he lives in a poor country: but he knows how to suck the best out of it. The blood in him is wormy and he fattens on decay. True son of his father, he extracts a thousand per cent ... I can smell a Jew, though, and in Ireland there's something rotten.[17]

Sinn Féin also carried advertisements emphasizing the Irish ethos of firms by stating 'No Jews' are employed; this was especially prevalent in the garment business, and was designed to appeal to the growing national consciousness, which was Gaelic and Catholic.[18]

However, despite being surrounded by an emerging national consciousness, the Briscoes lived happily in Lower Ormond Quay through Bob's formative years. Like many of his Dublin-Jewish contemporaries, he attended Kildare Street National School and St Andrew's Presbyterian Preparatory School, before finishing his formal education at Townley Castle School, a private Jewish school in England.[19] When his schooling had finished, his father decided to expand his horizons by sending him and his brother Bert to Berlin in 1912. The two feisty teenagers were sent to stay with their aunt Hedwig, who Briscoe in particular developed a strong bond with.[20] This secure family base in the German capital facilitated the two brothers in their apprenticeship to the import-export house of Hecht Pfeiffer and Company, where Briscoe would spend the next two years in a city he described as one of 'gaiety' with a 'genuine lightness of heart'.[21]

He recalled the balmy summer of 1914 thus:

17 *Sinn Féin* (Hereafter SF), 1 December 1906.
18 Jewish Museum Dublin (Hereafter JMD). Box 1. Category 1.03.
19 Lukas Peacock, '"Breaking down Barriers": An Insight into the Political Career of Robert Briscoe' (MA thesis, University College Dublin, 2010), p. 6.
20 Briscoe and Hatch, *For the Life of Me*, pp. 26–28.
21 Ibid.

> I never took much interest in international politics until they forced themselves upon me. I did not even read the papers carefully. When Archduke Franz Ferdinand and his wife were assassinated in Sarajevo in June 1914, it meant nothing to me, nor to most of my German friends. Nor did we notice the building up of tensions during that long, beautiful July. While the statesmen of Europe exchanged angry notes and ultimatums, we went on picnics and listened to the band concerts in the public parks quite ignorantly, sure that it did not concern us.[22]

This may very well have been the case for the ordinary citizen, but the state of innocence would soon change in cities all over the globe as the politicians began the inexorable march towards war.[23] In this respect Dublin mirrored events in Berlin, London and Paris where even though the political classes were on high alert, its citizens were only slowly absorbing the mounting tension emanating from central Europe.[24] As July turned to August, Briscoe's memory of halcyon summer jaunts would soon evaporate as the days of picnics and music gave way to the patriotic fervour and jingoism of mounting national tensions.[25]

Although detached from real-time events in Dublin by distance, Briscoe was developing a national consciousness and awareness of the small republican movement. This is not surprising; he had been brought up to be a proud patriot steeped in the revolutionary traditions of Wolfe Tone by his father, who had always emphasized that Judaism was his 'religious faith' and 'not his race'.[26] Having said that, the fact that he was still in Berlin as war began strongly indicated that despite Abraham's patriotic rhetoric about the need for his adopted country to be independent, his commitment did not extend as far as allowing one of his beloved sons join an increasingly militaristic republican movement.

22 Ibid., p. 29.
23 Seán McMeekin, *July 1914: Countdown to War* (Icon Books Ltd, London, 2013), pp. 7–42.
24 Richard English, *Irish Freedom: The History of Nationalism in Ireland* (Macmillan, London, 2006), pp. 250–265.
25 Hall Gardner, *The Failure to Prevent World War One: The Unexpected Armageddon* (Ashgate Publishing Ltd, Farnham, 2015), pp. 2–10.
26 Briscoe and Hatch, *For the Life of Me*, p. 17.

Abraham had not found this an easy prohibition to enforce, although Briscoe accepted paternal discipline; he was as previously mentioned, experiencing an awakening republican consciousness, and unlike his pacifist father, he firmly subscribed to the belief that only by a physical-force insurrection 'could the Irish break free from British domination'.[27] This conviction was reinforced as Briscoe observed events in Dublin from Berlin, he watched the increasingly militaristic ethos of Irish nationalism, and enviously saw his contemporaries flock to join the Irish Volunteers in 1913.[28]

However, his enthusiastic if detached support for the incipient independence movement was rudely interrupted as the prosaic implications of war impinged on his previously gilded existence in pre-war Berlin. The conflict was only weeks old when Briscoe was scheduled for internment as an enemy alien by the German authorities. He was, whether he liked it or not, classified as a British citizen and in a desperate attempt to evade incarceration, he managed to secure an American passport from the pro-allied United States ambassador in Berlin.[29] This allowed him to join his parents in Carlsbad Austria, where his father had been recuperating after suffering a major heart attack. After a number of weeks, he was allowed to return to Ireland after giving his a pledge not to take up arms against the 'Central Powers', a promise he was more than happy to give as he 'had no desire whatsoever to take part in England's wars'.[30] Although his time in Berlin was at an end, it would have a profound influence on Briscoe's future political and personal endeavours. It had improved his German to the point of bilingualism, a talent that would impact on his future Sinn Féin engagement as a Berlin-based arms procurer, and equally if not more importantly, on his 1930s Jewish immigration advocacy.

27 Ibid., p. 19.
28 Eunan O'Halpin, 'The Army in Independent Ireland', in Thomas Bartlett and Keith Jeffery (eds.), *A Military History of Ireland* (Cambridge University Press, Cambridge, 1996), pp, 406–408.
29 Briscoe and Hatch, *For the Life of Me*, p. 30. There is a facsimile of Briscoe's 1914 American passport in the Jewish Museum Dublin, Box 35, Cat 38.01–38.04.
30 Ibid.

CHAPTER 2

1915–1921
Nationalist Awakening: A Republican Formation in Jewish Dublin, Revolutionary New York and Weimar Berlin

When Briscoe returned to Dublin from Berlin in the autumn of 1914, he had assumed a cosmopolitanism that separated him from the majority of his fellow citizens. However, despite the fact his father Abraham was a proud supporter of Irish independence, it did not mean he was a supporter of violent rebellion. He had brought his children up in the first decade of the twentieth-century to believe that 'freedom for Ireland' was only virtuous if it was achieved by 'constitutional means'.[1] His young native-born son disagreed; Briscoe was fired with the vigour and enthusiasm of youth and had the certainty that independence could only be achieved through a direct confrontation with Britain.

Having said that, although Briscoe was moving towards an active republican involvement, he was still not ready to defy his father's wishes, and reluctantly agreed to his request to relocate to New York in December 1914.[2] Once again Abraham clearly hoped that by removing his son from a republican environment in wartime Dublin and immersing him in the business community of New York, his inclination to pursue an active revolutionary engagement would dissipate. Initially it could be said that Abraham's ambition was partly successful, as Briscoe quickly established a thriving network of contacts in both the Jewish and Irish Diasporas of New York before establishing a highly profitable factory producing Christmas tree

---

1   Briscoe and Hatch, *For the Life of Me*, pp. 18–19.
2   McCarthy, 'Exploring the Zionist Evolution of Robert Briscoe', pp. 38–42.

lights.³ However, as Briscoe financially prospered over the next two years and proved his abilities as an entrepreneur, it did not as his father had hoped, distance him from republican circles.

During his leisure time he became intimately involved in the Irish-American republican movement, and as the winter of 1915 turned into the spring of 1916, Briscoe became increasingly 'concerned for [his] homeland'.⁴ He was associating with John Devoy, and although Briscoe not aware of it at the time, Devoy was already one of the main instigators of the forthcoming rebellion in Ireland. Devoy was a prominent member of the Irish-American revolutionary movement Clan na Gael and former Irish Republican Brotherhood (IRB) organizer.⁵ Also unbeknownst to Briscoe who had frequently encountered Devoy in the early months of 1916, he had already played an instrumental role in the formulation of plans to support an armed insurrection in Dublin by carrying plans from James Connolly to America to pass on to Count Bernstorff, the German ambassador in Washington.⁶ These plans rapidly accelerated American involvement in New York, as the following extract from Devoy's communiqué to Bernstorff on 10 February proves.

> Delay disadvantageous to us. We can now put up an effective fight. Our enemies cannot allow us much more time. The arrest of our leaders would hamper us severely. Initiative on our part is necessary ... We have therefore decided to begin action on Easter Saturday.⁷

Thus began the first, but certainly not last German involvement in internal Irish revolutionary politics; throughout the war years there would be a number of German attempts to foster discontent and destabilize Ireland

3   Ibid.
4   Briscoe and Hatch, *For the Life of Me*, p. 42.
5   Terry Golway, *Irish Rebel: John Devoy and America's Fight for Ireland's Freedom* (St Martin's Press, New York, 1999).
6   Briscoe and Hatch, *For the Life of Me*, p. 36.
7   Tim Coates (ed.), *The Irish Uprising, 1914–1921: Papers from the British Parliamentary Archive* (The Stationary Office, London, 2000), pp. 55–56.

with the sole intention of weakening the British forces on the Western Front.[8]

However, there was immediate confusion when Devoy miscommunicated with his colleagues at home, indeed in many respects confusion could be said to be the defining imperative of the whole tenuous collaboration between Devoy and the American revolutionaries of Clann na Gael, the leadership in Ireland, and Imperial Germany.[9] This was replicated in Ireland as the presumptive revolutionaries waited for Devoy's promised aid from Germany; they were still waiting on the morning of Easter Sunday 1916. From his cell in Mountjoy Jail, Padraig Pearse would wistfully record that 'the help I expected from Germany failed', to arrive.[10] Briscoe had watched developments in anguish as the volunteers took to the streets of his beloved home city in a heroic, but ultimately doomed military confrontation with the forces of the British Crown. Watching this tragedy unfold from New York proved to be a difficult experience; there was no way of knowing the full extent of the carnage as the 'accounts of them in the American papers were inaccurate and slanted towards the British'.[11]

The New York papers were also full of the exploits of Éamon de Valera, an American born revolutionary who had led the Third Battalion of the volunteers in Boland's Mill, and in doing so had 'became the hero of the new nation and of Irishmen around the world'.[12] Briscoe had never heard of de Valera prior to the rising; however, as the trials and execution by firing squad of the captured leaders of the failed rebellion continued, de Valera's reprieve helped to galvanize the city's disparate and oftentimes internally confrontational republican community.[13] On hearing of the executions, Briscoe confessed to feeling as if his 'heart was torn' from his body; however,

8   Paul McMahon, *British Spies and Irish Rebels; British Intelligence and Ireland, 1916–1945* (The Boydell Press, Woodbridge, 2008), pp. 10–30.
9   Russell Rees, *Ireland, 1905–1925: Text and Historiography* (Colourpoint Books, Newtownards, 1998), pp. 202–210.
10   Coates, *The Irish Uprising*, p. 69.
11   Briscoe and Hatch, *For the Life of Me*, p. 43.
12   Ibid.
13   Seán Enright, *Easter Rising 1916: The Trials* (Merrion, Kildare, 2014), chapters 2–7.

he also instantly realized that it 'was the worst mistake England [could have possibly] made, for it aroused a fire-storm of resentment in Irishmen throughout the world'.[14] That being said, it did not prevent a wave of despair washing over these exiled republicans who fulminated at their impotence to directly engage with the old enemy. In an effort to retain some sense of cohesion, Clan na Gael began to organize a series of public talks by senior republicans who had managed to escape from Dublin to New York.[15]

It was at one of these meetings that Briscoe met Liam Mellows, an English born republican who had participated in the Easter Rising.[16] Mellows was one of a small cadre of republicans who, when they eventually made it to America, saw it as their duty to reorganize and re-energize their despairing colleagues of the diaspora.[17] However, Mellows was not merely organizing, he was also undergoing a personal political evolution which would in the fullness of time, see him progress far beyond the confines of conventional republicanism, to adopt socialist and anarchist, principles.[18] This evolution was in part driven by a friendship with socialist agitators like James Connolly's daughter Norah, who had arrived in America on the *Baltic*, the same ship that brought Briscoe to America, and it was through their mutual friendships with Nora that Briscoe and Mellows became fast friends.[19]

By the spring of 1917, Mellows's charismatic retelling of the Gaelic foundational narrative of as an-yet undeclared Irish republic, had completely seduced an awe-struck Briscoe. Almost immediately he decided to forgo

---

14   Briscoe and Hatch, *For the Life of Me*, p. 43.

15   For an insightful examination of Clan na Gael's strategy after the executions see: Michael T. Foy and Brian Barton *The Easter Rising* (The History Press, Stroud, 2011), pp. 284–328.

16   For further reading see: C. Desmond Greaves, *Liam Mellows and the Irish Revolution* (Lawrence & Wishart, London, 1971).

17   Dan Lainer-Voss, *Sinews of the Nation: Constructing Irish and Zionist Bonds in the United States* (Polity Press, Cambridge, 2013), p. 33.

18   Emmet O'Connor, 'Communists, Russia, And The IRA, 1920–1923', *The Historical Journal*, Vol. 46, No. 1 (2003), pp. 115–116.

19   Bruce Nelson, *Irish Nationalists and the Making of the Irish Race* (Princeton University Press, Princeton NJ, 2012), p. 222.

the opportunity of opening a subsidiary of the Christmas light bulb factory in Japan, and decided that a return home to engage in the republican struggle was going to be his next move.[20] He returned to Ireland in August 1917; this predated Mellows's return by three years, however, inspired by their friendship and imbued with a new sense of national destiny, he immediately joined Fianna Éireann, the republican revolutionary youth movement.[21]

Briscoe immediately set about establishing himself as a serious Sinn Féin activist, and within twelve months he had become a proficient gun runner using the pseudonym of Captain Swift.[22] In this role Briscoe proved a resourceful and imaginative operator, for example, Barney Mellows, Liam's brother recalled that alongside Éamon Martin, his future best man, Briscoe had established 'a clothing factory near the old fire station which ... [enabled us] to get small arms'.[23] This so impressed Michael Collins who was now head of a ruthlessly effective intelligence operation that he soon appointed Briscoe as a permanent member of his personal staff, a decision that would move him into the higher echelons of the republican movement.[24]

Although Briscoe was now a dedicated member of Sinn Féin, he still had time to woo and marry Lily Isaacs with whom he would have seven children, as well as becoming a loyal and devoted 'companion' in the stressful years to come.[25] It was not an easy courtship; he had to overcome the objections of her father Joseph, 'a red, white and blue Unionist', who was deeply committed to Ireland remaining part of the empire.[26] This did not deter Briscoe; he persevered with the courtship and eventually secured Isaacs's blessing. The wedding took place on 30 April 1919 with Éamon Martin as his best man, and was attended by a number of 'dangerous rebels' who took the opportunity to alleviate the stresses of the 'war with England'

20 Briscoe and *Hatch, For the Life of Me*, pp. 44–45.
21 Ibid., p. 45.
22 Rivlin, *Shalom Ireland*, p. 195.
23 IMA MSPC 34 Ref 297. Sworn deposition of Barney Mellows, 24 January 1935.
24 Briscoe and Hatch, *For the Life of Me*, pp. 60–64.
25 Ibid., pp. 65–76.
26 Ibid.

by celebrating the marriage of one of their comrades.[27] As a newly-wed, Lily did not have an easy time of it; her marriage to Briscoe meant that she was immediately drawn into the clandestine world of the IRA. As a consequence, their home at 181 Rathgar Road, and the Briscoe's business at 9 Ashton Quay were consistently raided by Britain's auxiliary militia, the Black and Tans.[28]

It was shortly after his marriage that Briscoe was first introduced to de Valera by Éamon Martin, he recalled it thus:[29]

> He had the indomitable determination of a Washington; the militant faith of St Paul and the moral grandeur of the Prophet Elijah ... Though I am not short, I felt small before him. He took my hand in a firm grip, and shook it silently. I was too awed to speak at all. Nor did I have to. Our eyes meeting for those few seconds said all that was needed.[30]

Meeting de Valera for the first time clearly had a profound impact on Briscoe; however, for now, he was still a member of Michael Collins staff, and his evolving republican narrative would be dominated by a direct order from Collins, which dispatched him to Berlin as an IRA gun-runner.[31] This decision was taken by Collins when he faced the stark reality that a long-running and debilitating guerrilla campaign had sapped the will of civil society to resist.[32] This was reinforced by Collins's astute recognition that as things stood, the IRA was struggling to maintain its fighting capacity as its 'military strength' had been eroded to a point of virtual oblivion by more than two years of armed struggle.[33] Consequently, it was clear that

---

27   Ibid.
28   Ibid.
29   McCarthy, 'Éamon de Valera's Relationship with Robert Briscoe', pp. 166–168.
30   Briscoe and Hatch, *For the Life of Me*, pp. 59–60.
31   IMA MSPC 24 Ref 297. Sworn deposition of Robert Briscoe, 18 January 1935.
32   Arthur Mitchell, 'Alternative Government: "Exit Britannia" – The Formation of the Irish National State, 1918–1921', in Joost Augusteijn (ed.), *The Irish Revolution, 1913–1923* (Palgrave Macmillan, London, 2002), pp. 70–86.
33   Paul McMahon, 'British Intelligence and the Anglo-Irish Treaty, July–December 1921', *Irish Historical Studies*, Vol. 35, No. 140 (November 2007), pp. 529–530.

if a secure and consistent supply of arms was not immediately secured, the organization's ability to wage war against the world's omnipotent superpower was in serious jeopardy.[34]

In order to rectify this threat to the fighting capability of the IRA, Collins dispatched a number of secret emissaries' to Berlin in November 1920 to secure a steady supply of arms and munitions, with Briscoe assuming the senior role. Collins's choice of Berlin was a logical one; in the immediate post-war period, Weimar Germany was awash with surplus military ordinance from the recent 'war to end all wars', and was justifiably described as 'Europe's illegal arms bazaar'.[35] Collins's choice of Briscoe as lead emissary was just as logical; Barney Mellows recalled the level of interest at HQ when they realized that 'with Bob's people being both Austrians and Germans ... he had a good bit of influence' there.[36] Moreover, if Collins had harboured any doubts about appointing Briscoe as lead emissary, it was dispelled on the strong personal recommendation of individuals whom he trusted implicitly. Liam Mellows, who was now the Director of Purchases for the IRA, had no hesitation in recommending Briscoe, whom he implicitly trusted to the point of administering the republican oath in November 1920.[37] Mellows's recommendation was reinforced when the only other senior Jewish Sinn Féin activist, the solicitor Michael Noyk, also confirmed that Briscoe was the right man for the job.[38] Noyk, a contemporary of Briscoe's from the Dublin-Jewish community had earned Collins's implicit trust after defending numerous Sinn Féin members such as Seán MacEoin during the bitter War of Independence years.[39]

34 Paul McMahon, *British Spies and Irish Rebels: British Intelligence and Ireland, 1916–1945* (Boydell Press, Woodbridge, 2008), p. 126.

35 Emmet O'Connor, *Reds and the Green: Ireland, Russia and the Communist Internationals 1919–1943* (University College Dublin Press, Dublin, 2004), p. 48.

36 IMA MSPC 24 Ref 297. Sworn deposition of Barney Mellows, 24 January 1935.

37 IMA MSPC 24 Ref 297. Sworn deposition of Robert Briscoe, 18 January 1935.

38 Rivlin, *Shalom Ireland'*, p. 193.

39 Tim Pat Coogan, *The Man Who Made Ireland: The life and Times of Michael Collins* (Palgrave, New York, 2002), p. 181.

Once Collins had made the decision to trust Briscoe, whom he affectionately called his *Jewman*, he dispatched him to Germany in the summer of 1920 where he was immediately immersed in the complex illegal arms market of Weimar Germany.[40] However, it was not the carefree Berlin of Briscoe's youth; the emissaries were soon mixing with 'Indian revolutionaries' who were advocating a combined front of 'Irish, Indians, Egyptians and Mesopotamian Revolutionaries for the purpose of taking a unified action against the British'.[41] Briscoe, by his own admission, found this a strange and unsettling experience, he described many of 'our own people in Germany' as 'a weird lot'.[42]

He was referring to John T. Ryan, an Irish-American who used his prominent position in Clan na Gael to be appointed as the organization's unofficial representative in Berlin.[43] Briscoe was also instantly suspicious of John Dowling, his immediate superior and resident Sinn Féin representative in Berlin, whom he believed to be defrauding the IRA, a misgiving he personally reported to Collins on a brief visit home to Dublin.[44] However, it appears Dowling was guilty of nothing more than naïveté; he had apparently handed over a £10,000 deposit to a supposed German shipping broker called Jergens who was in fact nothing more than a black-marketeer who disappeared with the money.[45] This took place in the harsh winter of 1920 and integrated Briscoe even deeper into Collins's inner circle, especially when he recovered the money a few weeks later by holding a gun to Jergen's head.[46] Moreover, Briscoe confirmed Collins's belief that although guns were relatively easily sourced in Berlin, they were proving extremely difficult to successfully transport back to Ireland. Indeed like his colleagues, Briscoe had in his desperation come up with a number of seemingly harebrained schemes, which included hiding single revolvers in 'plaster statues' of the

40   McMahon, *British Spies and Irish Rebels*, p. 126.
41   McMahon, 'British Intelligence and the Anglo-Irish Truce', p. 531.
42   Briscoe and Hatch, *For the Life of Me*, p. 81.
43   Lainer-Voss, *Sinews of the Nation*, p. 33.
44   McMahon, *British Spies and Irish Rebels*, p. 125.
45   IMA MSPC 34 Ref 297, 18 January 1935.
46   Ibid.

Virgin Mary and rifles inside pianos and farm machinery, all of which were turned down by headquarters.[47]

This problem was bedevilling the IRA and Briscoe was dispatched on a nationwide survey to define the exact ordinance requirement of each brigade commander. This turned out to be a complex operation as he tried to match the varied requests to his supply in Berlin. It was also a mission with humorous moments; on one occasion Briscoe became engaged in a dialogue about the pervasive influence of world Jewry with a young volunteer who earnestly believed there were more Jews in the world than any other race. When Briscoe disputed this and told him 'I happen to be a Jew, the young man resolutely refused to believe him saying 'don't try to pull the leg of a poor country lad, you're no Jew ... I know what they're like, and you're not him'.[48]

Nevertheless, despite these problems, his visit home had reinvigorated Briscoe who returned to Berlin enthused by the heavy responsibility of securing guns for his comrades, especially as Collins had decided to recall the unfortunate Dowling and appoint Briscoe as lead agent.[49] The success of the gun mission was evident not just to his colleagues, but also to the British agents, who seethed as an emissary of the IRA gunmen who were being 'feted as heroes' on the streets of Dublin, openly scoured the German capital for guns to rearm them with.[50] As well as reporting to Collins, Briscoe maintained close links with Mellows as he formed a small but tightly knit group of trusted allies As well as Éamon Martin, this circle included Séamus Robinson whom he had briefly met on his visit to Dublin and now proceeded to become close friends with.[51] Robinson, who had participated in the Easter Rising, would return to Ireland to lead the Third Tipperary Brigade of the IRA in the War of Independence before taking the anti-Treaty side in the Civil War.[52]

---

47   Ibid.
48   Briscoe and *Hatch, For the Life of Me*, pp. 83–90.
49   IMA MSPC 34 Ref 297, 18 January 1935.
50   McMahon, 'British Intelligence and the Anglo-Irish Treaty', p. 529.
51   Briscoe and Hatch, *For the Life of Me*, pp. 103–117.
52   IMA MSPC 34 Ref 147. Sworn deposition of Seámus Robinson, 30 June 1938.

This group had a strong socialist ethos, which given Mellows radical background was not at all surprising, so the fact that they approached James Connolly's son, Roddy, and asked him to use his communist contacts to facilitate an introduction to Soviet agents in Weimar Germany is also not surprising.[53] Roddy Collins confirmed this in 1936 when he claimed that Briscoe was his main contact in Berlin, and also confirmed that his role was 'to introduce them [the IRA arms procurers to] any parties who were likely to sell arms'.[54] However, despite Briscoe's best efforts, he was not able to keep up with the demand for an ever-increasing supply of guns from Dublin. This led to Collins demanding an increased intensity in the varied smuggling operations and initiated Briscoe's first seaborne endeavour as he sourced a number of ships to ferry the guns to Ireland.[55]

Now fully in charge of the gun-running endeavour, Briscoe appointed Charlie McGuinness, a master mariner, who used the pseudonym Mr Thompson, to secure a small fishing vessel the *Anita*.[56] However, this was not a successful endeavour; the British Secret Intelligence Service (SIS) was closely monitoring the operation, and aided 'by the poor security of the Irish arms smugglers', tipped off the German authorities who intercepted the vessel.[57] Briscoe managed to escape, but McGuinness was arrested and sentenced to a substantial jail term. However, according to Briscoe the German authorities were sympathetic to Irish aspirations and connived to not only release McGuinness, but to also return the shipment of guns to him.[58]

Briscoe and McGuinness remained undaunted, and they quickly sourced another ship, the *Frieda*, which successfully landed the returned

53   Emmet O'Connor, *Reds and the Green: Ireland, Russia and the Communist Internationals 1919–1943* (University College Dublin Press, Dublin, 2004), p. 48.
54   IMA MSPC 34 Ref 38900, 31 December 1936. Roddy Connolly's statement in support of a pension claim for active service in the War of Independence and Civil War.
55   McMahon, *British Spies and Irish Rebels*, pp. 126–127.
56   McMahon, 'British Intelligence and the Anglo-Irish Treaty', pp. 532–533.
57   Ibid.
58   Briscoe and Hatch, *For the Life of Me*, pp. 98–102.

cargo of arms in Waterford in November 1921.[59] This success emboldened the gun-runners, and they subsequently embarked on their most ambitious smuggling operation to date. This followed an order from Mellows to expand the operation, an order Briscoe and McGuinness undertook gleefully as they purchased the *City of Dortmund* and manned her with an IRA crew.[60] This operation was a resounding success, and for the next twelve months, Briscoe, McGuinness and various IRA mariners transported a variety of goods, including guns, to ports all along the Irish coast.[61] The *City of Dortmund* was eventually sold by the IRA on 18 August 1922 for the princely sum of £10,000 which was used to supplement the existing arms fund.[62] The directive to sell the ship had come from Mellows who although by then a prisoner of the Free State forces, was still directing IRA purchases from Mountjoy jail.[63]

Briscoe's involvement in the shipment of goods and arms from Germany transcended the War of Independence; it would continue throughout the truce period as the negotiators sought to define a political framework for an Irish state acceptable to the British.[64]

> All this happened on the eve of the Truce with England-the Truce which they begged of us; and the Treaty that brought not peace but a more terrible war. Had I known the use to which these weapons would finally be put, I would have been heartsick.[65]

Briscoe's recollection of this pivotal juncture in the centuries long Irish struggle for independence is also clearly tinged with a melancholic hue at the realization the very guns he so valiantly struggled to import, would soon be used by both sides of the ideological divide to slaughter each other in an internecine civil war.

59   Bureau of Military History, 1913–21. Michael Mansfield, Witness Statement 1188, 14 June 1955.
60   O'Connor, Communists, Russia, And the IRA', p. 120.
61   Briscoe and Hatch, *For the Life of Me*, pp. 109–111.
62   O'Connor, 'Communists, Russia And The IRA', p. 127.
63   Ibid.
64   English, *Irish Freedom*, pp. 288–290
65   Briscoe and Hatch, *For the Life of Me*, p. 117.

The starting point for this tragic episode was the fracture in a previously unified republican movement, which Briscoe had initially observed
from Berlin. He watched as the Irish plenipotentiaries engaged in a series
of fractious negotiations with Lloyd George, the British Prime Minister,
in an effort to secure a peaceful settlement to the War of Independence.[66]
At this point Briscoe was already convinced that the proposed settlement
should be rejected, and had made a personal commitment to support the
rejectionist stance of de Valera. He watched as 'the Chief' conducted affairs
of state from a small room in Merrion Square, where despite the difficulties
of disguise due to his 'tall lean figure, bold jutting nose, and brilliant eyes,
he managed to bicycle around Dublin without discretion.'[67]

The ongoing conflict was draining the will and energies of both participants in the five-year-long conflict dating back to the Easter Rising, a
fact that contributed to the controversial and ultimately tragic signing of
the Anglo-Irish truce on 9 July 1921.[68] Although it was broadly welcomed
by a civil society that had been enduring the political, social and cultural
consequences of war, it finally precipitated a split between the men and
women who had been prosecuting the republican military action.[69] This
dichotomy was symptomatic of a national schizophrenia that F. S. L. Lyons
famously described as 'an anarchy in the mind and in the heart, an anarchy
that forbade not just unity of territories, but also unity of being, an anarchy that sprang from the collision within a small and intimate island of
seemingly irreconcilable cultures, unable to live together or to live apart'.[70]

The conflict with Britain finally concluded when the Anglo-Irish Treaty
was signed on 6 December 1921. It brought to an end nearly three years of
official conflict that had started on 21 January 1919 when the first session

66   Jason A. Knirck, 'The Dominion of Ireland: The Anglo-Irish Treaty in an Imperial
      Context', *Éire-Ireland*, Vo. 42, Nos 1 & 2 (Spring/Summer 2007), pp. 229–255.
67   Briscoe and Hatch, *For the Life of Me*, p. 118.
68   Knirck, 'The Dominion of Ireland', pp. 232–234.
69   Cornelius O'Leary and Patrick Maume, *Controversial Issues In Anglo-Irish Relations
      1910–1921* (Four Courts Press, Dublin, 2004), pp. 120–122.
70   F. S. L. Lyons, *Culture and Anarchy in Ireland, 1890–1939* (Oxford University Press,
      Oxford, 1982), p. 177.

of Dáil Éireann had approved a provisional constitution and declared its independence, in a Message to the Free nations of the World.[71] The signing had followed the previous day's meeting between British Prime Minister Lloyd George and Michael Collins, where a highly agitated Collins had demanded that George secure a positive reply from the Unionist leader William Craig on 'essential unity'.[72] Collins had been somewhat placated when George 'expressed a view that this might be put to Craig, and if so the safeguards would be a matter for working out between ourselves and Craig afterwards'.[73] The treaty that officially ended a British presence in Ireland, or at least the southern 26 counties, was signed the following day and the initial precursors of a republican split were codified in article 18, which demanded ratification by 'the members elected to sit in the House of Commons of Southern Ireland'.[74]

As the republican camp split into pro and anti-Treaty factions, Briscoe was still a central actor in the Berlin arms mission; however, even though the news was slow to reach the German capital, he recalled a sense of foreboding as Collins, whom he believed to be a 'man of steel', appeared to buckle under the pressure exerted by the prime minister.[75] More worryingly from the perspective of the Berlin mission, an immediate division in the formerly cohesive structure of the Army Command manifested as Mellows and Collins began to countermand each other's orders.[76] This was the source of a deep anguish for Briscoe, the fact he was in Berlin as essentially Collins's man was increasingly being challenged by his friendship with Mellows, and a deepening conviction that de Valera was the man to save Ireland.

He quickly became disillusioned by Collins's apparent surrender to British demands, and fully subscribed to the prevailing consensus in the

---

71 treaty.nationalarchives.ie/timeline/
72 Éamon Phoenix, 'Michael Collins: The Northern Question 1916–1922', in Gabriel Doherty and Dermot Keogh (eds.), *Michael Collins and the Making of the Irish State* (Mercier Press, Cork, 1998), p. 99.
73 National Archives of Ireland Department of Defence/4/5/7, 5 December 1921. (Hereafter NAI DE).
74 National Archives of Ireland Taoiseach, 2002/5/1. 6 December 1921. (Hereafter NAI TAOIS).
75 Briscoe and Hatch, *For the Life of Me*, p. 124.
76 Ibid.

anti-camp that Collins had bowed his knee to George when he threatened an 'immediate and terrible war' if the treaty was not accepted by the plenipotentiaries.[77] Briscoe's reaction to the treaty was a visceral one, he read the agreement 'with despair', and concluded that the negotiators had conducted themselves 'such misfeasance as to be criminal negligent'.[78]

The antipathy was immediately clear when the Second Dáil began to debate the agreement barely a week after the plenipotentiaries returned to Dublin on 14 December 1921. An anti-Treaty faction coalesced around de Valera who unequivocally rejected Lloyd George's demands; he explained his objections in an open statement to the Irish people:

> The terms of the agreement are in violent conflict with the wishes of the majority of this nation, as expressed freely in successive elections during the past three years. I feel it is my duty to inform you immediately that I cannot recommend the acceptance of this Treaty either to Dail Eireann or to the country.[79]

As the debates became ever more divisive, radical republicans like Cathal Brugha and Austin Stack who had been vocal in their condemnation of any type of negotiations with the British, flocked to de Valera's side.[80] In Berlin, Briscoe had also made his choice. He committed to follow de Valera with a conviction that was absolute as he reaffirmed a 'pledge of utter devotion to him and to the cause he served'.[81]

It was clear that attitudes were becoming increasingly entrenched as the fledgling Dáil began to debate the merits of the Treaty, they would soon solidify to such an extent that a complete sundering of the republican movement became inevitable. John M. Regan has described the three week debate that started on 14 December 1921 as a complex debate, which was defined by a 'latticework of parochial and metropolitan loyalties and

---

77   Briscoe and Hatch, *For the Life of Me*, p. 125.

78   Ibid., p. 127.

79   www.generalmichaelcollins.com/on-line-books/michael-collins-his-life-times/9-2 [accessed 19 September 2015].

80   Jason A. Knirck, *Imagining Ireland's Independence: The Debates Over the Anglo-Irish Treaty*, pp. 122–124.

81   Briscoe and Hatch, *For the Life of Me*, p. 60.

feuds'.[82] This contextualizes the backdrop for the debates by emphasizing the political immaturity of the participants; Briscoe reinforced this impression as it is clear his focus was also on the rhetoric of rejection rather than the substance.[83] His recollection was full of the florid pronouncements of Cathal Brugha who by turn lambasted Michael Collins as being 'specially selected by the press and the people to put him into a position he never held' as 'a romantic figure, a mystical character'.[84]

The pro-Treaty argument was marshalled by Collins who explained his position to the anti-Treaty deputies on 9 January 1922:

> Hardly anyone, even those who support it, really understands it ... and the immense powers and liberties it secures. This is my justification for having signed it, and for recommending it to the nation. Should the Dáil reject it, I am, as I said, no longer responsible. But I am responsible for making the nation fully understand what it gains by accepting it, and what is involved in its rejection.[85]

As he pleaded for its acceptance, Collins was convinced that the proposed Boundary Commission would eventually deliver the lost counties to the Free State when it realized that they were an unviable economic and political unit.[86] Yet the subtleties of Collins argument seemed to totally escape Briscoe who could only see betrayal by his former hero.

> But Collins, our man of steel and granite, our fearless fighting leader, trusted and beloved; what strange malaise had weakened [him]? Had it been the strain of those long conferences for which this man of action was unused and ill-prepared? Had the practical subtleties of the English diplomats seduced his mind? Was there some personal reason or physical illness? Or could he have betrayed his country for personal reasons? We could not understand the man at all.[87]

82 John M. Regan 'The Politics of Reaction: The Dynamics of Treatyite Government and Policy, 1922–1933', *Irish Historical Studies*, Vol. 30, No. 120 (November 1997), p. 543.
83 Briscoe and Hatch, *For the Life of Me*, pp. 130–136.
84 Dáil Éireann Debates, Vol. 2, Col. 326, 7 January 1922. (Hereafter DÉD).
85 DÉD, Vol. 3, Col. 32. 19 December 1921.
86 English, *Irish Freedom*, pp. 315–317.
87 Briscoe and Hatch, *For the Life of Me*, pp. 133–134.

De Valera on the other hand rejected any form of compromise, instead he proposed an alternative strategy in what has come to be known as Document No. 2 which acknowledged the principle of External Association with Britain.[88] He told the Dáil during a particularly fraught exchange that:

> We would put up our counter proposals and show the worlds and see are the British going to make war on us because we won't give an oath to their King. Because that is what it amounted to … If we could get this external thing-external association-my whole hope was that I would be fighting not on this side but on the side of the plenipotentiaries for acceptance.[89]

When it became apparent that this type of conciliatory argument was not going to prevail, de Valera attempted to take the moral high ground by issuing a plea in *Poblacht Na hÉireann* to deputies on the pro-Treaty side to find an inner fortitude and reject the Treaty.

> Do not enter upon a compact which in your heart you know in your heart can never be kept in sincerity and truth. Be bold enough to say NO to those who ask you to misrepresent yourselves. If there was not a gin nor an ounce of lead in Ireland you should say it.[90]

However, his attempt to carry the Dáil by the sheer force of his personality did not work, and on 7 January 1922 the Treaty was accepted by a majority of seven.[91]

Briscoe was not in the Dáil when the vote was taken, but when he heard the result he likened the shock to being hit with 'a .45 calibre bullet in the belly'.[92] Events began to unfold with a rapidity that left Briscoe and his fellow rejectionists stunned; on 9 January de Valera resigned as President, telling the Dáil that the vote would 'subvert the independence of the country'.[93]

---

88   Knirck, *Imagining Ireland's Independence the Debates Over the Anglo-Irish Treaty of 1921* (Lanham, Rowman & Littlefield Publishers Inc, 2006, pp. 115–121.
89   DÉD, Vol. 3, Col. 137. 14 December 1921.
90   *Poblacht Na hÉireann*, 5 January 1922.
91   Lee, *Politics and Society*, p. 54.
92   Briscoe and Hatch, *For the Life of Me*, p. 137.
93   DÉD, Vol. 3, Col. 349. 9 January 1922.

It was done, the Treaty had been accepted and the realization of what was to come hit Briscoe like a whirlwind when he somewhat melodramatically stated that 'the war of Irish brothers could have started right there with a holocaust of the people's representatives shooting it out in the Council Chamber'.[94] The first steps to a tragic Civil War where brother would fight brother had just been taken.

94   Briscoe and Hatch, *For the Life of Me*, p. 138.

CHAPTER 3

1922–1926
The Irish Tragedy: Internecine Civil War, Anti-Semitism, Exile and Wilderness

The Dáil recommendation to accept the Treaty would be put to the people in an election in June 1922; this would effectively amount to a national referendum where people would pass judgement on both pro- and anti-Treaty positions. The intervening six-month period would prove to be a crucial time for the republican movement as the former comrades in arms began to frequently engage in violent confrontations as both factions sought to gain an advantage.[1] This scenario was replicated in Berlin where Briscoe tried to continue his arms mission; however, as he would almost immediately realize, this would now be a far more difficult proposition as the former comrades split into their respective factions.[2] These disputes were not always defined by the Treaty split, and for the first time in Briscoe's republican engagement, he began to encounter opposition tinged by a particular type of republican anti-Semitism.[3] This manifested in an infamous Berlin encounter with Charles Bewley who had been appointed to the position of temporary Consul in October 1921.[4] Bewley was as fervently pro-Treaty as Briscoe was anti-Treaty, so it was perhaps inevitable that the two men would clash; however, the incident had a much more unseemly

1   McMahon, *British Spies and Irish Rebels*, p. 130.
2   For further reading see: Mervyn O'Driscoll, 'Irish-German relations 1929–39: Irish reactions to Nazis', *Cambridge Review of International Affairs*, Vol. 11, No. 1 (1997), P. 295.
3   McCarthy, 'Exploring the Zionist Evolution of Robert Briscoe', pp. 53–57.
4   J. P. Duggan, 'An Undiplomatic Diplomat: C. H. Bewley (1888–1969)', *Studies: An Irish Quarterly Review*, Vol. 90, No. 358 (Summer 2001), pp. 208–210.

aspect to it than the normal, if robust and at times violent dispute between former comrades.[5]

The relationship between the two men was not initially confrontational, and Briscoe recalled that when Bewley arrived in Berlin it did not take long before 'they were soon on friendly terms', often sharing a coffee together at a table at the Tauenzien Palast where they placed a miniature tricolour so everyone would know they were Irish.[6] However, their previously cordial relationship abruptly ended when Briscoe was approached by the tavern's Jewish owner, who informed him that Bewley had launched an anti-Semitic tirade with particular emphasis on Briscoe the previous evening.[7] This outraged Briscoe, who although essentially a secular and assimilated Jew, was still a proud member of his faith. Moreover as a proud Irishman he was morally offended that an official representative of the Provisional Government would behave in such a way, and had immediately demanded an apology.[8] Briscoe was a pugnacious individual who described himself in the following terms, 'I am not the meek, mild suffer-in-silence sort of person which those Jews who have lived in a ghetto have been forced to become. I was roaring mad that a fellow Irishman should behave in such a way'.[9]

Briscoe's outraged and forceful response seemed to cow Bewley, who seemed contrite and immediately offered the proprietor of the Palast an apology. However, this was not the end of the matter, as both men sent their own highly personalized versions of the incident to George Gavan Duffy, the Provisional Government Minister for Foreign Affairs.[10]

5   Mervyn O'Driscoll, "The 'Jewish Question', Irish Refugee Policy and Charles Bewley, 1933–39." https://www.academia.edu/1065493/The_Jewish_Question_Irish_Refugee_Policy_and_Charles_Bewley_1933-39
6   Briscoe and Hatch, *For the Life of Me*, p. 259.
7   Andreas Roth, *Mr Bewley in Berlin: Aspects of the Career of an Irish Diplomat, 1933–1939* (Four Courts Press, Dublin, 2000), pp. 13–17.
8   Ibid.
9   Briscoe and Hatch, *For the Life of Me*, p. 260.
10   Mervyn O'Driscoll, 'Inter-war Irish-German Diplomacy: Continuity, Ambiguity and Appeasement', in Michael Kennedy and Joseph Morrison Skelly (eds.), *Irish Foreign Policy 1919–1966: From Independence to Internationalism* (Four Courts Press, Dublin, 2000), p. 77.

On 21 January 1922 Briscoe wrote to Gavan Duffy expressing his belief that Bewley's appalling behaviour in Berlin was not due to the internal republican split, but an innate anti-Semitism.

> Mr Bewley arrived ... in a rather advanced stage of intoxication, and on my name being mentioned burst forth into a string of most abusive and filthy language. His chief point argument as an excuse for this attitude was my religion. His expressions about me in connection with my faith were evidently of so strong and so vile a nature as to warrant his forcible ejection.[11]

A week later Gavan Duffy received Bewley's version of the incident; it was a strange synthesis of pro-Treaty antipathy towards an unrepentant anti-Treaty supporter reinforced by a nasty undercurrent of anti-Semitism. His comment 'that it was not likely a Jew of his type would be appointed' to such an exalted position, revealed the baser side of a flawed individual who evidently viewed Briscoe with contempt.[12]

This juncture marked the entrance of Ernest Blyth, Bewley's direct superior to the debate, he wrote to Gavan Duffy on 16 February, commenting that 'Briscoe was a decidedly ... shady character' who was on the make'.[13] He continued his correspondence with Gavan Duffy on 11 March by questioning whether the incident with Bewley actually occurred at all.

> There is no proof that this incident occurred further than the statement made by Mr Briscoe. You are aware of the character which this gentleman bears and I need scarcely point out to you that little weight should be attached to any statement made by him.[14]

Gavan Duffy's response to Blythe was informative, he was commenting on whether Bewley was suitable for a permanent appointment despite admitting that his:

11 Ronan Fanning, Michael Kennedy, Dermot Keogh and Eunan O'Halpin, (eds.), *Documents on Irish Foreign Policy, Volume 1: 1919–1922* (Royal Irish Academy, Dublin, 1998), pp. 374–375. 21 January 1922.
12 Ibid.
13 Quoted in Keogh, *Jews in Twentieth-Century Ireland*, p. 75.
14 Ibid.

Semitic convictions are so pronounced that it would be very difficult for him to deal
properly with all the persons and questions within the scope of Envoy to Berlin,
where the Jewish element is very strong.[15]

It is clear from the correspondence that Gavan Duffy was aware of Bewley's
casual anti-Semitism, it is also clear that Blyth was deeply suspicious of
Briscoe's personal character based on nothing more than his religious affiliation. Consequently, in a jarring example of early twentieth-century Irish
religious attitudes towards Jews, it was apparent both men did not see anything untoward in Bewley's behaviour. Consequently he was not recalled
to Dublin for any type of sanction, a decision that would have profound
long-term implications for Briscoe and the German-Jewish community.

Despite Gavan Duffy's negative response to his complaint about
Bewley, Briscoe remained in Berlin and attempted to the best of his ability to keep a steady supply of guns flowing back to Ireland. However, his
time there would come to an abrupt end on the night of 13 April 1922, when
Liam Mellows and his fellow anti-Treatyites seized Dublin's Four Courts,
and a two and a half month long siege began.[16] Once Briscoe learned that
Mellows was in the Four Courts alongside other radical republicans like
Rory O'Connor and Ernie O'Malley, he returned to Dublin and immediately went to join his comrades in the siege. However, despite Briscoe's
determination to remain at Mellows's side, his stay in the Four Courts
would be relatively brief.[17]

Mellows decided Briscoe was of more use to the cause by continuing
with his Berlin arms operation, rather than being simply another foot-sol-
dier in the prolonged siege, and with a heavy heart Briscoe returned to the
German capital to continue his gun running.[18] However, if Briscoe's stay in
the Four Courts was short, it would have profound long term implications

15   Fanning, et al, *Documents on Irish Foreign Policy: 1919–1922*, pp. 416–417. 28 March
      1922.
16   Murray, *The Irish Boundary Commission*, pp. 125–127.
17   Richard English, *Ernie O'Malley IRA Intellectual* (Oxford University Press, Oxford,
      1999), pp. 16–20.
18   Briscoe and Hatch, *For the Life of Me*, pp. 153–154.

due to a reintroduction to Seán Lemass, his future constituency colleague and Táoiseach.[19] Having said that, it was not, according to Briscoe the most civil of meetings, he described Lemass as 'a pugnacious young cock', a remark most likely made after Lemass had him arrested for a breach of discipline in the Four Courts.[20] According to Briscoe, it took all of Mellows's considerable powers of persuasion to have him released, and was perhaps facilitated by Lemass's considerable and 'long-lasting fondness', for Briscoe's republican mentor.[21]

The siege was eventually ended in late June 1922 when Michael Collins reluctantly ordered his troops to retake the Four Courts.[22] His decision was in part prompted by the assassination of Field Marshal Sir Henry Wilson, a staunch and recalcitrant Unionist who was assassinated in London on 22 June by two anti-Treaty gunmen.[23] This prompted the British authorities to demand action against the anti-Treaty forces; they had not minded so much when republicans were killing each other, but when one of the most senior British army officers was murdered, they demanded retribution.[24] The bombardment was devastating; the siege came to a brutal conclusion in only three days, and Briscoe's dearest friend Liam Mellows was imprisoned by the pro-Treaty forces in Mountjoy jail alongside Peadar O'Donnell and the other leaders of the garrison.[25] Mellows was tragically executed on 8 December 1922 in retaliation 'for the assassination of Seán Hales TD' as the Civil War reached a vicious climax.[26] Briscoe heard the devastating news in Berlin, he watched aghast as the inexorable sequence

19   John Horgan, *Seán Lemass: The Enigmatic Patriot* (Gill & Macmillan, Dublin, 1997), p. 23.
20   Ibid., p. 155.
21   Bryce Evans, *Seán Lemass: Democratic Dictator* (The Collins Press, Cork, 2011), p. 31.
22   Mitchell, *Revolutionary Government in Ireland*, pp. 331–333.
23   Murray, *The Irish Boundary Commission*, p. 93
24   Keith Jeffrey, *Field Marshal Sir Henry Wilson A Political Soldier* (Oxford University Press, Oxford, 2006), pp. 280–284.
25   Donal Ó Drisceoil, *Peadar O'Donnell* (Cork University Press, Cork, 2001), pp. 25–26.
26   O'Connor, 'Communists, Russia, and the IRA', p. 127.

of events plunged Ireland towards chaos before he decided that he must abandon his mission in Berlin and return to Dublin.

The siege of the Four Courts was punctuated by the General Election of 16 June which saw the hopes of the anti-Treatyites dashed as the Irish people rejected de Valera's arguments and voted 56 of 66 pro-Treaty Sinn Féin candidates in, while only 35 of 59 anti-Treaty nominees were elected.[27] This was by no means an overwhelming mandate for peace, on closer inspection, it probably reflected the wishes of a civil society that wanted to embrace 'the considerable material benefits' that the Treaty seemed to offer.[28] Briscoe was not surprised at the outcome he believed the population 'did not fully understand the implications' of the Treaty, 'or realise what had been lost', in part he ascribed this scenario as an illusory creation of a print media that was set on pushing its own pro-Treaty agenda on the electorate.[29] He somewhat disparagingly described the papers of the day as being 'festooned with shamrocks and holly berries in green and red ... In that guise the Treaty seemed to glitter like the star of Bethlehem bringing glad tidings of peace on earth'.[30]

Nevertheless, the June election did deliver a severe blow to anti-Treaty aspirations and initiated an anti-democratic response from de Valera and the anti-Treaty faction. He proceeded to dispute 'the legitimacy of the pro-Treaty government formed after the election under the terms of a pact agreed' beforehand, any government formed by the pro-Treaty side afterwards, violated the agreement.[31] The pact had been agreed between Collins and de Valera in an attempt to circumnavigate the will of the people, by effectively not 'putting the Treaty before the electorate', in order to get their

27 Arthur Mitchell, *Revolutionary Government in Ireland: Dáil Éireann, 1919–1922* (Gill & Macmillan, Dublin, 1995), p. 332.
28 Regan, 'The Politics of Reaction', p. 543.
29 Briscoe and Hatch, *For the Life of Me*, p. 128.
30 Ibid., p. 228.
31 Michael Gallagher, *Political Parties in the Republic of Ireland* (Manchester University Press, Manchester, 1984), p. 4.

respective candidates rubber-stamped.[32] This strategy failed completely, and as the anti-Treatyites ramped up their oppositional campaign by introducing ever more violent acts, the country plunged towards the precipice and a conflict that would pit brother against brother, descended across the state.

Briscoe had followed the bombardment of the Four Courts from Berlin with a sense of disbelief, which quickly turned to despair as his colleagues had no alternative but to surrender.[33] In early August he deciding to immediately return to Dublin and was devastated at the sight of the once magnificent building as a bombed shell only heightened his sense of desperation, which was in turn reinforced by the utter confusion of his colleagues in the anti-Treaty faction.[34] Throughout July, Briscoe like many of his friends went from safe-house to safe-house in an attempt to avoid capture by the Free State forces. Eventually he made contact with Michael Cremin,[35] who decided the best use of Briscoe's unique skills was to return to Berlin via London and secure arms for what promised to be a long campaign of resistance.[36] However, like nearly all of the plans of the moment, this one was made in an ad hoc manner without consultation and consequently Briscoe found himself stranded in London for nearly two months.[37]

This was the cause of immense personal frustration as he observed the tragic events in Dublin, which he described as 'a sort of Gotterdammerung, with the great figures on both sides falling'.[38] Initially it was Harry Boland, the multi-talented revolutionary who as well as being a President of the Irish Republican Brotherhood, had also served as the American Envoy of the

32   Diarmuid Ferriter, *The Transformation of Ireland 1900–2000* (Profile Books, London, 2005), p. 252.
33   Briscoe and Hatch, *For the Life of Me*, p. 168.
34   For further reading see: Richard Dunphy, *The Making of Fianna Fáil Power in Ireland 1923–1948* (The Clarendon Press, Oxford, 1995), p. 74–82. Anne Dolan, *Commemorating the Irish Civil War History and Memory, 1923–2000* (Cambridge University Press, Cambridge, 2003), pp. 196–202.
35   McMahon, *British Spies and Irish Rebels*, pp. 13–28–132.
36   Briscoe and Hatch, *For the Life of Me*, p. 174.
37   McCarthy, 'The Zionist Evolution of Robert Briscoe', pp. 62–66.
38   Briscoe and Hatch, *For the Life of Me*, p. 178.

fledgling Republic of Ireland.[39] Then Arthur Griffith, technically still president of a disintegrating Dáil Éireann succumbed to a heart attack.[40] Briscoe who was clearly unaware of Griffiths personal anti-Semitism lamented his death even though on opposite sides of the Civil War divide, concluding he was as 'undone by the events of that black summer'.[41] Finally the death of Michael Collins; where Briscoe's apparent lack of grief appeared callous considering Collins had appointed him to a senior position within Sinn Féin. Perhaps however, this was indicative of the hostilities of an internecine civil war which would see Briscoe take decades before being able to acknowledge his personal sadness at Collins death, but even in that moment of reflection, he maintained the Fianna Fáil line that Collins was 'largely responsible for the split between Irishmen'.[42]

It was late August before Briscoe eventually arrived in Berlin, where he received orders which took him totally by surprise when Michael Cremin decided to send him to America, to 'organize a new source of arms'.[43] Briscoe was ordered to hand over republican funds to Seán MacBride, who had an illustrious republican pedigree as the son of Maude Gonne and Major John MacBride, one of the 1916 martyrs.[44] This created something of a personal dilemma as even though he believed the IRA 'was the only body of men left in Ireland, who were true to their oath to defend the Republic', Briscoe did not trust MacBride, whom he thought 'a very strange sort of man'.[45] Despite his personal reservations, Briscoe complied with this directive, and although unaware of it at the time, initiated a lifelong suspicion in

39   Andrew Brasier and John Kelly, *Harry Boland: A Man Divided* (New Century Publishing, Dublin, 2000), pp. 86–100.

40   Bryan Fanning, *Racism and Social Change in the Republic of Ireland* (Manchester University Press, Manchester, 2002), pp. 56–62.

41   Briscoe and Hatch, *For the Life of Me*, p. 179.

42   Ibid., p. 182.

43   McMahon, *British Spies and Irish Rebels*, p. 183.

44   Caoimhe Nic Dháibhéid, *Seán MacBride: A Republican Life* (Liverpool University Press, Liverpool, 2011), pp. 40–42.

45   Briscoe and Hatch, *For the Life of Me*, p. 184.

republican circles that he had personally profited through appropriating a portion of these funds for himself.[46]

On arriving in Berlin, Briscoe was effectively unemployed and his boredom was only relieved by a visit from his mother who helped him belatedly celebrate the birth of his son Billy who had been born in his absence. This lifted his spirits and set him up for the long and lonely journey to America where he eventually arrived in September, only to find a divided republican community which reflected the split back home in Ireland.[47] Briscoe was immediately embroiled in the internal dissention of the New York American Friends of Ireland, as a cadre of strong republican women immediately 'questioned his authority' thus making life quite 'difficult for him'.[48]

The prime source of tension came from Hanna Sheehy Skeffington, who had been so tragically widowed when her republican, though pacifist husband Francis was arrested and murdered by a renegade British officer on 26 April 1916.[49] She apparently tried to dissuade Briscoe from associating with John Finnerty, a leading New York republican supporter, whom she accused of being 'unfaithful to our cause', before Briscoe orchestrated a showdown where Sheehy Skeffington's accusations were proven to be spurious ones.[50] This led to a period of inactivity, save for observing the internal feuding of the disparate factions, before Frank Aikin, now second-in-command of the IRA contacted him with the order to wait for instructions.[51] This was very much the daily pattern of Briscoe's New York existence throughout the terrible events of the Irish Civil War; he helplessly observed from afar until an out-gunned, out-manoeuvred and

46 Fanning, *Racism and Social Change*, pp. 78–82.
47 Briscoe and Hatch, *For the Life of Me*, pp. 186–188.
48 IMA MSPC 34 Ref 297, 18 January 1935.
49 Margaret Ward, *Hanna Sheehy Skeffington: A Life* (Attic Press, Cork, 1997).
50 Briscoe and Hatch, *For the Life of Me*, pp. 187–188.
51 Matthew Lewis, *Frank Aikin's War: The Irish Revolution, 1916–1923* (University College Dublin Press, Dublin, 2014).

out-led anti-Treaty surrender in May 1923, when Aikin gave the order 'to cease fire and dump arms'.[52]

Briscoe's activities during the intervening months are difficult to precisely define except for one documented event. In the summer of 1923, he received orders from Ireland to occupy the offices of the Provisional Government Consul in New York.[53] Briscoe's version of events begins when he led twenty New York anti-Treaty republicans and seized the consular office, where Lynsey Crawford, the Free State representative was given a choice to remain there as a member of the 'Irish Republican Consulate', or to leave and never come back.[54] However, the evidence suggests that over the following months, Briscoe was more than prepared to work with Crawford, an Irish-Canadian.[55]

This cooperation was based on a need to promote Irish goods in the United States; Crawford had suggested that if this was to be successful, a two-way trade route would be necessary, and this is where his interaction with Briscoe seems to have originated.[56] The evidence suggests that despite their differences, the two men were prepared to engage in a business capacity, and although we know little of Briscoe's republican activities in New York other than from his own recollection, it seems clear that he had developed a considerable network of entrepreneurial contacts.[57] To this end, Crawford forwarded a letter from Briscoe to Joseph McGrath, the Minister of Industry and Commerce, inquiring if any 'special attractions' were being offered 'by the Government' to American firms that would open Irish subsidiaries.[58] However, before Briscoe could further this potential

---

52 Richard English, *Armed Struggle: The History of the IRA* (Macmillan, London, 2003), p. 35.
53 IMA MSPC 34 Ref 297, 18 January 1935.
54 Briscoe and Hatch, *For the Life of Me*, pp. 198–199.
55 Robert McLaughlin, *From Home Rulers to Sinn Féiners: the Transformation of Irish-Canadian Nationalist Identity, 1912–1925* (Department of English Winthrop University, Rock Hill S C, 2004), p. 31.
56 For further reading see: Gavin Foster, 'Class Dismissed? The Debate over a Social Basis to the Treaty Split and Irish Civil War', *Saothar*, No. 33 (2008), pp. 73–88.
57 IMA MSP 34 Ref 297, 18 January 1935.
58 National Archives of Ireland Department of Finance 1/3656, 10 July 1923. (Hereafter NAI FIN).

initiative, de Valera was released from jail by the Free State Amnesty of July 1924, and he made an immediate decision to return to Dublin.[59]

On arriving, Briscoe found Dublin was a far more threatening city than the one he had left; he knew 'that despite any act of amnesty, the position of a former member of the IRA ... would not be a happy one'.[60] His apprehension was justified; anti-Treaty supporters were effectively disenfranchised from the Free State, so Briscoe was more fortunate than most in that he had at least the opportunity of earning a steady income. His brothers Bert and Wolf were diversifying the family business in order to concentrate on their overseas interests, so they handed over control of the Briscoe Importing Company (BIM) to him. However, this was not as we shall see without complication, or indeed ulterior motive. The brothers had for a number of years been trying to separate Briscoe from his republican commitment, going so far as offering him the family subsidiary in Switzerland.[61] This had not gone unnoticed in republican circles, causing some of his fellow activists to wonder, 'did he join for patriotic reasons or to spite his own family?'.[62] However, the general consensus, among other republicans at least amongst those who knew him best, was that 'Bob was definitely alright'.[63]

His new role as Chief Executive Officer of the company immediately initiated a direct confrontation with General Richard Mulcahy; as the Cumann Na nGaedheal Minister of Defence instituted an inquiry into the financial conduct of the company in the recently ceased volatile and bitter Civil War. It appears that while Briscoe was in the United States furthering the cause of the anti-Treaty forces, his brothers had been supplying the pro-Treaty forces with various types of military equipment. This does not appear to have been a simple business transaction however, as the army finance officer quickly brought to Mulcahy's attention 'an extraordinary series of

59 Donnacha Ó Beacháin, *Destiny of the Soldiers: Fianna Fáil, Irish Republicanism and the IRA, 1926–1973* (Gill and Macmillan, Dublin, 2010), Chapter One.
60 Briscoe and Hatch, *For the Life of Me*, p. 210.
61 Ibid., p. 211.
62 IMA MSPC 24 Ref 297. Sworn deposition of Barney Mellows, 24 January 1935.
63 Ibid.

transactions', that had cost 'a total sum of £191,000 before concluding that 'the above statement of facts requires very serious notice'.[64]

After an investigation that lasted more than a year, the Department of Defence (DOD) official duly concluded that commitments from both parties (DOD and the BIM) had been honoured, and as far as he was concerned the matter was now closed. The conclusion to the inquiry appears to have been grounded in a compromise between the two disputing parties; the official on behalf of the Minister for Defence declared that 'the final sum found to be due to the firm, after allowing for all deductions, as shown below, has been paid to the firm'.[65] The official then proceeded to highlight the contentious nature of the inquiry, before giving Mulcahy the final settlement figure of £9410. 17. 8.[66] The final sum withheld from the Briscoe Importing Company was less than £10,000 from a total Civil War invoice to the Provisional Government of more than £275,000.[67] It is clear that there was considerable consternation within the ranks of the new Cumman na Gaedheal administration, they extensively investigated the firm for evidence of war-profiteering. In this, Briscoe's role in Berlin was highly pertinent to the context of the investigation considering the fact that it centred on the sale of military equipment to the state, indeed there was a persistent suspicion that Briscoe had remained an active member of the company even when he was a member of Liam Mellows's arms procuring team.[68]

Perhaps the antipathy of the new administration was also underpinned by the fact that Briscoe was now using the company as a haven for disaffected anti-Treaty IRA members. Agents of the new Criminal Investigation Division periodically raided the company, in a sustained effort to locate any 'ammunition ... that might incriminate me or some member of the

64   NAI FIN 1/3365, 21 October 1922.
65   Ibid.
66   Ibid.
67   Francis M. Carroll, *Money for Ireland: Finance, Diplomacy, Politics and the First Dáil Éireann* (Praeger Publishers, Westport CT, 2002), pp. 31–68.
68   IMA MSPC 34 Ref 297. Sworn deposition by Commandant Alec Thompson, 14 September 1936.

staff'.[69] The harassment continued for a number of months and became so bad that the firm started to lose custom, so much so that Briscoe was compelled to personally address the campaign of intimidation by visiting the College Green Police accompanied by some his employees in the BIM, who intimated that if the threats and disruption by the police did not cease, they would return 'with a gun in one hand and a bomb in the other'.[70] As the months passed, a semblance of normality imposed itself on Briscoe's chaotic existence as tensions between the former comrades simmered rather than boiled. However, no sooner had a sense of equilibrium been restored when a slowly prospering business life once more became a secondary concern as Briscoe responded to de Valera' clarion call to protect anti-Treaty republicanism by founding Fianna Fáil (Soldiers of Destiny), as an alternative republican political party.

Like many of his colleagues this is what Briscoe had been waiting for; as a businessman he understood better than most that a disenfranchised anti-Treaty republican underclass had been abandoned by the abstentionist policy of Sinn Féin.[71] Prior to de Valera's political initiative, this cohort had been left without a voice as Sinn Féin, its representatives had refused to take their seats in Dáil Éireann due to the passing of the Anglo-Irish Treaty on 20 January 1922. This had required all members of the Dáil to accept a reduced Irish Free State of twenty-six counties that remained within the British Commonwealth as a self-governing dominion, a position that demanded its parliamentary members swear an oath of allegiance to the British Crown.[72] This was an impossible imposition for anti-Treaty Sinn Féin who, wedded to the Easter Proclamation of 1916, were prepared to accept nothing but an independent and unified Irish Republic.

This had allowed Cumann na nGaedheal to ride roughshod over the ineffective opposition of a directionless Labour Party to implement a series

---

69   Briscoe and Hatch, *For the Life of Me*, p. 214.
70   Ibid.
71   Brian Girvin, *Between Two Worlds: Politics and Economy in Independent Ireland* (Barnes and Noble Books, Savage MD, 1989), pp. 58–60.
72   Gemma Clark, *Everyday Violence in the Irish Civil War* (Cambridge University Press, Cambridge, 2014), pp. 2–4.

'of illegal and ruthless acts of suppression', which outraged Briscoe.[73] The dictatorial nature of the pro-Treaty government, as Briscoe saw it, merely intensified when it became apparent that the Collins's belief that the missing six-counties of Ulster would prove politically or economically unviable turned out to have been a naïve one.[74] Briscoe took a far harsher view; he had always reflected the grassroots, anti-Treaty rejection of partition, and fully subscribed to the belief that by accepting the dictates of the treaty, Cumann na nGaedheal had sold 'Tyrone ... Fermanagh and the large Catholic city of Derry ... into British bondage'.[75]

He was therefore not at all surprised when the Boundary Commission initially recommended very little change to the status quo, beyond a proposed land swap South Armagh for a part of East Donegal.[76]

This was due in large part to the intransigent stance of a recalcitrant contingent of Ulster Unionists, who, superbly marshalled by Sir James Craig, rejected any notion of a unified Ireland.[77] This resistance was codified on the 3rd of December 1925 'article twelve of the Anglo-Irish Treaty of 1921 ... was revoked' and 'the border between Dublin and Belfast ... remained unchanged'.[78] This new reality forced a reappraisal in the previously inflexible rejectionist position of the anti-Treaty faction; they were faced with a choice of whether to resume the armed struggle, or 'to compromise with principle for the sake of real political power'.[79]

The new reality of Northern Ireland was ruthlessly exploited by de Valera who lambasted the government for its failure to secure a united Ireland, and in the process became the de-facto spokesman on the injustice

---

73   Briscoe and Hatch, *For the Life of Me*, p. 223.
74   Murray, *The Irish Boundary Commission*, pp. 136–142.
75   Briscoe and Hatch, *For the Life of Me*, pp. 223–224.
76   J. J. Lee, *Ireland 1912–1985: Politics and Society* (Cambridge University Press, Cambridge, 1989), p. 145.
77   Éamon Phoenix, 'Michael Collins-The Northern Question 1916–1922', in Gabriel Doherty and Dermot Keogh (eds.), *Michael Collins and the Making of the Irish State* (Mercier Press, Cork, 1998), pp. 98–100.
78   Stephen Kelly, *Fianna Fáil, Partition and Northern Ireland 1926–1971* (Irish Academic Press, Dublin, 2013), pp. 21–22.
79   Briscoe and Hatch, *For the Life of Me*, p. 224.

of partition by assuming the role of 'guardian of nationalist Ireland'.[80] This prompted an abrupt rupture within the previously unified abstentionist mindset as a number of Sinn Féin deputies began to argue that the party should now enter the Dáil, if only to 'vote against the boundary commission bill'.[81] This group was supported from outside of the Dáil by de Valera's supporters including Briscoe, and his old gun-running comrades from Berlin, Éamon Martin and Seámus Robinson.[82] This was the first breach in a previously united policy of dissention, and slowly but surely de Valera built a momentum that would culminate in a 1926 showdown between the growing body of Sinn Féin members who wanted to participate and the ideological rejectionists.

The confrontation between the Sinn Féin purists and the de Valera pragmatists came to a head at the Árd Fheis in March 1926, when de Valera proposed the following motion that 'provided the oath was abolished, Sinn Féin should regard entry into the Dáil as a matter of tactics rather than principle'.[83] When this was narrowly rejected by the delegates, de Valera understood that the doctrinarian position of those rejecting the proposal meant that only a new republican party could adopt 'a realistic attitude on political matters' and in March 1926 he founded Fianna Fáil.[84] The first meeting of the new party was in Dublin's La Scala theatre, and Briscoe like all those attending, was mesmerized as de Valera carried them on a wave of euphoria.

> The speech he made was a hard thing to pull off … But by the transparent integrity of the man, even more than by the carefully brilliant logic of his words, he won his audience and led them from doubt to triumphant enthusiasm for his new party of political action.[85]

---

80 Kelly, *Fianna Fáil, Partition and Northern Ireland*, p. 22.
81 Ibid., pp. 22–23.
82 Briscoe and Hatch, *For the Life of Me*, p. 224.
83 Lee, *Politics and Society*, p. 151.
84 Kelly, *Fianna Fáil, Partition and Northern Ireland*, p. 23.
85 Briscoe and Hatch, *For the Life of Me*, p. 228.

It had not taken much for de Valera to carry his core support base
into an absolute support for the new party; however, he also had instantly
understood that Fianna Fáil could not achieve its ambition to replace
Cumann na nGaedheal as the state's major political force, if it did not
abandon abstentionism.[86] De Valera and his advisors knew this would not
be either an easy or quick objective to implement. On top of that, the more
progressive members of the Executive Council like Seán Lemass knew that
the anti-Treaty constituency still needed to be persuaded that Fianna Fáil
was a credible alternative to Sinn Féin. One way of addressing this problem
was by highlighting the 'economic grievances' of this disenfranchised and
disaffected underclass.[87]

From the moment of its inception, the Fianna Fáil party realized that
this marginalized cohort was its natural constituency, and the more pragmatic members of the party, especially Lemass, pushed the more conservative elements on the Executive Committee to accept that social justice, or
at least a visible attachment to it, had to be a central plank in their electoral
strategy.[88] In February 1926 *An Phoblacht* published a report where Lemass
had urged his colleagues to spread the message that 'National Independence'
meant 'real concrete advantages for the common people'.[89] This radical new
republican approach manifested in a pragmatic approach to balancing the
economic and social aspirations of a deeply underprivileged underclass
far better than its Sinn Féin predecessor.[90] Consequently, from its inception, Fianna Fáil was able to secure a steady stream of financial donations
which set it apart from the established parties in terms of liquidity; Briscoe
observed this 'reckless generosity' with a delighted, if almost disbelieving
sense of euphoria.[91]

---

86   Kelly, *Fianna Fáil, Partition and Northern Ireland*, pp. 28–32.
87   Ferriter, *The Transformation of Ireland*, p. 311.
88   Evans, *Seán Lemass: Democratic Dictator*, pp. 54–55.
89   *An Phoblacht*, 5 February 1929. (Hereafter *AP*).
90   J. Peter Neary and Cormac Ó Gráda, 'Protection, Economic War and Structural
      Change: The 1930s in Ireland', *Irish Historical Studies*, Vol. 27, No. 107 (May 1991),
      p. 250.
91   Dunphy, *The Making of Fianna Fáil*, p. 79.

Although surprised at how easily and quickly Fianna Fáil entered the hearts, and indeed pockets of the anti-Treaty faction, Briscoe, as a founding member of the National Executive began tirelessly traversing Ireland in an effort to secure support for the following year's election due in June 1927.[92] He enthusiastically disseminated Lemass's vision of a socially just and inclusive society, this was met with an overwhelmingly positive reaction from a marginalized core republican cohort, even when the meetings were the focus of attack from pro-government supporters.[93] That Briscoe spoke of social justice with such passion was not really surprising given his previous exposure to socialist radical republicans like Liam Mellows and Peádar O'Donnell. However, despite a deep personal commitment to building a strong electoral foundation for Fianna Fáil, Briscoe was in many respects an unknown quantity in the wider anti-Treaty republican movement. He had not gained a national prominence during the independence struggle, and unlike many members of the new party was not a defecting Sinn Féin TD. Over the course of a tumultuous summer, Briscoe determined that his future lay not in the business world, but as an integral part of de Valera's new political endeavour; however, to do this he realized he had to join his colleagues as a TD.

Making the decision to enter the political arena was one thing; successfully doing so would prove to be an entirely different proposition, and even though Briscoe was part of de Valera's inner-circle, he still had to negotiate a number of obstacles before he could join his new colleagues as an elected representative of the party. Foremost amongst these was a lingering suspicion that he had personally profited[94] from his time as one of Mellows's–Collins's designated arms procurers in Berlin between November 1920 and February 1922.[95] However, despite the fact that Briscoe had always strenuously denied any wrongdoing, rumours of financial gain had persisted, and

92   Briscoe and Hatch, *For the Life of Me*, pp. 226–227.
93   Ibid.
94   See pp. 38–44.
95   Emmet O'Connor, *Reds and the Green: Ireland, Russia and the Communist Internationals, 1919–1943* (University College Dublin Press, Dublin, 2004), pp. 46–52.

before he was deemed to be a suitable candidate to represent the new party, Seán Lemass initiated an investigation to see if there was any substance to the allegation.[96] Although Briscoe found this to be a thoroughly unpleasant experience, he understood the fragility of the new party meant every prospective TD had to be beyond reproach not just in a moral sense, but also in a financial one.[97]

Ultimately Briscoe was completely exonerated of any charge of profiteering; however, so volatile and persistent was the suspicion that close friends like Seámus Robinson, time and again had to publicly defend him from these rumours 'which were absolutely unfair and unfounded'.[98] Although Lemass now deemed Briscoe a suitable electoral candidate for Fianna Fáil, and perhaps just as importantly to be a potential constituency colleague in Dublin South, he still had to be elected. He had not, unlike many of his peers on both sides of the ideological divide, developed a high public profile during either the War of Independence or the Civil War. In effect, the Irish electorate knew next to nothing about him as an individual, much less as an integral part of Collins's personal staff. This was clearly a situation that needed to be rectified if Briscoe was going to stand any chance of being elected to Dáil Éireann.

In the overtly nationalist context of the moment, there was no better way of redressing his relative anonymity than by participating in high-profile issues that emphasized his republican connection. Less than two months after the foundation of Fianna Fáil, Briscoe was presented with a golden opportunity to insert himself into the public consciousness. In July and August of 1926 the IRA decided to embark on a high profile campaign against the scourge of the working-class, Dublin's numerous moneylenders.[99] However, this campaign cannot be examined in isolation; it has to be

96   Evans, *Seán Lemass Democratic Dictator*, p. 52.
97   Eunan O'Halpin, 'Parliamentary Party Discipline and Tactics: The Fianna Fáil Archives, 1926–32, *Irish Historical Studies*, Vol. 30, No. 120 (November 1997), p. 589.
98   IMA MSPC, 18 January 1935.
99   Ó Gráda, *Jewish Ireland in the Age of Joyce*, pp. 61–71.

viewed against the template of a deepening parochialism that was driven by a reactionary Catholic hierarchy.

This was increasingly manifesting as a deep-rooted mistrust of everything foreign; for example, in May, Archbishop Gilmartin of Tuam spoke about the link between foreign music and dance and the ever-growing 'craze for pleasure – unlawful pleasure'.[100] As part of the national project, the archbishop insisted on the benefits native song and dance had on young people, suggesting it had an anaesthetizing effect, thus soothing the raging hormones of young people who if they listened to foreign music, would surely become degenerates.[101] The following year Bishop McNamee of Ardagh suggested that 'in many respects the danger to our national characteristics was greater now then ever. The foreign press was more widely diffused amongst us: the cinema brought very vivid representations of foreign manners and customs: and the radio would bring foreign music and the propagation of foreign ideals.'[102]

Consequently, in the poverty-ridden, priest-dominated enclaves of working-class Dublin, the foreign-dominated moneylenders of Dublin became a prime cultural as well as political target. Briscoe's involvement also needs to be contextualized; the whole concept of moneylending, especially if its source was a Jewish one, was a highly emotive at a personal level.[103] Like many of his Irish co-religionists he abhorred both the exploitative aspect of the profession, and the inevitable Christian assumption that Jews were the main beneficiaries of usury (loaning money at exorbitant rates of interest).

The IRA was still capable of capturing the public imagination, and the choice to focus on the moneylending profession was an inspired one; it justified the decision 'to suppress the practice of moneylending at usurious rates of interest' because it was 'unjust, parasitical, and a flagrant social

---

100 Dermot Keogh, 'The Catholic Church and the Irish Free State 1923–1932,' *History Ireland*, Vol. 2, No. 1 (Spring 1994), p. 48.
101 Ibid.
102 J. H. Whyte, *Church and State in Modern Ireland 1923–1970* (Gill and Macmillan, Dublin, 1971), p. 25.
103 Briscoe and Hatch, *For the Life of Me*, pp. 16–18.

scandal.'[104] The type of rhetoric emanating from the Army Council was met with widespread approval from a disaffected republican generation, and was skilfully orchestrated by Peadar O'Donnell, who had been appointed editor of *An Phoblacht* in 1926.[105] The army council resolutely denied that the action had anti-Semitic undertones, although it is implausible to suggest that the intellectual leadership of the organization did not, in part at least, share the view that Jews were an alien presence in a homogeneously Christian state.[106]

It was at this point that Briscoe entered the debate and forcefully defended the IRA position, by arguing that the campaign was not anti-Semitic, but pro-working class.[107] This was an especially clever move given the Catholic-nationalist demographic profile of his potential constituents, and in an open letter to *An Phoblacht* shortly after the commencement of the campaign he asserted that 'I ... would like ... to make it quite clear that these raids were not for one moment interpreted by me as an attack on the Jewish community.'[108] Briscoe concluded his initial letter of support for the IRA by publicly expressing his 'appreciation on this first move, at least to curb if not to eventually put out of business this rotten trade'.[109] By the end of Briscoe's letter-writing campaign, he was no longer an unknown political entity.

This was not the only substantive aspect of his involvement, for he had also renewed his friendship with O'Donnell, and this would last far beyond the contentious IRA campaign against moneylending. It was clear that the two men, although known to each other before the moneylending campaign, had developed their friendship during these contentious months. It deepened as O'Donnell came up with a compromise that

104 *Irish Times*, 21 August 1926. (Hereafter *IT*).
105 Brian Hanley, *The IRA: 1926–1936* (Four Courts Press, Dublin, 2002), p. 76.
106 Neil R. Davison, *James Joyce, Ulysses, and the Construction of Jewish Identity: Culture, Biography, and 'the Jew' in Modernist Europe* (Cambridge University Press, Cambridge, 1998), p. 21.
107 Hanley, *The IRA*, pp. 75–76.
108 *AP*, 16 July 1926.
109 Ibid.

allowed the IRA 'to save face' and withdraw from the campaign.[110] Briscoe had helped O'Donnell in this endeavour, and in the post-campaign months the two men acted as observers to ensure that the dispute did not flare up again.[111]

110 Hanley, *The IRA*, p. 76.
111 Tom Mahon and James J. Gillogly, *Decoding the IRA* (Mercier Press, Cork, 2008), p. 98.

CHAPTER 4

1927–1931

Republican Renaissance: Fianna Fáil and de Valera, the Voice of an Anti-Treaty Underclass

Although Briscoe was now deemed to be a suitable Fianna Fáil constituency candidate, the new party still had a number of obstacles to surmount if it was to engage in the political process. Firstly and most importantly was the need to circumnavigate the oath of allegiance to the British monarch, an imposition from the detested 1921 Anglo-Irish Treaty. As long as Fianna Fáil was tied to the Sinn Féin abstentionist policy, de Valera understood that Fianna Fáil would remain as a peripheral party 'but without the purity of soul of Sinn Féin'.[1] In order to achieve its objective, the party mounted a campaign to gain the necessary 75,000 signatures that would force a constitutional referendum on the retention or rejection of the oath.[2] The party focused on highlighting the 'evils of the oath' in an attempt to force the issue; this strategy was highly effective and was reaching a climax prior to the June 1927 General Election.[3] However, the decision on whether or not a referendum would occur was essentially taken out of de Valera's hands by the brutal assassination of Kevin O'Higgins in August 1927.[4]

1   J. Bowyer Bell, *The Secret Army: The IRA* (Transaction Publishers, New Brunswick NJ, 2008), p. 58.
2   Lee, *Politics and Society*, p. 152.
3   Richard Sinnott, *Irish Voters Decide: Voting Behaviour in Elections and Referendums Since 1918* (Manchester University Press, Manchester, 1995), p. 31.
4   Eileen O'Reilly, 'Modern Ireland: An Introductory Survey', in J. J. Lee and Marion R. Casey (eds.), *Making the Irish American: History and Heritage of the Irish in the United States* (New York University Press, New York, 2006), p. 129.

As Minister for Justice, O'Higgins had been in the forefront of the Provisional Government's attack on the anti-Treaty forces. He had over-seen the execution of an estimated seventy Anti-Treaty IRA members, which included Briscoe's closest friend in the republican movement, Liam Mellows.[5] He heard the news of O'Higgins assassination when swimming in Dún Laoghaire harbour with his old friend from Berlin, Seámus Robinson, and immediately understood the potential implications for Fianna Fáil. They were under no doubt that 'reprisals' would follow, assuming that the 'Staters' would instinctively blame 'Fianna Fáil or the IRA' and not the 'Irregulars'.[6] Briscoe was not wrong in his assumption, a wave of mass arrests and harassment descended on de Valera's people.

The widespread revulsion at O'Higgins's murder allowed W. T. Cosgrave to introduce legislation demanding that any TD in Dáil Éireann took the oath; if they refused to do so then they would 'forfeit' the right to their seat.[7] In many respects this forced de Valera's hand, he knew if Fianna Fáil was to become a viable alternative to Sinn Féin then they had to embrace the political institutions of the state. However, if the party hierarchy was going to bring the rank and file membership with it, it would have to at least give the illusion of remaining vehemently opposed to the oath. This necessitated creative thinking on de Valera's part, and resulted in the infamous 'empty political formula', which saw the post-1927 election Fianna Fáil TDs sign their name 'in the book containing the oath', while the Bible was placed 'in the furthest corner of the room', thus alleviating the consciences of those participating.[8]

De Valera had not taken this position without reservation; he acknowl-edged that 'Fianna Fáil's decision to end its policy of abstentionism was 'painful and humiliating', but deemed it a necessary evil, arguing 'that to do otherwise would have led to a resumption of the civil war with Sinn Féin.[9] On 11 August 1927, the elected members of Fianna Fáil took their

5   Briscoe and Hatch, *For the Life of Me*, pp. 232–233.
6   Ibid.
7   Kelly, *Fianna Fáil, Partition and Northern Ireland*, p. 25.
8   Lee, *Politics and Society*, p. 155.
9   Kelly, *Fianna Fáil, Partition and Northern Ireland*, p. 26.

seats in Dáil Éireann; however, Briscoe was not present when 'The Chief' led his men into the chamber; he had in his own words been 'soundly trounced',[10] securing just 1,705 votes in the election.[11] Briscoe's despair did not last as long as he might have expected; he was given an unforeseen opportunity to try again in late August by-election occasioned by the death of Countess Markievicz, where he increased his percentage of the vote to 18,647.[12] Although unsuccessful, Briscoe adopted a sanguine approach to yet another defeat, and took no offence when the *Irish Independent* report on the by-election was headed by "We gave it to Bob."[13] This was a reference to his campaign slogan, and caused Briscoe to somewhat wryly remark that the electorate had, 'in the neck.'[14] However, the fact he had increased his core vote perhaps explains Briscoe's equanimity; it was clear to all in the party that he was now poised to finally win an election, he just had to bide his time and wait for an opportunity.

His chance came far sooner than anyone could have possibly imagined, when less than six weeks after losing the August by-election, Cosgrave called an unexpected election in September 1927. Briscoe finally followed de Valera into the Dáil when he won a seat for the first time in Dublin South with 5,570 votes.[15] However, once again the election had exposed the soft underbelly of a homogeneous Christian society when Briscoe had experienced an unsavoury rising anti-Semitism underpinned by allusions of global Jewish-Bolshevism.[16] On 13 September, the *Irish Independent* carried two reports, noting firstly that in a rally in Connemara, Fianna Fáil were attacked for fielding as a candidate 'Mac Giolla Briscoe ... agus na giollai

10   Briscoe and Hatch, *For the Life of Me*, p. 232.
11   Electionsireland.org/1541.
12   Ibid.
13   *Irish Independent*, 26 August 1927.
14   Briscoe and Hatch, *For the Life of Me*, p. 235.
15   Ibid.
16   Mártín Ó Catháin, *The Black Hand of Irish Republicanism? Transcontinental Fenianism and Theories of Global Terror*, in Fearghal McGarry and James McConnell (eds), The Black Hand of Republicanism: Fenianism in Modern Ireland (Irish Academic Press, Dublin, 2009), p. 137. (pp. 135–148).

iasachta eile' (Briscoe and the other alien ruffians).[17] While secondly the paper carried the first, although certainly not last, reference to 'Bobski Briski', an innuendo-laden appellation alluding to a widespread belief that like Jews everywhere, Briscoe was a communist.[18]

Nevertheless, despite some less than savoury anti-Semitic under-tones during the election, Briscoe rejoiced in his success and recalled in a somewhat light-hearted manner how he approached the empty formula of taking the oath. Pointing to the Bible, he told the Dáil that as it was presently constituted the procedure had no relevance for him by arguing that 'even if I swore on that Book, I would not be bound, for it is not my testament'.[19] With that, he proudly followed de Valera by uttering one of political Ireland's most enduring phrases, 'I am not taking any oath. I am signing the document merely to gain admission to the Dáil', and took his place on the opposition bench.[20] It had been a tumultuous six months for Briscoe, but he was now where he had always wanted to be, at de Valera's side as Fianna Fáil adapted quickly to opposition politics.[21] Now with a relent-lessness born of the bitter memories of the Civil War defeat, the new party began to stalk 'Cumann na nGaedheal and hunter became [the] hunted.'[22]

It was a time for learning, both individually and collectively as Briscoe and his colleagues set about securing the stability of Fianna Fáil in Dáil Éireann, and the physical safety of their friends in what was after all, still in many respects the era of the gun-man.[23] Briscoe recalled these early months as a nearly legitimate liberal democrat as one 'of bombings and violence [where] the authorities were inclined to lay every happenings of this sort like a dead cat on our doorsill'.[24] It was also a period where the innuendo

---

17   *Irish Independent*, 13 September 1927. (Hereafter *II*).
18   Ibid.
19   Briscoe and Hatch, *For the Life of Me*, p. 236.
20   Ibid.
21   McCarthy, 'Éamon de Valera's Relationship with Robert Briscoe', pp. 165–187.
22   Lee, *Politics and Society*, p. 155.
23   J. Bowyer Bell. *The Gun in Politics: An Analysis of Irish Political Conflict, 1916–1986* (Transaction Publishing, New Brunswick NJ, 2009).
24   Briscoe and Hatch, *For the Life of Me*, p. 238.

about Briscoe's links with Judeo-communism which had started in the autumn elections, started to really take hold. He was oftentimes in earshot when a loaded comment was made, such as 'Briscoe must go to Moscow'.[25] This sense of vulnerability was reinforced by the constant raiding of his home and reached a climax in early December 1927, when on his way home an unmarked car drew level with his, and a number of shots were fired.[26]

With all this going on at home, it was no wonder that Briscoe was not aware of an investigation that was occurring in the British Mandate of Palestine, where the findings of *The Shaw Commission* would have far more impact on his life over the next decade than the parochial infighting afflicting Irish republicanism.[27] The significance of the Shaw report from Briscoe's perspective, was that it for the first time addressed Jewish immigration to Palestine as a problem for the indigenous Arab population.[28] This would have implications for European Jews which no one could have foreseen in the latter years of the 1920s, as British policy makers heard Shaw's report that Arab representatives:

> Told us of a growing apprehension and alarm due to the conviction that the policy of the Zionists in regard to land and immigration must inevitably result in the complete subordination of the Arabs as a race and the expropriation of their people from the soil.[29]

This was picked up by a number of the Irish newspapers, with the *Irish Times* reporting that Jewish settlers work the land not necessarily through choice but because they 'possess no means, direct or indirect, of expropriating the natives'.[30] The Shaw Report laid the groundwork for increasingly restrictive immigration quotas for Jewish immigration to Palestine;

25   Ibid., p. 239.
26   Ibid.
27   Michael J. Cohen, *Britain's Moment in Palestine: Retrospect and Perspectives, 1917–48* (Routledge, Abingdon, 2014), pp. 212–244.
28   Walter Laqueur, *The History of Zionism* (I. B. Tauris, London, 2003), 227.
29   Report of the Commission on the Palestine Disturbances of August 1929. Command Papers; Reports of Commissioners. Paper Number [Cmd. 3530] Vol. XVI. 675.
30   *IT*, 15 March 1928.

commenting on an early draft on 9 May 1930, Lord Passfield Secretary of State for the Colonies suggested that:

> The question of a temporary suspension of immigration is under examination: and legislation is to be introduced with the object of controlling the disposition of agricultural lands in such a manner as to prevent the dispossession of the indigenous agricultural population.[31]

No one, least of all Briscoe, was aware what this would mean for Germany's Jews, who in 1929 were the most assimilated and prosperous Jewish community in Europe.

The second aspect of the commission that would directly impact on Briscoe, was the glowering presence of Vladimir [Ze'ev] Jabotinsky a bombastic nationalist and sophisticated intellectual, who was arguing the Zionist position.[32] Jabotinsky was the leader of the revisionist movement; founded in 1925 as an alternative to the pragmatic pioneering vision of David Ben-Gurion and Chaim Weizmann's Zionist Labour Movement.[33] The practical Zionism of Ben-Gurion and Weizmann was grounded in a slow colonization of Palestine, and focused on a gradually evolving homeland and a modus vivendi with the Arabs.[34] Jabotinsky rejected this approach; he believed that only an immediate and large-scale immigration of Jews to Palestine, with the 'direct intervention of the government', would secure a future Jewish state.[35] Briscoe was aware of none of this in 1929, as he readily admitted a number of years later, 'I had not thought very deeply about the world position of Jewry or the ambition of my people to

31   National Archives of Great Britain CAB/24/212, 9 May 1930. (Hereafter TNA CAB).
32   Zouplna, 'Revisionist Zionism: Image, Reality and the Quest for Historical Narrative', pp. 1–22.
33   Alon Gal, *David Ben-Gurion and the American Alignment for a Jewish State* (The Magnes Press, The Hebrew University, Jerusalem, 1991), 15–67.
34   Ibid.
35   Mordechai Sarig (ed.), *The Political and Social Philosophy of Ze'ev Jabotinsky Selected Writings* (Vallentine Mitchell, London, 1999), p. 44.

regain their homeland Zion', in 1929 his awareness of Zionism was limited to regarding it as nothing more than 'a magnificent inspiration'.[36]

The Shaw Commission was being conducted simultaneously with one of Briscoe's earliest political crises. In early 1929 he became involved in the case of Albert Armstrong, a constituent who was embroiled in a dispute with irredentist republicans. The basis for the disagreement centred on the still strong attachments of the Protestant community to a British identity, which oftentimes manifested around the display of symbols like the poppy or flying the Union flag.[37] This was anathema to the majority of republicans in the 1920s, and was depicted as not just rejecting their new identity as citizens of a newly independent Irish state, but as actively anti-Irish.[38] Over the next two years the effort to remove the Union Flag from Dublin intensified, and culminated in the trial of four IRA men who had seized the flag from the Royal Insurance Company where Armstrong worked. He had witnessed the removal of the flag, and despite receiving repeated warnings not to do so, had proceeded to give evidence against the four men.[39] Armstrong's resistance to intimidation was rewarded with a bullet when he was murdered by unknown assailants soon after the trial finished.[40]

Briscoe's involvement in the case occurred when he was summoned as a witness by the prosecution in a case that Armstrong's father had taken against the gardái after a decision to withdraw his son's protection.[41] It marked a far from pleasant reacquaintance with Charles Bewley, who in his incarnation as a King's Council, was representing the police officers against Armstrong senior's action. Bewley mounted a vigorous defence on behalf of the gardái, which was based on evidence given by the deceased man's

36   Briscoe and Hatch, *For the Life of Me*, p. 258.
37   Ferriter, *The Transformation of Ireland*, p. 282.
38   Fearghal McGarry, *Republicanism in Modern Ireland* (University College Dublin Press, Dublin, 2003), p. 68.
39   Bowyer Bell, *Secret Army*, p. 76.
40   Ibid.
41   *IT*, 16 March 1929.

brother.[42] Briscoe had attempted to clarify his role with Armstrong in an extensive interview with a senior member of the gardái on 23 April 1929.

> I knew the late Mr Albert Armstrong intimately in the course of business and as a friend ... I remember the prosecution against four men, Fox, Kinsella, Stapleton & Lyons, in which Mr Armstrong was a witness for the State .... Mr Armstrong ... told me that he was receiving police protection ... I told him that I could not believe that anything serious could happen under such circumstances ... Kinsella came to my shop about 3 days later ... I asked Kinsella if he thought there was going to be any further trouble in connection with the case. Kinsella said ... as far as he was concerned he was finished with the matter ... I met Armstrong later and told him as far as I could judge there was no danger, but that if anything did happen to him he should communicate with me ... Kinsella never met Armstrong in my presence ... I have never seen or heard Armstrong speak to Fox, Stapleton, Lyons or Kinsella.[43]

Briscoe here clearly denied that a meeting between the four charged men and Armstrong had ever taken place, at least to his knowledge. Just as clearly, Chief Superintendent Brennan, the investigating officer, believed him.

> I am of the opinion, however, that Mr Briscoe knows nothing of the suggested meeting of the deceased with any of the four men ... although he did endeavour to ascertain from Kinsella whether the later had any intention to cause violence to deceased.[44]

However, despite Brennan's statement, Briscoe continued to be harassed by the Criminal Investigation Division (CID) of the gardái, and his home remained under constant surveillance, a situation which distressed his wife and children. The raids became so frequent that the day after he gave his lengthy statement to the gardái, Briscoe felt compelled to raise the issue in the Dáil when he accused the Minister for Justice, James Fitzgerald-Kenny, of directing the Garda Síochána to specifically target his home and business premises. He asked Fitzgerald-Kenny:

---

42   David McCullagh, *The Reluctant Taoiseach A Biography of John A. Costello* (Gill and Macmillan, Dublin, 2010), p. 65.
43   NAI TAOIS/ S 5862, 26 April 1929.
44   Ibid.

> If it is a fact that Guards in plain clothes, amongst whom was a detective officer, entered 27 Dawson Street ... and took from Miss Florence McCarthy shorthand notes and typewritten sheets containing the evidence of the police court proceedings in the case of Brendan O'Carroll v. Detective Officer Pluck, when that officer was finned in the amount of £ 2 for assault.[45]

A clearly irritated Fitzgerald-Kenny responded that the raids were a consequence of Briscoe associating with individuals who were guilty of offences against the state:

> It is well known that the persons who frequent these offices are responsible for the various anti-state activities and for the intimidation of jurors and for incitement to assassination of various persons.[46]

The implication was clear; Briscoe had been associating with recidivist physical force republicans who were involved in serious crimes against the state, and by doing so, he could expect to be targeted. Fitzgerald-Kenny placed a particular emphasis on developing a public perception that Fianna Fáil was somehow a puppet of the Jewish-Bolshevists in Moscow.[47] The tenuous basis for this political opportunistic strategy was the moribund IRA War of Independence connection to the Comintern, which had briefly viewed the organization 'as the trigger of revolution in Ireland'.[48] Fitzgerald-Kenny reinforced the notional link at every opportunity, even though Moscow's interest in the IRA as a vehicle for communist insurrection had waned after 1922.[49] If the charge had any factual basis, it was grounded in the recent attempt by the IRA to project 'a more plebian hue' in an effort to stem the increasing flood of defections to Fianna Fáil's

45   DÉD, Vol. 29, Col. 742, 24 April 1929.
46   Ibid., Cols. 742–743.
47   André Gerrits, *The Myth of Jewish Communism a Historical Interpretation* (P. I. E. Peter Lang S. A. Éditions Scientifiques Internationles, Brussels, 2009), pp. 52–60.
48   Emmet O'Connor, 'Bolshevising Irish Communism: The Communist International and the Formation of the Revolutionary Workers Groups, 192731', *Irish Historical Studies*, Vol. 33, No. 132 (November 2003), p. 454.
49   Ibid.

economic nationalism.[50] The governing party was increasingly alarmed by the swelling ranks of Fianna Fáil and Fitzgerald-Kenny was intent on undermining this surge of support by playing on the pervasive Catholic fear of atheistic Jewish-led Bolshevism, which enabled him to foster a 'Red Scare' depicting Fianna Fáil as a crypto-communist organization.[51] That so many disparate people who would otherwise have had no ideological link to Cumann na nGaedheal paused for thought, illustrates how successfully a new Irish identity which was grounded in a slavish subservience to a conservative Catholic hierarchy had taken hold in the Irish psyche.[52]

Consequently, given Briscoe's supposed connection to Moscow, it was no surprise that he had to consistently defend his reputation from pejorative innuendo in the parochial hotbed of Irish politics. In 1931 the *Irish Times* carried a report where Briscoe highlighted a concern that he was being harassed because he was a Jew, and therefore in some minds, also a communist.

> While I am amazed by this unexpected act on the part of the Minister for Justice against a public representative. I would not be surprised if the next thing they did was to connect me with some communist plot, as I am not a Christian, but a Jew.[53]

Throughout this period the raids on Briscoe's home continued, and once again shouts of 'Bobski Briski' were heard, which were more often then not, accompanied by a veiled insinuation that he was 'importing Russian aliens' to the state, or acting as a subversive agent for Moscow.[54] If he had not previously been aware that his background made him politically vulnerable, these experiences quickly disabused this naïve belief that a

50   Emmet O'Connor, *Reds and the Green: Ireland, Russia and the Communist Internationals, 1919–1943* (University College Dublin Press, Dublin, 2004), p. 128.
51   Mahon and Gillogly, *Decoding the IRA*, p. 248.
52   Keogh, '*The Catholic Church and the Irish Free State 1923–1932*', p. 47.
53   *IT*, 12 November 1931.
54   *United Irishman*, 12 November 1932.

Jewish politician would go unnoticed in a corporate confessional Catholic Irish state.[55]

Despite conducting a fledgling political career in an oftentimes hostile environment, Briscoe reinforced an increased Dáil prominence by being elected to Dublin Corporation.[56] His success was yet another indication that Fianna Fáil's brand of nationalism was prompting 'an electoral realignment … along a left-right axis'.[57] His election clearly indicated that social concerns were slowly starting to take precedence over the old enmities, as much to the chagrin of both the IRA and Cumann na nGaedheal, poverty-stricken citizens started to put economic advancement over rigid nationalist orthodoxies.[58] Briscoe's time as a member of the corporation was not, at least in the early years, a particularly pleasant one. On one occasion he had to vociferously defend himself from a pejorative-laden assault by Paddy Belton, which nearly resulted in a physical assault.[59] In the near future Belton would become a leading actor in the Irish state's fascistic Blueshirt movement, as well as being a founding member of the overtly xenophobic Irish Christian Front (ICF).[60] Briscoe was only saved by the intervention of Sean T. O'Kelly, a future Irish president, who faced down Belton, by ridiculing his threat to 'pummel' Briscoe 'to smithereens'.[61]

Yet despite the intense and intimidating atmosphere in Dublin, it soon became clear that Briscoe's attention was increasingly directed towards events in Germany, which was rapidly descending into the political, economic and social abyss.[62] He watched with increasing concern how Hitler focused his hatred on his German co-religionists, he also learned this hatred

---

55 Eugene Broderick, 'The Corporate Labour Policy of Fine Gael, 1934', *Irish Historical Studies*, Vol. 29, No. 113 (May 1994), pp. 88–99.
56 Briscoe and Hatch, *For the Life of Me*, p. 241.
57 Ibid.
58 Ferriter, *The Transformation of Ireland*, p. 311.
59 Briscoe and Hatch, *For the Life of Me*, p. 243.
60 Colette Mary Cotter, 'Anti-Semitism and Irish Political Culture, 1932–1945' (M. Phil thesis, University College Cork, 1996), pp. 12–14.
61 Ibid.
62 Detlef Mühlberger, *Hitler's Voice, the Völkischer Beobachter, 1920–1933: Organisation and Development of the Nazi Party* (Peter Lang AG, Bern, 2004), pp. 355–365.

was not opportunistic but a primordial ideological psychopathy stretching back a decade.[63]

> Do not imagine that you can combat a sickness without killing what causes it, with-
> out annihilating the germ; and do not think that you can combat racial tuberculosis
> without taking care to free the people from the germ that causes racial tuberculosis.
> The effects of Judaism will never wane and the poisoning of the people will never
> end until the cause, the Jews are removed from our midst.[64]

As a politician Briscoe understood the appeal of the Nazis to a downtrodden German people, although even he was astounded at the rapid
momentum of the Nazi success. Throughout the summer of 1930, he
observed unprecedented electoral which came to fruition in the September
election, an achievement Ian Kershaw describes as 'the most remarkable
result in German parliamentary history'.[65] Briscoe watched with foreboding
how emboldened by this astounding increase, Hitler, started to immediately ratchet up the level of vitriol and physical targeting of German Jews.
This did not surprise him, he was convinced the Nazis were a direct threat
to German Jews and felt with a certainty born of desperation that Hitler
had merely been biding his time prior to the election due to 'uncertainty
about domestic opinion and concern that foreign disapproval might result
in economic reprisals.'[66] Briscoe's prescient understanding of the threat
to the Jewish community of Germany was based not only on his experience of living there for two years before the Easter Rising, but also on the
report of Professor Daniel A. Binchy, Irish Minister Plenipotentiary and
Envoy Extraordinary to the Weimar Republic.[67] He had spent more than
a decade there, and dissented from the consensus, by arguing that 'the

63   Briscoe and Hatch, *For the Life of Me*, pp. 260–261.
64   Cited by Peter Longerich, *The Unwritten Order: Hitler's Role in the Final Solution* (Tempus Publishing Ltd, Stroud, 2003), p. 32.
65   Ian Kershaw, *Hitler* (Penguin Books, London, 2008), p. 204.
66   Jeremy Noakes and Geoffrey Pridham, *Documents on Nazism: 1919–1945* (Viking Press, New York, 1975), p. 460.
67   Daniel A. Binchy, 'Adolph Hitler', *Studies: An Irish Quarterly Review*, Vol. 22, No. 85 (March 1933), pp. 29–47.

content of Hitler's speech had not changed', it was still according to Binchy, 'an extremely repetitive and conspiratorial attack of Marxists, "the October Criminals", and Jews'.[68] Briscoe was now fully aware that the initial phase of the Nazi determination to dismantle the fragile liberal-democracy of the Weimar Republic had also marked the start of the Jewish tragedy.

68   Mervyn O'Driscoll, 'Irish-German relations 1929–1939: Irish reactions to the Nazis', *Cambridge Review of International Affairs*, Vol. 11, No. 1 (1997), p. 293.

CHAPTER 5

1932–1934
Zionist Awakening: The Nazi Machtergreifung and Jewish Persecution

Although the rise of Hitler had jolted Briscoe out of a dislocation from global Jewish concerns, he was forced to refocus on parochial concerns by the forthcoming Irish election scheduled for February 1932. He was determined to not merely hold his own seat, but ensure Fianna Fáil win the election by tirelessly extolling the benefits it would bestow on the poverty stricken and neglected working-class, telling his constituents that 'Fianna Fáil would tackle the housing problem' and provide accommodation at affordable rents'.[1]

After a bitter campaign that was grounded in an extraordinary level of personal vitriol between the candidates, the General Election was held on 16 February 1932. It was a momentous one for Fianna Fáil, as it underscored the meteoric rise of the organization, which secured 44 per cent of first-preference votes which secured an extra fifteen seats on its performance in the 1927 election.[2] Despite its phenomenal electoral success, the party was still five seats short of the magical figure of seventy-seven that would have given it an overall majority. De Valera overcame this deficit by securing the support of a drastically reduced Labour Party, and Fianna Fáil was for the first time in its short history, set to govern.[3] On 9 March 1932 Briscoe, who had retained his seat in Dublin South with a slight increase

---

1 *Irish Press*, 29 January 1932. (Hereafter *IP*).
2 Dunphy, *The Making of Fianna Fáil*, pp. 145–146.
3 Kieran Allen, *Fianna Fáil and Irish Labour: 1926 to the Present* (Pluto Press, London, 1997), pp. 55–57.

in his personal vote to 10.31 per cent, sat on the government backbench and listened as South Mayo TD Michael Kilroy nominated De Valera as the President of the Executive Council.[4] Kilroy was effusive in his proposal speech, and reflected the reverence the rank-and-file Fianna Fáil deputy felt towards 'The Chief' by telling the Dáil that 'I pray that God will give him health and strength to carry out the program he has so long and so valiantly fought for'.[5]

This was a pivotal moment in the life of every party member; the election had been a fractious one, which had been defined by the Cumann na nGaedheal strategy of depicting Fianna Fáil as 'a communistic ... party ... intent upon Bolshevising the structures of the Irish State'.[6] Despite this, the electorate, or at least enough of them, had ignored the attack in order to give Fianna Fáil a majority; however, it was evident that a Pandora's box had been opened. The 'red scare' had been introduced to a public consciousness and it would not, as de Valera and Briscoe would find out, be easily removed.[7]

This was proved much to Briscoe's discomfort only two months after the joy at finally being a member of a Fianna Fáil government, when he was the target of an international campaign designed to reinforce the supposed Jewish–communist plot for global domination. The fact that the attack originated in France should not be surprising; Paris perhaps more than anywhere else in Western Europe, was home to a plethora of ideological publications.[8] It emanated from the perfume manufacturer-turned-

---

4   ElectionsIreland.org/?1541
5   DÉD, Vol. 41, Col. 27. 9 March 1932.
6   Dermot Keogh, *Twentieth-Century Ireland: Nation and State*, (St Martin's Press, New York, 1995), pp. 59–60.
7   Seán Hutton, 'Labour in the Post-Independence Irish State: An Overview', in Seán Hutton and Paul Stewart (eds.), *Ireland's Histories: Aspects of State, Society and Ideology* (Routledge, London, 1991), pp. 54–60.
8   William I. Braustein, *Roots of Hate Anti-Semitism in Europe Before the Holocaust* (Cambridge University Press, Cambridge, 2003), pp. 128–134. Braustein highlights how *L'Ami du Peuple* was one of a suite of right-wing publications including *L'Action Francaise, Gringorie, Au Pilori, la vielle and Je suis Partout* that manifested a virulent anti-Semitic ethos.

newspaper magnate Francois Coty, who was determined to disseminate to the widest possible audience, the virulent anti-Semitic conspiracy theories that had turned fin de siècle France into one of Europe's most xenophobic societies.[9] Coty was the proprietor of the French right-wing newspaper *L'Ami du Peuple* (the friend of the people), and in April decided to initiate a sustained attack on the Irish state's only Jewish parliamentarian.[10] He had founded the paper to provide the French working classes with an alternative rightist narrative to the leftist socialist papers like *L'Humanité, Vendredi* and *Regards*.[11]

In April 1932 *L'Ami du Peuple* carried the first article in a series that accused Briscoe of being a secret agent of Kuhn Loeb and Co, an American investment bank founded in the middle of the nineteenth century by two Russian-Jewish immigrants.[12] An editorial implying that Briscoe was some sort of Jewish secret agent for economic domination tried to establish a link between the bank and the struggle for Irish independence.

> Nobody dreams of asserting that the separatist movement in Ireland is the work of a secret agent of Kuhn, Loeb & Company, but the existence of this association is only too certain, and we are going to prove it.[13]

9   For a more detailed understanding of the prevailing multi-layered strands of cultural, social and political anti-Semitism see: Chad Alan Goldberg and Emile Durkheim, 'Introduction to Emile Durkheim's "Anti-Semitism and Social Crisis"', *Sociological Theory*, Vol. 26, No. 4 (December 2008), pp. 301–305. Jan Goldstein, 'The Wandering Jew and the Problem of Psychiatric Anti-Semitism in Fin-de-Siècle France', *Journal of Contemporary History*, Vol. 20, No. 4 (October 1985), pp. 521–523.

10 Ralph Schor, 'Xenophobia and the Extreme Right: 'L'Ami du Peuple', 1928–37', *Revue d' Histoire Moderne & Contemporaine*, Vol. 23 (January 1976), p. 118.

11 George L. Mosse, 'The French Right and the Working Classes: Les Jaunes', *Journal of Contemporary History*, Vol. 7, No. 3/4 (July-October 1972), pp. 185–208.

12 Priscilla Roberts, 'Jewish bankers, Russia and the Soviet Union, 1900–1940: The case of Kuhn, Loeb and Company', *The American Jewish Archives Journal*, Vol. 49, No. 1 & 2 (1997), pp. 9–37.

13 National Archives of Ireland Department of Foreign Affairs/2/5/17, 21 April 1932. (Hereafter NAI DFA).

In order to support the accusation, Coty manufactured a profile that was, as far as the available evidence suggests, greatly exaggerated if not entirely imagined.

> The agent is a Zionist Jew ... named Robert Briscoe ... He joined at a very early hour in the most advanced Nationalist movement in Ireland. Knowing a good deal about finance, he became to a certain extent the treasurer of Mr, de Valera's party, and very soon complete reliance was placed on him for the purpose of procuring resources for the National movement.[14]

It was clear that Briscoe was only becoming aware of the global Zionist movement at this point in time, as for as joining the republican movement 'at a very early hour' it is evident that he was very much a late-comer having been sent to New York by his father to avoid joining the independence struggle. Coty used these tenuous links as a foundation for allegations that became even more outlandish:

> Officially these subsidies come from people of Irish origin ... But the exceptional abundance and the regularity with which these monies were supplied coincided with the moment when this Lithuanian Jew entered into relations with the banks of his co-religionists in America. Thanks to the money received from Kuhn, Loeb & Company, an important contraband ... of arms and ammunition was established by Briscoe himself.[15]

However, despite the fact that the accusations were completely without foundation, they were sulphuric enough to convince a sizable percentage of Catholic Ireland already predisposed to Jewish-communist conspiracy theories, that there was some merit to them. This cohort's reactionary Catholic worldview was reinforced by the Bolshevist hysteria promulgated by publications like the *Irish Messenger of the Sacred Heart*, which reflected traditional Catholic dogma depicting Jews as deicidists.[16] The following

14   Ibid., 25 April 1932.
15   NAI DFA/2/5/17. 26 April 1932. Copy of Coty article entitled 'Les Financiers qui minent le monde'.
16   Elizabeth Russell, 'Themes in Popular Reading Material in the 1930s', in Joost Augusteijn (ed.), *Ireland in the 1930s: New Perspectives* (Four Courts Press, Dublin, 1999), pp. 13–25.

letter was sent to the editor of the *Catholic Mind* which had on more than
one occasion taken de Valera to task for not being 'Catholic enough'.[17]

> Would you please read the enclosed articles and test if the sensational revelations
> about Mr Briscoe T. D. are true. If so it is a very sorry state of affairs for Catholic
> Ireland. I believe these articles ... written by Coty have ... appeared in the "figaro [sic]
> an important French paper ... It would be well to publish it in order to find out if
> there is any truth in the allegation.[18]

It is clear people were prepared to accept a link between the state's only
non-Christian parliamentarian and the supposed Jewish-Freemasonry
plot 'against the Church', on the say-so of an individual they had never
even heard of prior to the controversy.[19] This was reinforced in Cumann
nGaedheal ranks when *L'Ami du Peuple* carried an even more inflammatory
editorial stating 'that Briscoe was member of an extreme faction who condemned Collins and had him assassinated'.[20] Given the fractious nature of
the post-Civil War ideological split this was an incendiary charge. Collins
had assumed an almost mythical status for the recently defeated pro-Treaty
party, and it is was therefore only logical that Coty's new accusation would
result in a virulent reaction.

Although the controversy raged around Briscoe throughout the spring
and summer of 1932, it is important to emphasize he was also aware the
Dáil was in the process of introducing the first in a series of legislative
acts, which would increasingly isolate the state from the global events
and make an already restrictive immigration criteria harder still, especially
for his German co-religionists.[21] When the restrictive ownership criteria
of the Control of Manufactures Act of June 1932 was introduced, it was
immediately clear to Briscoe that it would disproportionately impact on

17 Lee, *Politics and Society*, p. 167.
18 NAI DFA/2/5/17, 1 May 1932.
19 Whyte, *Church and State in Modern Ireland*, p. 73.
20 NAI DFA/2/5/17, 30 May 1932.
21 Mary E. Daly, 'An Irish-Ireland for Business?: The Control of Manufactures Acts,
    1932 and 1934', *Irish Historical Studies*, Vol. 24, No. 94 (November 1984), pp. 259–261.

the potential immigration of German Jewish industrialists.[22] The Act
stipulated that any new company must have as majority shareholders
Irish citizens:

> Such business, is, at the time such thing is done, owned by a body corporate the issued
> shares of which are at that time to an extent exceeding one-half (in normal value)
> thereof in the beneficial ownership of a person who is or of two or more persons each
> of whom is at that time either a national of Saorstát Éireann or a body corporate the
> issued shares of which are at that time to an extent exceeding one-half (in nominal
> value) thereof in the beneficial ownership of nationals of Saorstát Éireann.[23]

It was evident that this would impose a set of ownership principles that
most potential Jewish migrants would find almost impossible to meet,
moreover, it made the already complex and stressful cultural adjustments
of the few Jewish immigrants who had succeeded in gaining entry to
the state even more precarious as they wondered if they would now face
expulsion.[24]

This was clear from the moment the act became operational on 29
October 1932, when Briscoe was immediately inundated with queries from
frantic Jewish industrialists who approached him to see if they would be
affected by the new immigration/ownership criteria. So as well as dealing
with an unprecedented political assault from external right-wing, anti-
Semitic factions in France, it was clear that Briscoe's status as the state's
only Jewish TD was inexorably leading to a pivotal role as the de-facto
representative of his German co-religionists as Hitler's Jew-hatred would
precipitate an emigration crisis of unimaginable proportions.

So as the summer of 1932 turned to autumn, it was increasingly clear
that Briscoe was under enormous stress as he fought for his personal and
political survival and had to contend with multiple pleas for help from terrified German Jews desperate to escape Hitler's persecution. His predicament
reached a climax when Cumann na nGaedheal seized the opportunity to ask

22   Ibid.
23   http://www.irishstatutebook.ie/eli/1932/act/21/enacted/en/html
24   John Brannigan, *Race in Modern Irish Literature and Culture* (Edinburgh University
     Press, Edinburgh, 2009), pp. 152–154.

a succession of Dáil questions based on Coty's spurious accusations. This set the scene for an ugly exhibition of political bias which was laced with an anti-communist, anti-Semitic undercurrent as the opposition sought to taint de Valera through his association with Briscoe.

The interrogation was conducted by Patrick McGilligan, the former Minister for Industry and Commerce, who had never made any effort to disguise that his political worldview was guided by a 'staunch Catholicism'.[25] Briscoe's ordeal began when McGilligan made an opaque reference to 'a certain Deputy' that left little doubt to whom he was referring.[26] This dexterous method of interrogation had all the hallmarks of a skilful cross-examination, as McGilligan, a practising barrister, adroitly referred to Coty's allegation that Briscoe was part of a global communist conspiracy.

> The point in question, and upon which the whole article has been written, was whether or not a particular deputy had touch with a certain organisation, the alleged purpose of which was to spread Communism in all countries. The implication, of course, was that that Deputy was being used as an agent for the spread of Communistic activities in this country.[27]

Once he had laid out the broader accusation, McGilligan pointedly focused on Briscoe as an individual by suggesting that the gardaí were in possession of a letter that supported Coty's allegations. He followed this by directly asking de Valera if he was aware of this, and suggested that if he was not, then he would be 'surprised' if he did not change his 'opinion of the Irish patriotism of this particular Deputy' after reading it.[28] However, de Valera refused to rise to the bait, and angrily refuted McGilligan's allegation by telling the Dáil that he was more than 'satisfied' with the Deputy's explanation.[29] It is to de Valera's credit that he had not abandoned Briscoe at any point during the Coty affair showing a commendable loyalty that

---

25   Elaine A. Byrne, *Political Corruption in Ireland 1922–2010* (Manchester University Press, Manchester, 2012), pp. 38–40.
26   DÉD, Vol. 44, Col. 1135, 4 November 1932.
27   Ibid., Col. 1136.
28   Ibid.
29   Ibid., Col. 1148.

would over the forthcoming decades be repaid by Briscoe. However, by defending him de Valera also made a clear statement that he would not be railroaded by the outraged sensibilities of a conservative Catholic group. Of course it must also be acknowledged that de Valera saw it as part of a broader political strategy designed to challenge any allegation that linked Fianna Fáil to communism.

At the same time Briscoe was the subject of an intense Dáil debate, events in Germany were rapidly and inexorably leading to a situation where every previous Jewish fear of Nazi persecution would lapse into insignificance as Hitler seized absolute power in a series of elections that occurred with bewildering speed. Firstly, despite a resounding success in July that had made the NSDAP the single largest party in the state, Hitler was still in opposition, so in the November election he decided to sideline the purely ideological platform of July and concentrate on a platform of 'Work and Bread', which promised to eradicate 'unemployment [and deliver] fully-paid work for each and every jobless German'.[30]

However, much to the surprise of a confident Hitler, the NSDAP suffered an electoral set back. It lost 34 seats and although still the largest party was momentarily in disarray. However, an unlikely alliance with a conservative faction offered Hitler an unexpected route to his ultimate goal of absolute political domination. This group was determined to reinstate Fritz Von Pappen and his 'Cabinet of Barons', to power after a reluctant Hindenburg had appointed Kurt Von Schleicher as Chancellor to forestall a wave of social discontent.[31] A fortuitous meeting between Pappen and one of Hitler's wealthy conservative supporters, the Cologne banker, Kurt von Schroeder, initiated a series of secretive meetings between Pappen and Hitler.[32] This cabal thought it could control Hitler: it could not and Hindenburg, who had been alienated by Von Schleichter's agricultural cen-

---

30   Jürgen W. Falter, 'How Likely Were Workers to Vote for the NSDAP?', in Conan Fischer (ed.), *The Rise of National Socialism and the Working Classes in Weimar Germany* (Berghahn Books, Providence RI, 1996), p. 37.
31   Kershaw, *Hitler*, p. 245.
32   Catherine Epstein, *Nazi Germany: Confronting the Myths* (John Wiley & Sons Ltd, Winchester, 2015), p. 40.

trist focus, 'demanded and received' his resignation, and on Von Pappen's recommendation appointed Hitler as Chancellor on 30 January 1933.[33] On this day there were 523,000 German Jews. By the end of World War Two on 8 May 1945, less than 20,000 remained in hiding.[34] Although Briscoe was aware through his contacts in Berlin that if Hitler seized power, it would mean devastation for his central European co-religionists, even he could not, distracted as he was by parochial politics, have envisaged the forthcoming slaughter.

The complex juxtaposition of Briscoe's increasingly dualistic commitment was evident when he finally succeeded in bringing the 1929 co-sponsored private member's moneylending bill to a conclusion.[35] He had been brought up with an abhorrence of moneylending; his father had vehemently denounced this practice lamenting the innate association between it and Judaism.[36] He had first attempted to eradicate one of the more exploitative blights of contemporary society in the 1926 IRA campaign against moneylenders. Then in early 1930, he set about regulating a profession that was effectively uncontrolled in Ireland by introducing a private members bill telling the Dáil that:

> I must say that I have instances of harshness, unreasonableness and blackmail which really were shocking and which fortify me in asking this House to give support to a measure which will protect borrowers from the impositions which are attempted by these usurers called moneylenders.[37]

However, it had taken four years of constant effort to secure the passage of the bill; he only succeeded when Fianna Fáil secured an overall majority in the snap election of 1933 securing seventy-six seats meaning that the party

33   Henry Ashby Turner, *Hitler's Thirty Days to Power: January 1933* (Basic Books, New York, 1997), pp. 1027.
34   Peter G. Pulzer, *Jews and the German State: The Political History of a Minority, 1848–1933* (Blackwell Publishers, Hoboken NJ, pp. 338–350.
35   http://acts.oireachtas.ie/zza36y1933.1.html
36   Briscoe and Hatch, *For the Life of Me*, p. 16.
37   DED, 20 February 1930, Vol. 33, Col. 680.

no longer needed the support of the seven Labour deputies.[38] Briscoe was re-elected in Dublin South securing the third seat; however, his percentage of the popular vote decreased from the 10.31 per cent of the previous year, to 8.05 per cent.[39]

Yet despite the fact that the passage of the bill was now ensured due to Fianna Fáil's overall majority, two of Cumann na nGaedheal's more reactionary individuals attempted to embarrass Briscoe by highlighting how a number of Jewish moneylenders had supposedly Hibernicized their names in an effort to blend in.[40] James Fitzgerald-Kenny, Briscoe's long time nemesis, made a contribution to the final debate on the act that exhibited a narrow worldview bordering on the anti-Semitic. During the final stage of the debate he wondered if 'any moneylenders who may come down here from Belfast would be of the Celtic race?'[41] His party colleague James Dillon reinforced the xenophobic undertone by suggesting that 'at least, any moneylenders who came here from Belfast would have acquired a Celtic veneer' and 'have wrapped the green flag around him'.[42] Given the rampant xenophobia of the moment, it was perhaps not surprising that members of Dáil Éireann should follow suit; it was not, as Briscoe knew, an isolated incident and variations on the theme would be repeated in the years to come.

The increasing restrictions on immigration coincided with an upsurge in requests for help from German Jews who were desperate to escape the increasing Nazi persecution; oftentimes these people had already fled Germany and were already living as refugees in mainland Europe.[43] On

---

38   Ferriter, *The Transformation of Ireland*, pp. 364–365.
39   ElectionsIreland.org/1541
40   Donal Ó Drisceoil, 'Jews and Other Undesirables: Anti-Semitism and the Second World War', in Ethel Crowley and Jim Mac Laughlin (eds.), *Under the Belly of the Tiger Class, Race and Culture in the Global Ireland* (Irish Reporter Publications, Dublin, 1997), pp. 74–75.
41   DÉD, Vol. 49, Col. 330. 20 July 1933.
42   Ibid.
43   For a comprehensive overview of Briscoe's Immigration initiative see: McCarthy, 'An Introduction to Robert Briscoe's Extraordinary Immigration Initiative, 1933–1938', pp. 80–90.

10 August 1933, Briscoe wrote to Paddy Rutledge, the Minister for Justice, explaining that the chief rabbi, Isaac Herzog had asked him to secure, if possible, an entry visa for Irene Dozialosgrynsk, a young Jewish translator presently residing in Paris. He outlined the specific qualities that this person had, which, in Herzog's opinion, could not be found in Ireland, specifically the ability to translate 'Hebrew into various languages and translation into Hebrew from other languages'.[44] The response from the department was not encouraging; Briscoe received the following query, is it 'not possible for you to obtain the services of a suitable person in the Irish Free State to act in this capacity'?[45] When he replied in the negative, the department, in an early display of understanding, granted the request, and Briscoe was able to dispatch a handwritten note to Herzog, informing him that the young lady in question had been granted permission to enter Ireland, and that the 'permit' would be 'delivered' later that month.[46]

Briscoe followed up this initial success by petitioning the department on behalf of a young Jewish doctor who was looking to further his studies in Ireland. Herzog had been contacted by this young man who, after being initially granted permission to follow a course of post-graduate study, had for some unexplained reason had this permission rescinded. It appears from Briscoe's adroit handling of the case, that he had quickly acquired the necessary negotiating skills to secure an extension. He emphasized that 'Dr Sommer is not interfering in any way with the livelihood of Saorstat Nationals, and ... that he maintains himself ... at no cost to the ... Irish State.'[47]

By addressing these two issues, he pre-empted questioning about potential cost to the state, or the possibility that he would compete for a job with Irish doctors. On 20 November he received the following reply, the 'Minister for Justice ... will raise no objection to this alien's remaining in the Saorstat for a period of twelve months', providing it is 'for the purpose

44   Robert Briscoe Private Papers (Hereafter RBPP). 10 August 1933.
45   Ibid., 11 August 1933.
46   Ibid., 14 August 1933.
47   Ibid., 16 November 1933.

of study only.'[48] These two successful interventions by Briscoe would be the exception rather than the rule in his forthcoming role as a Jewish refugee advocate. As the decade unfolded, the department would adopt a hard line interpretation of increasingly restrictive immigration criteria.[49] This raises the intriguing possibility that Briscoe's early interventions were successful because Justice was 'a novice department' and 'new to the scenario of creating and implementing refugee centred policy extracted from a general "aliens" policy.[50] If so, this position would not last long.

The reality of the Nazi ascension to power would have 'major implications for the Saorstát in terms of cultural relations, refugee policies, foreign relations and commerce'.[51] In a broader sense, it is important to emphasize that all of Briscoe's refugee representations would be conducted against the backdrop of Irish-German relations. However, the extent of the impact on refugee policy was not initially apparent; it was a period of political chaos in Berlin, which from the perspective of an evolving Irish immigration policy would only become more complicated due to the August 1933 appointment of Charles Bewley, Briscoe's nemesis from 1922, as Minister Plenipotentiary and Envoy Extraordinary.[52]

Irish refugee policy in Germany had been initially designed by Leo T. McCauley, Bewley's immediate predecessor who informed Dublin of his strategy in April 1933.

> The Department will be interested to know that many inquiries and applications for visas have been received by the Legation within the past week from Jews desiring to leave Germany and take up their residence in the Irish Free State ... As far as possible the legation has discouraged such persons from going to Ireland, as they are really

48   Ibid., 20 November 1933.
49   Clair Wills, *That Neutral Island: A Cultural History of Ireland During the Second World War* (Faber and Faber Ltd, London, 2007), pp. 394–398.
50   O'Connor, 'Irish Government Policy', p. 120.
51   Mervyn O'Driscoll, *Ireland, Germany and the Nazis: Politics and Diplomacy, 1919–1939* (Four Courts Press, Dublin, 2004), p. 95.
52   Ibid.

only refugees; and it assumes that this line of action would be in accordance with the Department's policy.[53]

On appointment to Berlin, Bewley did not simply enforce McCauley's policy but enthusiastically set about reinforcing it to the point that it became almost impossible for German Jews to meet his self-determined criteria. In his capacity as minister, Bewley wielded extraordinary power in deciding who was suited to enter the Irish state from Germany. Irish immigration policy dictated that any foreign national first had to apply for an entry visa through the Irish mission in his/her host country.[54] Bewley's anti-Semitism led him to immediately interpret policy in the strictest possible fashion, believing it to be inordinately liberal by facilitating the entry of the wrong class of people, by this he meant criminals, communists and Jews.[55]

It is clear therefore that Briscoe's initiative was confronting hostile forces in Berlin, a position that was unfortunately reinforced by a considerable anti-Semitic resentment in Irish civic society. The letter pages in a number of Irish broadsheets featured commentary that was receptive to the supposed Judeo-Bolshevik plot for global political and economic domination. This was the cause of considerable consternation in the Irish-Jewish community, and after a period of reflection, a decision was made to fight back against the wave of innuendo by offering a reasoned, factual counter-narrative. This was not an easy decision to make; by inclination the community tended to keep a low-profile, however, it was clear in leadership circles that they could no longer ignore the wave of anti-Jewish hysteria. It was decided that Isaac Herzog, given his prominent position as chief rabbi, would be best placed to challenge a discriminatory public discourse.

53   National Archives of Ireland Department of External Affairs102/9, 7 April 1933. (Hereafter NAI DEA).
54   Katrina Goldstone, "'Benevolent Helpfulness'? Ireland and the International Reaction to Jewish Refugees, 1933–9 in Michael Kennedy and Joseph Morrison Skelly (eds.), *Irish Foreign Policy 1919–1966 From Independence to Internationalism* (Four Courts Press, Dublin, 2000), p. 123.
55   Mervyn O'Driscoll, 'The 'Jewish Question': Irish Refugee Policy and Charles Bewley, 1933–39', https://www.academia.edu/1065493/The_Jewish_Question_Irish_Refugee_Policy_and_Charles_Bewley_1933-39.

In April 1934 the chief rabbi sent a scathing letter to the *Irish Press*; he attempted to systematically dismantle the notion that Jews were disproportionately represented in the communist movement by arguing that it was just as likely that Christians would be followers, as Jews.

> This ... is one of the most groundless and most outrageous libels ever invented by human wickedness. Its sole object is to discredit the Jewish community, and pave the way for anti-Semitism. There are men and women born of Jewish parents who happen to be Communists, or who are sympathetic towards that dangerous atheistic creed, but their communism, or Communistic sympathy, has as much to do with the fact of their Jewish birth as the communism or Communistic sympathy of the members of other races has to do with the fact that they were born in the Christian faith.[56]

Although Herzog's logic seems flawless, it did no go unchallenged; this was evident when an outraged letter appeared in the *Irish Independent* ten days later. The respondent to Herzog's logical dissection of the prevailing Jewish-communist dogma claimed that:

> Unless Bolshevism is nipped in the bud immediately, it is bound to spread in one form or another over Europe and the whole world, as it is organised by Jews, who have no nationality, and whose one object is to destroy, for their own ends, the existing order of things.[57]

He continued his critique of Herzog's acclamation by suggesting, without foundation, that:

> A Jew is the Commander–in-Chief of the Ukrainian army; a Jew is President of the State Bank; Jews occupy almost all important ambassadorial positions of the Soviet Union. The Universities, professions, the Judiciary, and Administration ... have now a greater percentage of Jews than of any other nationality.[58]

This type of statement is exactly what Herzog had been referring to; he knew that as long as this type of falsehood went unchallenged, no matter its origin, then bigoted individuals would keep repeating it.

56   *IP*, 2 April 1934.
57   *II*, 12 April 1934.
58   Ibid.

Briscoe eventually got drawn into the debate as the 1932 Coty incident was reintroduced by Herzog's critic, who asked if Herzog had read 'the correspondence-files and ledgers of Messrs. Kuhn Loeb and Co?', and used this to assert a definitive link between the state's only Jewish parliamentarian and communism.[59] The letter finishes with the self-satisfied assertion that as Herzog has been conspicuously absent from the debate since his initial letter, then the writer can only surmise that:

> In the absence of any reply from Dr Herzog, may I conclude that he has withdrawn his former statement, and that it is no libel, but the absolute truth to declare that Jews are in close association with Russian Communism.[60]

If this sense of vulnerability was apparent in the native Irish-Jewish community, it was far more pronounced in the small number of recently arrived Jewish immigrants. This cohort became increasingly concerned about their residency status as an increasingly xenophobic discourse emerged during the Dáil debate on the second Control of Manufactures Bill in 1934.[61] The state's newest Jewish residents listened as the bureaucratic language of the debate clearly defined them as somehow different, it was patently obvious that the new arrivals were being targeted by some of the state's senior politicians, even if the term Jew, or Jewish was never used.[62] By adopting this type of coded referential system, it offered the contributor a degree of protection from any accusation that they were being overtly anti-Semitic.[63]

---

59   Ibid.
60   Ibid.
61   Mary E. Daly, 'Cultural and Economic Protection And Xenophobia in an Independent Ireland, 1920s–1970s', in Borbála Faragó and Moynagh Sullivan (eds.), *Facing the Other* (Cambridge Scholars Publishing, Newcastle, 2008), pp. 6–19.
62   Katrina Goldstone, 'Christianity, conversion and the tricky business of names: Images of Jews and Blacks in the nationalist Irish Catholic discourse', in Ronit Lentin and Robbie McVeigh (eds.), *Racism and Anti-Racism* (Beyond the Pale Publications, Belfast, 2002), p. 170.
63   Martin Reisigi and Ruth Wodak, 'The Discourse-Historical Approach (DHA)', in Ruth Wodak and Michael Meyer (eds.), *Methods of Critical Discourse Analysis* (Sage

The queries about ethnic origin were phrased in a way that emphasized the non-Christian origin of the individual; for example General Richard Mulcahy,[64] demanded to know how many factories had been opened by people with names like 'Gaw', 'Matz' or 'Yaffe' in the previous twelve months.[65] When Seán Lemass, who was determined to modernize a moribund Irish indigenous manufacturing sector,[66] responded with the required information that only four factories had been opened in the period in question, a Cumann na nGaedheal deputy inquired 'whether Mr Gaw. Mr Silverstein or Mr Hastello' had 'a competent knowledge of Irish?'[67] As the debate continued James Dillon, a future Fine Gale leader, who had an illustrious political pedigree as the son of John Dillon, the last leader of the Irish Parliamentary Party demanded to know if the following named individuals could even be described as citizens.[68] As Dillon listed the names, it was crystal clear to all those present that they were Jewish:

> I should like to know if in the following cases any provisions of the Control of Manufactures Act have operated to preserve the factories referred to for predominant control by Irish nationals and whether he will say if the names Matz, Gaw, Lucks, Galette, Keye, Wigglesworth, Vogel, Witstan or Whizton, Caplan or Caplal,

---

Publications Ltd, London, 2009), pp. 87–122. This is a highly theoretical approach, but essentially it argues that there are five critical stages in defining newcomers as the other. 1] How are persons named and referred to linguistically? 2] What traits, characteristics, qualities and features are attributed to them? 3] By means of what arguments and argumentation schemes do specific persons or social groups try to justify and legitimize the exclusion, discrimination, suppression and exploitation of others? 4] From what perspective or point of view are these labels, attributions and arguments expressed? 5] Are the respective utterances articulated overtly? Are they intensified or are they mitigated?

64 Maryann Gialanella Valiulis, *General Richard Mulcahy and the Founding of the Irish State* (University Press of Kentucky, Lexington KY, 1992).

65 DÉD, Vol. 50, Col. 346, 22 November 1933.

66 Horgan, *The Enigmatic Patriot*, p. 72.

67 Ibid.

68 The most informative available monograph on Dillon remains: Maurice Manning, *James Dillon: A Biography* (Wolfhound Press, Dublin, 2000).

Hastello, Silverstein, Mendelberg, Levins, Michaels, Greiw, Levy, Mennel and Yaffe are Irish nationals within the meaning of the Act?[69]

It was perhaps inevitable that Briscoe would eventually be a target of the increasing hostility toward Jews from the Irish political elite, this is not surprising given the context of the era and his unique status as the Dáil's only Semitic deputy. However, what is perhaps surprising is that the negativity was not confined to his political opponents; he received the following letter from a clearly chagrined Fianna Fáil deputy:

> The Fianna Fail party is too well able to look after its own affairs without having blocks of the "Laurel and Hardy" type messing up things for it. I suppose you are after a "job". People of your ilk always are, particularly when they rush into help ministers and Bishops-the snail helping the lion with its "great big horne". [Sic] Well, sonny, take a tip and mind the job you have ... Moreover, if you are wise, you will let us speak for ourselves for the future, or you will be told publicly to mind your own business. We want xxx to avoid being bracketed in any way with you or your family.[70]

This was a coded reference to Briscoe's increasingly high profile, which had clearly offended some of the more reactionary elements within Fianna Fáil; a situation that would only be exacerbated by the increasing anti-Semitic innuendo being directed at Éamon de Valera.

In the spring of 1934 de Valera confronted his political opponents in a strongly worded refutation of a sustained campaign of political/religious vilification. In many respects he had no choice as the onslaught had taken on elements of a crusade, therefore, if his authority as President of the Executive Council was not going to be undermined, he could not allow it to continue. The chance to face down his accusers came in February 1934 when James Fitzgerald-Kenny, the former Minister for Justice, suggested that he had 'Communistic supporters' with ambitions that 'Catholicism should be driven out of this country'.[71] This statement was made in a debate on the Wearing of Uniforms Bill, where Fianna Fáil was attempting to

69   DÉD, Vol. 50, Col. 248, 22 November 1933.
70   Briscoe Papers National Library of Ireland Ms, 26, 445, 3305, 19 February 1934. (Hereafter BPNLI).
71   DÉD, Vol. 50, Cols. 2253–2254. 28 February 1934.

84

introduce an act that restricted the wearing of military style uniforms to
the official forces of the state.

This was a response to the growing popularity of the Blueshirts, a
quasi-military organization that had been founded in early 1933, by the
time the act was proposed it was clear the movement had become a real
threat to the state's stability.[72] The organization had embraced the trap-
pings of the European fascistic movements, the stiff-arm salute, the para-
military uniform, and had an overwhelmingly Catholic membership.[73]
This was reflected in the criteria for joining the movement, which limited
membership 'to citizens of Irish birth ... who profess the Christian faith'.[74]
It seems clear that the clause excluding non-Christians in the provisional
constitution was inserted specifically to exclude members of the Jewish
faith. This was yet another concern for Irish Jews, who by and large were
convinced that if the Blueshirts had actually managed to seize power they
would have been deprived of citizenship and/or expelled.[75]

The fact that de Valera was trying to limit the appeal of the Blueshirts
had been enough for Fitzgerald-Kenny to accuse him of being anti-Catholic
with pro-communist sympathies. De Valera's rebuttal was clinical. Firstly
he highlighted the political opportunism of Fine Gael by pointing out that
they were exploiting the public paranoia about the Jewish-Bolshevik plot.

> Now this thing of Communism was worked up to such a stage in the country that
> there is a background, for the people on the benches opposite, on which they can
> stand, and work on the fears of the multitude, and they have never been slow to
> avail of that.[76]

72   Lee, *Politics and Society*, pp. 178–182.
73   Mike Cronin, Catholicising Fascism, Fascistising Catholicism? The Blueshirts and
     the Jesuits in 1930s Ireland', *Totalitarian Movements and Political Religions*, Vol. 8,
     No. 2 (June 2007), p. 401.
74   NLI, Eoin O' Duffy Papers. Ms 48, 286/7. Acc 5694. Provisional Constitution of
     the National Guard. 1933.
75   John Newsinger, 'Blackshirts, Blueshirts, and the Spanish Civil War', *The Historical
     Journal*, Vol. 44, No. 3 (2001), p. 839.
76   DÉD, Vol. 50, Cols. 2511–2512, 2 March 1934.

He extended his refutation to include an angry denial of any link to Jewish-Bolshevism.

> Now their filthy propaganda has not stopped at that. The same type of whispering, the same type of propaganda is going on now as in 1922. I have here in this House had to speak on a personal matter. I did it, not that I cared a snap of my fingers about what anybody says about me personally but I am jealous, as long as I occupy this particular position, that my antecedents and my character shall not be attacked. Before they went and soiled the steps of God's Altar; the same campaign in another guise is going on now and I know that in order to get some basis for their Communistic attack upon us they are suggesting that I am of Jewish origin.[77]

It was a clever strategic move by de Valera, although all the evidence suggests that he was personally philo-Semitic, he understood that the overwhelming Catholic belief of the era linked Jews to communism.[78] This was underscored by a further denial of Jewish antecedents, which de Valera emphasized with a religious rhetoric that reflected the dominant Christian view of Jews as deicidists.[79]

> There is not, as far as I know, a single drop of Jewish blood in my veins ... I know originally that they were God's people; that they turned against Him and that the punishment which their turning against God brought upon them made even Christ himself weep ... I say that on both sides of me I come from Catholic stock ... I was baptized in a Catholic Church. I was brought up in a Catholic home.[80]

De Valera's political pragmatism was evident in this statement. It was clear that he was willing to do whatever it took to put a stop to the rumours of a Jewish-communist link.

Listening to de Valera's Dáil pronouncement only reinforced the concerns of a Jewish community already living in fear at the rise of Ireland's

---

77   Ibid., Cols. 2513–2514.
78   Benjamin Keatinge, 'Responses to the Holocaust in Modern Irish Poetry', *Estudios Irlandeses*, Vol. 1, No. 6 (2011), pp. 22–23.
79   E. Brian Titley, *Church, State, and the Control of Schooling in Ireland 1900–1944* (Gill and Macmillan, Dublin, 1983), pp. 3–31.
80   DÉD, Vol. 50, Col. 2514. 2 March 1934.

own home-grown fascist organization.[81] The community was so concerned
by the perceived anti-Semitic ethos of the Blueshirts that they contacted
Ernest Blyth to express their fears; he replied as follows:[82]

> I wish to assure you that your apprehensions concerning the attitude of the United
> Ireland Party towards the Jewish community in the Irish Free State are quite
> unfounded. This party as you are no doubt aware, has always stood for toleration
> and full liberty for all law abiding citizens of every denomination. It has never dis-
> criminated between persons of different religious beliefs in their treatment as citi-
> zens, and never intends to do so, holding that every person who conforms to the
> law of the State is entitled to full enjoyment of the privilege of citizenship without
> any discrimination whatsoever against him. The rumour that this party intends to
> propagate a campaign of victimisation against the members of any community is
> absurd and malicious.[83]

This bland response did nothing to calm the fears of Irish Jews; as a community they had experienced enough discrimination over the preceding
decade to understand the precarious nature of their communal position.
They had not forgotten de Valera's Dáil April statement and knew that as
a community, they were at the disposal of Irish politicians to use as a point
of pejorative reference.

81   Ó Grada, *Jewish Ireland in the Age of Joyce*, p. 91.
82   For a comprehensive overview of the interaction between Irish political parties and
     the Blueshirts see: Mike Cronin, *The Blueshirts and Irish Politics* (Four Courts Press,
     Dublin, 1997).
83   JMD Box 1. Category 1.06. Limerick No.s 1–7. 29 October 1934.

CHAPTER 6

1935–1937
Political Reality: Immigration Failure, League of Nations and the New Zionist Organisation (Revisionists)

Ireland's political direction continued to become increasingly insular in the immediate aftermath of de Valera's Dáil address, so much so that it was decided to introduce a new Aliens Act in March 1935. Prior to the introduction of the 1935 act, travel and immigration into Ireland had been controlled by legislation passed in the pre-independence period when the country had been an integral part of the United Kingdom. Siobhán O'Connor insightfully suggests that the 1935 act was yet another building-block, albeit a foundational one, in de Valera's long-term project to 'define' the Irish state as an independent entity with 'borders ... distinct from the previous union' with Britain.[1] In many respects the act built on the circum-scribed ownership criteria of the 1932 and 1934 Control of Manufactures Acts, and the already limited opportunities for inward migration were dealt a further blow.[2]

De Valera strongly asserted the right of the state to determine its own policy on citizenship in his opening statement on the second reading of the Aliens Bill saying:

> I do not know whether it is necessary to enter into any detailed explanation of this bill or to give any special reason for its introduction ... It is obvious that having changed the basis of citizenship ... we need in defining as a non-citizen to have a

1   O'Connor, 'Irish Government Policy', p. 74.
2   Mary E. Daly, Irish Nationality and Citizenship since 1922', *Irish Historical Studies*, Vol. 32, No. 127 (2001), pp. 392–393.

bill like this. [This bill] is to provide for the control of aliens and for other matters relating to aliens.[3]

Yet logical as this sounds, it seems clear that the Irish definition of citizenship shared the social Darwinism that underpinned the exclusionist immigration policies of the former British colonies, which were determined to remain white and Christian. People of colour and those groups outside the wider Christian family were not welcome; this was oftentimes disguised by the economic arguments of the era, but in reality this stance was in fact secondary to the prevailing orthodoxy that Jews were 'alien', and therefore not assimilable.[4] This proposition is reinforced when some of the pejorative Dáil commentary in the final debate on the act is examined.[5] In a loaded comment, Patrick McGilligan, Briscoe's chief prosecutor in the Coty inquiry of 1932, resurrected the anti-Semitic undertones from the 1934 Control of Manufactures debate that Jews were Hibernicizing their names.

> Say you have a gentleman called Wassenfeldt or some name of that kind, that he decides to Irishise his name, and that he becomes The O'Maguire on a particular date. If it is later than the 6th December, 1922, he may continue as the O'Maguire, and later he may find that there are too many O'Maguires in the country, and he can change the name to something else. I wonder is that what is intended?[6]

The response from civic society tended to reflect the discriminatory stance of the state's political class; however, there were a number of honourable exceptions. For example the overwhelmingly generous response of Frank Duff, who became one of Irish Judaism's foremost advocates; he had founded the influential Catholic-lay organization the Legion of

---

3   Seanad Éireann Debates, Vol. 19, Col. 1376. 20 March 1935.
4   Goldstone, 'Benevolent Helpfulness'?, p. 118.
5   Gisela Holfter, 'Some Facts and Figures on German-Speaking exiles in Ireland, 1933–1945', in Mathias Schulz, James M. Skidmore, David G. John, Grit Liebscher, and Sebastian Siebel-Achenbach (eds.), German Diasporic Experiences Identity, Migration, and Loss (Wilfrid Laurier University Press, Waterloo ON, 2008), pp. 181–185.
6   DÉD, Vol. 54, Col. 2034, 14 February 1935.

Mary and consistently objected to the bigoted ramblings of virulent Irish anti-Semites.[7] As Duff became increasingly concerned about the fate of Europe's persecuted Jews, he founded the *Pillar of Fire Society* to aid their Irish relatives and friends in any way possible.[8] Given the anti-Semitic mood of the moment this was a courageous and principled stand, and although it would bring the everlasting gratitude of Irish Jews, it would also bring down the wrath of the most influential member of a conservative Irish hierarchy on his head.[9] This is perhaps not surprising, it was inevitable that Duff's attempt to foster a dialogue with Jews, would bring him to the attention of the soon-to-be Archbishop of Dublin, John Charles McQuaid.[10] Duff's attempt to aid a persecuted people initiated a far from Christian response, and the depths of McQuaid's antipathy towards his initiative was summarized by his use of pejorative terminology when referring to the *Pillar of Fire* initiative. Exercising his ecclesiastical authority, he prohibited Duff and the society from having any further 'contact with Jews', and cautioned him against having any further 'discussions with Atheistic Communists'.[11]

One of Duff's prime motivations for founding the *Pillar of Fire* was to counteract the anti-Semitic narrative that had being constructed by some of the state's more bigoted commentators. This included the virulently anti-Semitic, but thankfully short-lived publication *Aontas Gadeheal* (Unity of the Gaels). This paper had an editorial remit that rejected any non-Christian group as alien; it made no pretences about its agenda, the front page had the word 'ALIENS' writ large beside a sweeping brush, and it outlined ten primary objectives all designed to emphasize that Ireland

---

7   Dermot Keogh, 'Irish Refugee Policy, Anti-Semitism and Nazism at the Approach of World War Two', *German-Speaking Exiles in Ireland 1933–1945*. Ed. Gisela Holfter (Rodopi, Amsterdam and New Yor, 2006), p. 70.

8   León Ó Broin, *Frank Duff* (Gill and Macmillan, Dublin, 1982), p. 63.

9   Finola Kennedy, 'Frank Duff's Search for the Neglected and Rejected', *Studies: An Irish Quarterly Review*, Vol. 91, No. 364 (Winter 2002), p. 386.

10 Ferriter, *The Transformation of Ireland*, p. 522.

11 John Cooney, *John Charles McQuaid Ruler of Catholic Ireland* (Syracuse University Press, Syracuse NY, 2000), pp. 177–178.

was a homogeneously Christian state.[12] The editorial argued that this objective could only be achieved by ensuring that 'all traders' traded 'under their actual names', in 'a state, based on Christian principals'.[13] This did not go unnoticed in the wider Jewish world, and the *Jewish Telegraphic Agency* carried a banner headline of 'Erin Gets Its First Anti-Semitic Paper', and reprinted a map from *Aontas Gadeheal* showing an Irish state where Jerusalem replaced Dublin, and Tel Aviv replaced Cork.[14]

Although the rabid anti-Semitism of Aontas Gaedheal only appealed to a minority within Irish society, its insidious and xenophobic message could sometimes slip through editorial oversight and be repeated in the mainstream press. In February 1935 the *Irish Independent* featured a report from their special correspondent in Central Europe that carried the following unqualified statement, 'the Jew is usually more nimble-witted than the German'.[15] This correspondent then proceeded to repeat the type of propaganda that was usually more associated with individuals like Charles Bewley, by informing his readership that the reports of anti-Semitic acts in Germany 'cannot be believed'.[16] However despite the generally apathetic response to the plight of Germany's Jewish citizens, the small Irish community did have its champions. Briscoe received the following letter from a fellow Irishman outraged that *Aontas Gaedheal* was even published.

> As a patriotic Irishman and a Jew fighting for the cause of our beloved country you are to be greatly admired I note that during the last week a paper was published in Dublin condemning your race. As an Irishman I have every sympathy towards those in minority and consider this scandalous outrage should be stopped immediately.[17]

---

12   *Aontas Gaedheal* was only published five times, and although it clearly appealed only to a minority belief system it made an already insecure Irish-Jewish community even more frightened. For further reading see: R. M. Douglas, *Architects of the Resurrection*: Ailtiri na Aiséirghe and the Fascist 'New Order' in Ireland (Manchester University Press, Manchester, 2009), pp. 37–40.
13   JMD, 23 June 1935.
14   *Jewish Telegraphic Agency*, 31 May 1935. (Hereafter *JTA*).
15   *II*, 27 February 1935.
16   Ibid.
17   BPNLI Ms. 26, 442 Acc. 3305, 17 May 1935.

However, the anti-Semitism exhibited by extremist publications in Ireland would soon seem of little consequence as the Nazis continued to strip the essential rights of citizenship from Germany's Jews.

The level of Nazi hatred towards German Jews did not surprise Briscoe. He was a frequent visitor to Germany throughout the early years of the decade; as well as having family there, he was also involved in a business partnership with a German beef-baron. He had invested in a Roscrea processing plant after becoming aware from his time in Germany between 1912 and 1914 that there was an insatiable demand for high-quality beef.[18] He then secured investment from a German friend of his, Hans Fasenfeld, who owned a cattle processing plant in Breman. Briscoe described Fasenfeld in the following way:

> Herr Fasenfeld was a Christian, but by no means a Nazi. While staying with him I discovered his friendship for many unfortunate Jewish people whom he helped to escape to Holland from Hitler's insane persecutions which were just getting into high gear. These things he did at considerable personal danger. Even having me in his house was a risk.[19]

This may very well have been so, however, Fassenfeld's investment in the Roscrea factory was as much a consequence of Briscoe's help in securing the backing of the Irish government for the enterprise, as a humanitarian gesture. Briscoe had apparently used his friendship with de Valera to help Fasenfeld secure a license to 'manage ... the quota of 6,000 cattle to be sent to Germany in 1933'.[20] Briscoe had spent the spring of 1934 in Berlin with Fassenfeld, and in order to get the necessary export permits, Fassenfeld and Briscoe had to negotiate with high ranking Nazi bureaucrats at the Foreign Office, and although they treated him with the utmost courtesy as a visiting politician, Briscoe was not fooled for one moment about their intent regarding German Jews.[21]

18   Briscoe and Hatch, *For the Life of Me*, p. 261.
19   Ibid.
20   O'Driscoll, *Ireland, Germany and the Nazis*, p. 103.
21   Briscoe and Hatch, *For the Life of Me*, p. 261.

Briscoe's fears for his German co-religionists were reinforced over the spring and summer of 1935 when a series of laws were introduced banning Aryan Germans from marrying 'members of alien races' on the pretext that these were 'detrimental to the German people'.[22] The Nazis had initiated the final legal step in the process of Jewish exclusion by stripping German citizenship from its Jewish population.[23] These laws collectively became known as the Nuremberg Laws, and classified Jewishness by familial lineage, based on quasi scientific degrees which started with full Jewishness before steadily becoming more draconian with half Jew and quarter Jew before the degrading term mischling was introduced for more distant ancestry.[24] This implementation of secondary status appalled Briscoe, who 'desperately begged [his] Jewish friends to flee at all costs'; however, although many chose to heed his words, many more did not and settled into the twilight zone of existing within, but not being part of German society.[25]

Those that did listen to the warnings of far-sighted individuals like Briscoe, immediately began making the necessary preparations to leave Germany; however, the implementation of the alien's act in March had an immediate impact on Jews who were attempting to gain entry visas for Ireland. One specific case seems to have particularly affected Briscoe, although it was one of only hundreds he was to receive over the next four years. He received the following request for help from a lady by the name Angela Anders on 6 April 1935, just four days before the Aliens Act was written into law.

> Dear Sir, I got your adress {sic} through a Danish lady ... who was sure of the possibilities for Jews in the Irish Free State. I am myself a Jew ... and I am trying to find a shelter anywhere. I used to be a secretary of a German corporation ... I would be very grateful to you if you could give me these informations [sic] or any other which

---

22   Peter Longerich, *Holocaust: The Nazi Persecution and Murder of the Jews* (Oxford University Press, Oxford, 2010), pp. 52–70.

23   Sarah Gordon, *Hitler, Germans, and the 'Jewish Question'* (Princeton University Press, Princeton NJ, 1984), pp. 170–174.

24   Stephen Brockmann, *Nuremberg: The Imaginary Capital* (Boydell & Brewer Limited, Woodbridge, 2006), pp. 152–154.

25   Briscoe and Hatch, *For the Life of Me*, p. 263.

might be of any use for me. As I think that you know the position on German emigration I hope that you won't mind me bothering you.[26]

This plea for help never achieved even applicant status, Briscoe understood that the alien's act meant this unfortunate lady did not have a hope of meeting the new immigration criteria. The Nazis had successfully created 'the most undesirable class of refugee imaginable', they were 'often penniless but more importantly' from the perspective of any state that might offer a temporary sanctuary, they were 'stateless' and could not return to their country of origin.[27]

The schizophrenic nature of Briscoe's life in the mid-thirties is perfectly encapsulated by his involvement in one of the more bizarre episodes of an already parochial nationalist discourse. Although he was already a central actor in the impending Jewish tragedy, he was trying to juggle this with aspects of a complicated personal business life and political career as a backbench TD. These micro-narratives were at times competing ones, where an involvement in one exposed a vulnerability in another.[28] The dichotomous aspects of his political life collided in a perfect storm in May 1935, when Briscoe and a fellow Fianna Fáil party colleague Senator Patrick Comyn were accused of using their political connections to secure the lease to 2,000 acres of the Wicklow countryside. Apparently there was a widespread belief that this region contained considerable deposits of gold-ore, and according to reports, the two men believed that by securing the mining rights they would make a financial killing.[29] It appears that Briscoe had first become aware of a potential gold mine in the early 1930s, and had over the subsequent years invested 'considerable sums of money' developing the project.[30] This statement had formed part of his testimony before a contentious Dáil Select Committee, which had been established

26 BFJITA 7/253 0, 6 April 1935.
27 O'Connor, 'Irish Government Policy', p. 83.
28 Ó Gráda, *Jewish Ireland in the Age of Joyce*, p. 190.
29 McCullagh, *The Reluctant Taoiseach*, pp. 121–122.
30 *IP*, 12 September 1935.

to investigate if the two men had used their membership of Fianna Fáil to influence the awarding of the leases.

The formation of the committee had reinforced the lingering Civil War antipathy which defined the Dáil chamber during this period. Fine Gael had nominated Patrick McGilligan, Briscoe's nemesis from the *L'Ami du Peuple* controversy of 1932, as a member, but Seán Lemass had refused this on the basis that it was McGilligan who had made the initial complaint about Briscoe and Comyn. Lemass justified this by arguing that the committee had been 'set up in the first instance to try Deputy McGilligan ... to find out if he had any foundation for his allegations'.[31] This decision precipitated a fractious confrontation between McGilligan and Lemass that dominated the Dáil debate on the process.[32] McGilligan forcefully brought forth the charge of corruption by suggesting that the 'prospecting lease ... was made to Senator Comyn and Deputy Briscoe because they were political associates of the Minister'.[33] Lemass forcefully denied McGilligan's accusation and suggested that it was 'the most disgusting motion that has ever appeared on the Order paper in this House'.[34]

In many respects the charge against Briscoe was subsumed as Lemass and McGilligan sought to inflict as much political damage on each other as possible. However some of the metaphor directed at Briscoe clearly damaged him politically, and the charge that he had secured the leases for 'personal benefit' was one of the lasting legacies of a much broader Fine Gael attack.[35] This was particularly relevant given the lingering rumours of Briscoe's financial malfeasance during the truce period preceding the Civil War. The label of profiteer was one that Briscoe found impossible to shake off, it emerged periodically, oftentimes, it must be said, as a consequence of his own somewhat naïve involvement in financial transactions/adventures. The increasingly bizarre nature of Briscoe's political experience was

31   DÉD, Vol. 57, Cols. 776–785. 25 June 1935.
32   Byrne, *Political Corruption in Ireland*, pp. 37–42.
33   DÉD, Vol. 57, Col. 744. 25 June 1935.
34   Ibid., Col. 748.
35   Ibid., Col. 769.

illuminated once more, as he appeared to seamlessly transition from the relative absurdities of a mythical gold mine to a tentative Zionist engagement.

It is clear that the events of 1935 were a pivotal point in Briscoe's Zionist evolution; his immersion in the Jewish emigration crisis had deepened as a consequence of Nazi persecution. All that being said, it was apparent that as late as November 1935 Briscoe still did not have the slightest idea of what type of engagement to pursue in order to fulfil an increasingly urgent desire to aid Germany's besieged Jews.

The first steps to remedy this state of affairs occurred after a fortuitous meeting with the Chief Rabbi, Isaac Herzog in November 1935. Herzog, the former leader of the Leeds Jewish community, was aware that the larger British Jewish community was far more active in the attempted rescue of their German co-religionists than the smaller and less vocal Irish one. Consequently he suggested to Briscoe that perhaps his future endeavours might be best served by making contact with a British organization.[36] He proceeded to initiate contact with Neville Laski, the president of the Board of Deputies of British Jews (BDBJ) on Briscoe's behalf.[37] The response was instantaneous, Herzog received a reply the following day from Laski's secretary saying that 'he would be delighted ... to dine' with Briscoe 'on the evening of the 26th' of November.[38] Given Laski's immediate response, it seems clear that Briscoe was already known to influential British Jews, which was perhaps not surprising given that his unique status as Ireland's only Jewish politician had been widely reported in the global Jewish press.[39]

---

36   Stephen E. C. Wendhorst, *British Jewry, Zionism and the Jewish State, 1936–1956* (Oxford University Press, Oxford, 2012), pp. 50–55.
37   BFJITA 7/253 0, 13 November 1935.
38   Ibid., 14 November 1935.
39   For further reading see: Stuart A. Cohen, 'Anglo-Jewish responses to Anti-Semitism', in Jehuda Reinharz (ed.), *Living with Anti-Semitism: Modern Jewish Responses* (Brandeis University Press, Dartmouth NH, 1987), pp. 90–94. David Ceserani, 'The Politics of Anglo-Jewry Between the Wars', in Daniel J. Elazar (ed.), *Authority, Power and Leadership in the Jewish polity: Cases and Issues* (University Press of America, Lanham MD, 1991), pp. 145–150.

From Laski's perspective the possibility of establishing a relationship with a Jewish politician with access to influential policy makers in his native land was bound to be of interest. It appears that Briscoe was just as eager to establish a dialogue, he accepted the invitation with alacrity, and only confirmed his status by requesting a different date for the meeting, as he 'urgently' needed 'to be in Dublin' on the proposed date for a governmental meeting.[40] This was a clever strategic move by Laski, and his initial decision to cultivate a relationship with Briscoe turned out to be a profitable one that would lead to an official audience in Dáil Éireann by de Valera.[41] However, if the relationship clearly benefitted Laski, the same cannot be said from Briscoe's perspective; the evidence suggests that he found the relationship a frustrating experience. Over the spring of 1936, he slowly realized his burgeoning Zionist vision was incompatible with the BDBJ political philosophy, which favoured maintaining the immigration status quo in Palestine.[42] This was confirmed in a secret memorandum presented to the British Cabinet as far back as 1934.

> I, and the Under-Secretaries during my absence, have had most useful and helpful talks with Mr Laski and Mr Lionel Cohen, Chairman and Legal Chairman of the Jewish Board of Deputies on this subject. They regard it as reasonable; indeed they made the same proposal themselves.[43]

It was clear that Briscoe was increasingly unsatisfied with the BDBJ perspective on a potential Jewish state, a position that slowly manifested as the organization's collusion with the British government to prevent 'illegal' Jewish 'immigration' to Palestine emerged.[44] It is also clear that Briscoe was initially unaware of this stance; however, if he had explored the underlying BDBJ philosophy, he may very well have realized far earlier that under Laski's presidency the organization was in fact anti-Zionist in thought and application, with a policy that reflected what was in the best interests of

---

40 BFJITA 7/253 0, 18 November 1935.
41 *JTA*, 2 December 1936.
42 Briscoe and Hatch, *For the Life of Me*, pp. 258–264.
43 TNA CAB/24/248, April 1934.
44 Ibid.

British Jewry instead of their persecuted German co-religionists.[45] This was perhaps not surprising when the elitist demographic profile of the organization is examined; it consisted of pillars of the Anglo-Jewish community who were Anglophile culturally as well as politically.[46] On every level this would have offended Briscoe's sensibilities; he had already confronted the might of the British Empire to secure the freedom of his beloved homeland, and if he had been aware that Laski had co-operated to exclude Jews from the British-controlled Mandate he would have been appalled.

Yet even though he had clearly started to seek an external engagement, it did not mean he had abandoned efforts to secure visas for German-Jewish immigrants to Ireland. It is clear that the emotional, yet fruitless appeal from Angela Anders in April had deeply affected him, and subsequently prompted him to adopt a proactive approach to the problem of making sure any potential refugee could not be depicted as a financial burden on the state. This approach was grounded in circumnavigating the restrictions by depicting potential immigrants as having a unique skill-set that no Irish citizen did. In order to further this objective, he started to contact acquaintances and constituents in the manufacturing industries to see if they would employ German Jewish craftsmen.

In December 1935 he wrote the following letter to the managing director of Green and Sons, a Dublin industrial concern, on behalf of an individual named Meidner.

> Mr Meidner has had a chat with me and as a result ... I wrote, as per enclosed copy, to the Department of Industry and Commerce. Mr Meidner is very keen on getting a permit enabling him to be employed in your concern and would be prepared to assist you develop new lines-One of which he mentioned to me and which appears

---

45 Stuart A. Cohen, 'Anglo-Jewish Response to Antisemitism', pp. 90–94.
46 For further reading see: David Cesarani, 'The Politics of Anglo-Jewry Between the Wars', in Daniel J. Elazar (ed.), *Authority, Power and Leadership in the Jewish Polity Cases and Issues* (University Press of America, Lanham Ma, 1991), pp. 148–150. Stephen E. C. Wendehorst, *British Jewry, Zionism and the Jewish State, 1936–1956* (Oxford University Press, Oxford, 2012), pp. 51–54.

to be a good one, since practically all of the raw materials required are used by you in the ordinary source of your business.[47]

Once Briscoe had made overtures to a potential employer and secured a job commitment, he then made as strong a case as possible to the Department of Industry and Commerce. In Meidner's case, he stressed three specific aspects of his application: he had unique skills, he would not be a burden on the state and he had the potential to create employment.

Providing he received a permit to be engaged, he could add to their existing lines of manufacture or, failing this, he would be prepared to get Irish Nationals to finance him ... I believe that if the application for a permit is favourably decided on for the purpose of being employed ... it would add to the number of their employees.[48]

Despite Briscoe's desperate attempts, the department rejected his argument and decided that Meidner did not meet the requirements, stating that 'the Minister is not prepared to agree to the issue of a permit in this case'.[49] By this point in time it was clear that Briscoe was not going to successfully secure even a small percentage of the required entry visas to the Irish state for his fellow Jews. It was therefore apparent that if he was going to remain an active participant in the search for a solution to the Nazi-propelled emigration crisis, then it would have to be as an external Jewish actor.

By the spring of 1936 Briscoe and Herzog were intensifying their efforts to secure refugee status for German Jews. The pressure that Briscoe was experiencing is evident from an ongoing correspondence with the chief rabbi that took place in 1936. This dialogue had a distinct pattern, it is clear that Herzog was oftentimes the first contact point for German Jews who were desperately trying to escape. When he received these entreaties, he passed them onto Briscoe in a series of emotive pleas imploring him to do everything in his power to secure refugee status for these people. The following letter is one example in this sequence.

47 RBPP, 31 December 1935.
48 Ibid.
49 Ibid., 17 February 1936.

Dear Mr Briscoe, Kindly note the contents of the enclosed letter [and?] your enquiries will of course be made on the [... wishes?] "ganz allge mein"? in general terms
without mention of name. I should feel obliged if you would kindly let me know
the results of your enquiries. Perhaps you might save me the trouble in my weak
state of health and reply direct to that unfortunate brother Jew in Nazi Germany?[50]

The emotional pressure that Herzog exerted would over time inevitably
extract a high price as Briscoe's unswerving commitment to Fianna Fáil
strained against the desperate plight of his German co-religionists. This
emotional pressure is apparent in Herzog's choice of phrase; he emphasized his 'weak state of health' and suggests that Briscoe respond directly
'to that unfortunate brother Jew in Nazi Germany'.[51] This is not a critique
of Herzog's actions; given the terrible persecution of Germany's Jews it
is perfectly understandable. He had become increasingly vocal about the
plight of his co-religionists, and he expressed his fears in a 1936 speech
on Yom Kippur (Day of Atonement), the most solemn day in the Jewish
liturgical calendar.

When one reviewed the present state of affairs in so far as they affected the Jewish
people, gloom in its very widest sense starred them in the face ... In Poland the plight
of three and a half millions of Jews was appalling in the extreme ... they were made
to suffer from the poisonous darts of Jew-hatred and Jew-baiting. In Germany the
Jewish position was going from bad to worse and systematic efforts were increasingly
made to make existence impossible for the 500,000 Jews still remaining there ... Alas!
the plague of Jew-hatred, the most wicked and at the same time the most senseless
phenomenon in this age of enlightenment was spreading.[52]

The tidal wave of European anti-Semitism Herzog was so terrified of
had consequences for the Irish state, which already had the Blueshirts, but
now manifested in a plethora of smaller fascist groups like 'the pro-Axis'
Craobh na hAiséirghe (Branch of the Resurrection).[53] Although these
groups were in the broadest possible sense fringe movements, they were the

50 RBPP, 16 June 1936.
51 Ibid.
52 *IT*, 28 September 1936.
53 Wood, *Britain, Ireland and the Second World War*, p. 73.

cause of a considerable amount of governmental concern. To this end, the Department of Justice was resolute in its determination to closely monitor the activities of these groups, and tasked the Garda Special Branch and G2, the military intelligence unit of the Irish army, to place them under close surveillance.[54]

One of the more ardent fascist supporters was Briscoe's old nemesis from the Dublin Corporation chamber, the Fine Gael TD Paddy Belton, who in August 1936, had founded the Irish Christian Front as a pro-Franco support group, in response to the success of the anti-clerical republican side in the Spanish Civil War, a state of affairs that had whipped a conservative Catholic Irish demographic into a frenzy.[55] This had been fermented by a series of lurid articles in the *Irish Independent* depicting the republican forces as priest-murdering atheists intent on desecrating Catholic Spain:

> Vivid accounts of their experiences in Spain were given by Mr H. L. Kerney, Saorstat Minister to Spain and his assistant, Miss M. Donnelly ... Miss Donnelly said that before the destruction of the great state of Our Lord outside Madrid, the inscription on it, "I am the Redeemer of the World," had place under it, "You believe that." Pictures appeared in the Irish Independent on Monday last showing a firing squad of "Reds" shooting at this statue, and the scene after the sacrilege had been completed, showing the ruined statuary.[56]

As the ICF President, Belton orchestrated a venomous anti-communist campaign that professed 'to stand against the crimes of Godless capitalism', a strategy that inevitably focused on the prevailing belief that Jews were the prime ideological force behind this assault on Christendom.[57]

---

54   NAI JUS/2011/25/714 (Garda File) and I/MA/G2/x/0040 (Military Intelligence File). For perhaps the single most informative examination of G2 see Maurice Walsh, *G2 in Defence of Ireland: Irish Military Intelligence, 1918–1945* (Collins Press, Cork, 2010).

55   R. A. Stradling, *The Irish and the Spanish Civil War, 1936–39: Crusades in Conflict* (Manchester University Press, Manchester, 1999), pp. 6–22.

56   *II*, 22 August 1936.

57   Keogh, *Jews in Twentieth-Century Ireland'*, p. 107.

The pressure on Briscoe and Herzog was reinforced by a Dáil discourse that at times was overtly anti-Semitic; Belton was whipping a conservative Catholic Irish population into a frenzy. In March 1937 under the pretext of querying Fianna Fáil industrial policy, his anti-Semitic agenda was quickly exposed.[58] He posed the following question, 'what' does 'industrialisation in this country really' mean? However, before any Fianna Fáil deputy even had the opportunity to respond, he answered it himself by arguing that 'it means that we are handing this country over to a gang of international Jews'.[59]

When a Fianna Fáil deputy finally got an opportunity to respond to Belton's anti-Semitic remarks, it was Briscoe's constituency colleague Thomas Kelly who labelled the comments as 'Rubbish'.[60] The two men proceeded to engage in a confrontational debate, before Belton accused the government of implementing an industrial policy that allowed 'these international Jews' to prosper on 'the sweat of the Irish people'.[61] As the debate continued it was evident that Belton's real target was not international Jewry, but recently arrived Jewish immigrants whom he labelled 'undesirable aliens' and 'outcasts' from abroad, before bemoaning the fact that they were 'getting full citizenship rights'.[62]

Seán MacEntee, the Minister for Finance and future Tánaiste (Deputy to the Taoiseach), entered the debate and injected an air of reality to the proceedings by insightfully asking Belton if the many millions of Irish emigrants who had left these shores seeking refuge from various forms of persecution, were not also 'outcasts'.[63] Conforming to type, Belton reiterated the stereotypical notion of the Jew as a financial parasite by comparing their supposed freeloading to the work ethic of the Irish emigrant. He

58 Cotter, 'Anti-Semitism and Irish Political Culture, 1932–1945', pp. 12–14.
59 DÉD, Vol. 65, Col. 1359, 4 March 1937. This is a possible reference to Seán Lemass' policy of granting visas if they established manufacturing concerns that offered employment to Irish citizens. See section 4.5.
60 Ibid.
61 Ibid. Col. 1360.
62 Ibid.
63 DED, Vol. 65, Col, 1360. 4 March 1937.

asked MacEntee if he was seriously comparing the Jew to 'the Irishman who, no matter what country he goes into, is prepared to take off his coat and work'.[64] MacEntee's reply showed a real and relatively rare empathy with the small number of German Jews who had successfully secured alien status, by commenting that 'the village of Nazareth has at least as much claims on humanity as Deputy Belton's birthplace'.[65] It appeared that this put-down did not bother Belton as he ignored MacEntee's biblical allusion and continued his pejorative attack on Ireland's recently arrived Jewish industrialists, by suggesting that they had a vice-like grip on the 'commerce' of the nation, having firstly taken control of 'industry'.[66]

Earlier in the same Dáil session, Paddy Ruttledge, the Minister for Justice, had given a precise breakdown of recent immigration figures; he had told the Chamber that as of 1 March 1937 the total number of resident aliens was '329', of these '70' were German, '55' were Czechoslovakian, '13' were Austrian, '7' were Polish and '7' were Russian.[67] It seems highly unlikely that Jews would have formed part of the 13-strong Chinese community, or indeed that the single Luxembourger was a Jewish immigrant.[68] When the evidence is examined, Belton's accusations are all the more fallacious; however, they are illustrative of the hostile anti-Semitic environment in which Briscoe was conducting his immigration campaign.

This was reinforced by the anti-Semitic rhetoric of Fr. Dennis Fahey, who sought to once again highlight the supposed linkages between Freemasonry and Jewish-Bolshevism as part of a satanic plot against the Catholic Church.[69] It has already been established that Fahey's virulent type of anti-Semitic invective only appealed to a minority group who were already predisposed to this bigoted worldview.[70] However, despite the fact

64   Ibid.
65   DÉD, Vol. 65, Col. 1360. 4 March 1937.
66   Ibid., Col. 1361.
67   Ibid., Col. 1228. 4 March 1937.
68   Ibid.
69   Whyte, *Church and State*, pp. 72–73.
70   Louise Fuller, *Irish Catholicism Since 1950: The Undoing of a Culture* (Gill and Macmillan, Dublin, 2004), pp. 7–8.

that Fahey's diatribes were unrepresentative of even the most conservative Catholic worldview, they terrified the small Jewish community who were already feeling increasingly vulnerable, as Nazi persecution approached a horrendous climax.

This concern is perfectly understandable when Fahey's public commentary is examined:

> Calvary … resulted from the clash between the outlook of the Jewish leaders and that of Christ, and the Jews programme of opposition to the supernatural Messiah continued … They regarded the French Revolution and the Reformation as serious steps in their advance, giving them dual citizenship. The Church, although condemning acts of violence against the Jews, and respecting their liberty of conscience and the freedom of their cult, strove always to keep Christians from contact with them. The Jews had endeavoured to use Russia as a lever to impose Communism on Europe.[71]

Fahey's public pronouncements were appearing at precisely the same time as de Valera was preparing to replace the 1922 constitution with one that reflected his personal worldview. On 11 January 1937, the third and final draft of the proposed new constitution entered the public domain despite the best efforts of all involved to keep it secret.[72] It included Article 44.1.3., an attempt by de Valera to broaden, but not diminish, the Christian ethos of the state.

> The State also recognises the Church of Ireland, the Presbyterian Church in Ireland, the Methodist Church in Ireland, the Religious Society of Friends in Ireland, as well as the Jewish Congregations and the other religious denominations existing in Ireland at the date of coming into operation of this Constitution.[73]

De Valera had to approach this issue with caution; he was aware that a sizeable percentage of the population maintained that Ireland was a de-facto

---

71   *IT*, 15 February 1937.
72   Dermot Keogh and Andrew McCarthy, *The Making of the Irish Constitution 1937: Bunreacht Na HÉireann* (Mercier Press, Cork, 2007), pp. 92–93.
73   http://www.taoiseach.gov.ie/eng/Historical_Information/The_Constitution [accessed 19 September 2015].

Catholic country, and that any group outside of this homogeneity was, and would remain, an alien presence.[74]

When the constitution was finally ratified in a referendum held on 1 July 1937, the same day as the General Election, Article 44.1.3. afforded the small and increasingly frightened Irish Jewish community a sense of security that was rapidly disappearing from European Jewish life. There is no doubt that Briscoe realized the importance of the new constitution for Irish Jews even though he acknowledged and welcomed the fact that Ireland was a Catholic country.[75] He did however deem it vitally important that minority faiths were accorded constitutional recognition.[76] This is understandable given the fact that the Nazis had stripped German Jews of their citizenship in the 1935 Nuremberg Laws, and fascist Italy was in the process of drawing up the Racial Manifesto that would disenfranchise Italian Jews in 1938.[77] Therefore in the context of the anti-Semitic moment, the new constitution's guarantee to its Jewish citizens of religious liberty was something the Irish state could be proud of.[78] The reality is of course that it was in many respects merely symbolic and would have effectively done nothing to protect Irish Jews from Nazi persecution if there had been an Axis invasion, however, that is immaterial to the fact that the clause was included.

While it is evident that Briscoe welcomed the inclusion of the article, the fact that he sought an external legal analysis of the constitution supports the proposition that he was not prepared to take it at face value. In this context his choice of counsel was interesting; he looked to America

74   Elizabeth Keane, *An Irish Statesman and Revolutionary: The Nationalist and Internationalist Politics of Seán MacBride* (I. B. Tauris, London, 2006), pp. 75–81.
75   O'Connor, 'Irish Government Policy', pp. 107–113.
76   Briscoe and Hatch, *For the Life of Me*, pp. 253–254.
77   For further reading see: Longerich, *Holocaust*, pp. 29–70. And Susan Zuccotti, *The Italians and the Holocaust Persecution Rescue & Survival* (University of Nebraska Press, Lincoln NE, 1987), pp. 28–51.
78   Joseph Lee, 'The Irish Constitution of 1937', in Seán Hutton and Paul Stewart (eds.), *Ireland's Histories Aspects of State, Society and Ideology* (Routledge, London, 1991), p. 83.

where he had long-standing and prominent contacts in the Irish and Jewish communities. He had met Algernon I. Nova, a prominent Jewish member of the judiciary, on one of his frequent trips to America, and it appears that they had developed a close enough relationship for Nova to visit him in Dublin in the summer of 1937 where Briscoe gave him a draft copy of the new constitution and asked for his legal opinion. However, it was a number of months before Nova responded, but when he did, he described it as 'a document' that was 'well prepared', and one that 'fully covers all that which could be within the contemplation of humans interested in democratic government'.[79] Nova expanded on his legal reasoning to Briscoe by praising the constitution as a fine example of democratic principles, and said that he was more than impressed with the conditions that Irish Jews enjoyed.

> Permit me also to embrace this opportunity by saying that I learned much from my conversation with you, more particularly as to how the Jew is cared for in your country. It is one of the few havens that the Jew has.[80]

Nova finished by including a fulsome praise for the government's policy regarding Jewish education.

> The subsidy on the part of the Government of your Hebrew school is one outstanding feature that I have spoken about on many occasions since I have come back home. There is so much more that I would like to write, but time does not permit.[81]

Nova's legal interpretation of the constitution was a great relief to Briscoe, however, although that is undoubtedly true, Briscoe's choice of Nova as a legal advisor was an interesting one. At the same time that he was fulsomely praising the constitution and the position of Jews in Irish society, Nova was actually under Federal investigation for owing more than $400,000 to various debtors.[82] It would eventually transpire that he had links to Frank Costello, the notorious New York Mafioso, who in the 1930s

79   BFJITA 7/253 0, 29 November 1937.
80   Ibid.
81   Ibid.
82   *New York Times*, 10 March 1938. (Hereafter *NYT*).

and 1940s, presided over 'one of the most openly corrupt periods in the city's history'.[83] Of course this has nothing whatsoever to do with his legal abilities; it does however, indicate that Briscoe was acquainted with some interesting individuals.

If Briscoe had concerns about the ramifications of the constitution for his fellow Jewish citizens, he also had more prosaic ones. De Valera decided that the constitutional referenda would be held simultaneously with the general election. For Fianna Fáil the two results aroused a contrasting reaction. The referendum to replace the 1922 Constitution with de Valera's new version was passed by 685,105 to 526,945 votes which was warmly received by the party faithful.[84] However, the result of the election was a shock for the Fianna Fáil grassroots activists, as its share of the popular vote decreased by nearly 4.5 per cent, despite party activists fighting a frenetic campaign.[85] The party retained power with support from the Labour Party, but was nevertheless shaken out of a complacency that had led many deputies to believe that all they had to do to be elected was to actually stand.[86] Briscoe's personal electoral performance reflected that of the party, and his percentage of the popular vote continued a steady decline that had begun in 1933. The 1933 election had seen Briscoe secure 8.05 per cent of the vote, down from a high of 10.31 per cent in 1932; this downward trend had continued, and in the 1937 election he secured just 5.81 per cent, a drop of nearly 50 per cent since 1932.[87]

Briscoe's decreased vote was the result of a number of factors. Firstly, he was increasingly absent from his constituency in Dublin South as his refugee and embryonic Zionist engagement became ever-more time consuming. This was reinforced by parochial constituency concerns, which demanded attention to the small issues of daily urban Dublin life. Housing and job issues were the dominant issue for his voting base, and it most certainly

83   *New York Magazine*, 6 January 1975. (Hereafter *NYM*).
84   www.environ.ie/en/LocalGovernment/Voting/Referenda/Publications Documents/FileDownload.1894,en.
85   Sinnott, *Irish Voters Decide*, pp. 100–102.
86   Lee, *Politics and Society*, pp. 210–212.
87   www.ElectionsIreland.org/?1541

did not help when Briscoe was not there to facilitate them. Secondly, it has to be acknowledged that he was conducting his electioneering against the backdrop of an increased Irish and global anti-Semitic ethos. This secondary aspect was unique to Briscoe, and given the overt linkages that had been drawn between communism and its supposed Jewish command structure, it is only logical to infer that his decreasing electoral popularity was reinforced by the fact that the 1930s was the most manifestly anti-Semitic decade of the century so far.

So given the anti-Semitic upsurge, it was no surprise that Briscoe's increasingly visible involvement in the Jewish emigration crisis would impact his electoral effectiveness in a conservative, almost universally homogeneously Catholic voting enclave. This had become clear during the election when he had had to fight a campaign against the backdrop of an unprecedented level of anti-Semitic political innuendo. Charles Fagan, a former Blueshirt, was not slow to publically repeat Paddy Belton's anti-Semitic Dáil commentary of January 1937. The *Irish Press* carried a report where he promised that if he was re-elected he would make sure 'that Jews and other foreigners' would no longer be allowed 'to exploit the people'.[88] This was reinforced in civil society by fringe organizations like the small but vociferous Irish Christian Rights Protection Association (ICRPA), which, led by the overtly anti-Semitic George Griffin, was intent on highlighting the Jewish threat.[89]

Throughout the summer/autumn of 1937 the ICRPA had been conducting a vociferous anti-Semitic campaign that climaxed when Griffin targeted Dublin's Jewish community in the organization's political manifesto. This document was distributed around the streets of Dublin at precisely the same time that the Nazis were codifying the Nuremburg racial laws of 1935 and completing the disenfranchisement of German Jews.[90] Given the fact that a core tenet of Nazi anti-Semitic policy was predicated on turning Germany's Gentile population into a community that was willing to

88   *IP*, 19 June 1937.
89   O'Driscoll. *Ireland, Germany and the Nazis*, p. 253.
90   Longerich, *Holocaust*, pp. 95–122.

inform on their Jewish fellow citizens, one of the most loathsome clauses must surely have been the request for the citizens of Ireland to follow suit and turn on their non-Christian neighbours who were running small businesses.[91] The were asked 'to let us have a list of your trading firms in this city, other cities and towns in Ireland, and places abroad'; it was a truly sinister document, echoing as it did the Nazi expectation that Gentile German citizens would hand over their Jewish neighbours.[92] The fact that Griffin's anti-Semitic message was ignored by the vast majority of fair-minded Irish people suggests it only appealed to a minority; however, it is also clear that if the Nazis had ever been in a position to implement their virulently anti-Semitic racial policies in Ireland, then there would have been a body of willing collaborators to aid them in their endeavours, just as there was in the rest of occupied Europe.[93]

The far more common response to Griffin's obnoxious campaign was similar to the one expressed by some of Briscoe's Fianna Fáil colleagues who were quick to mount a staunch defence of Dublin's Jewish community.

> We condemn the activities of a secret ring styled the Irish Christian Protective [sic] Association and call upon the Government immediately to declare the Association illegal. The people of Dublin have always been the most tolerant of people and we call upon them to ignore the scurrilous propaganda directed against the Jewish people in our midst.[94]

This was a laudable statement, and it did go a long way to dampening down, though not entirely eliminating, the more overt displays of public anti-Semitism and illustrates that although the majority Irish population did indeed subscribe to the religious anti-Semitism of the Catholic Church,

---

91   Robert Gellately, *The Gestapo and German Society: Enforcing Racial Policy 1933–1945* (Clarendon Press, Oxford, 1991), pp. 130–158.

92   *IT*, 30 November 1937.

93   Wood, *Britain, Ireland and the Second World War*, pp. 72–74.

94   Cyrus Adler and Henrietta Szold (eds.), *American Jewish Year Book, Vol. 40* (American Jewish Committee, Miami, 1938), p. 170. It has proved impossible to attribute this statement to the relevant Fianna Fáil Cumann. The only source that I have been able to locate remains the Adler-Szold one.

they were not prepared to countenance the extreme anti-Semitic policies of the ICRPA.

The government were also determined to stamp out any nascent anti-Semitic mass movement, and issued a statement emphatically denying 'that there is any organized anti-Semitic movement in Éire'.[95] Briscoe quickly followed suit issuing a statement supporting the government position, he contacted the *Jewish Telegraphic Agency* (a wire service established in 1917 to report on Jewish affairs) and argued that Irish anti-Semitism was 'so insignificant' that 'the Government did not deem it worthy of notice'.[96] This was a clever tactic by Briscoe, and it paid dividends in terms of shoring up a rapidly dwindling personal Fianna Fáil vote which might have disapproved of his burgeoning Zionist activities. It was evident that this core constituency had been deserting Briscoe over the previous five years; however, it was also clear that while they may have subliminally absorbed the anti-Semitic ethos of the moment, they were not prepared to embrace it as overtly as Fagan might have imagined. Briscoe received the following letter from an exiled London party member the week before the election; as well as containing a donation for the electoral expenses of the party, the writer pointed the finger of blame squarely at Fine Gael telling Briscoe that 'I think anti-Semitism is creeping into Cosgrave's crowd, all the more reason why they should be dormant-it would be shameful if Eire were to emulate the Huns & the other decadent European slugs'.[97]

On 7 July, less than a week after the dual election/constitutional referendum in Dublin, Lord Peel (who had been appointed to investigate the 1936 Arab riots in the Palestine mandate) addressed the opening of the British Royal Commission on Palestine in London with the following words:

> Half a loaf is better than no bread is a peculiarly English proverb; and, considering the attitude which both the Arab and Jewish representatives adopted in giving evidence before us, we think it improbable that either party will be satisfied at first

95 Quoted in Keogh, *Twentieth-Century Ireland Nation and State*, p. 129.
96 *JTA*, 5 January 1938.
97 BPNLI Ms. 26,449 Acc.3305, 27 June 1937.

sight with the proposals we have submitted for the adjustment of their rival claims. For partition means that neither will get what it wants.[98]

Briscoe had until relatively recently been disengaged from the global Zionist world, however, by the time Lord Peel made his address, he had developed an insightful awareness that a Jewish homeland in the Palestine Mandate was essential, especially if the vulnerable Jews of Eastern-Europe were going to be saved.[99] Briscoe immediately understood that this objective faced its greatest threat from the tentative conclusions of the 1936 British Royal Commission as defined by Peel's opening statement. The commission established under the chairmanship of Lord Peel, was a response to the wave of Arab violence sweeping across the Mandate, which had started in April 1936.[100] There appeared to be three underlying reasons for the wave of unrest; the Arab leadership had demanded that the British implement '(a) total cessation of Jewish immigration into Palestine; (b) prohibit all sales of Arab land to Jews; and (c) the granting of independence to Palestine and the ending of the Mandate'.[101] The British response to these demands was the setting up of yet another commission to investigate the demographic and cultural imperatives behind the revolt; this did not address the Arab demands, and Palestine descended into an anarchic state.

The imposition of martial law had infuriated Jabotinsky and the Revisionists, and the commission's ultimate conclusion on Palestine's future drove them to the edge of despair. In response to wave after wave of inter-communal violence, the commission had tentatively concluded that if any

98   Itmar Rabinovich and Jehuda Reinharz (eds.), *Israel in the Middle East: Documents and Readings on Society, Politics and Foreign Relations, Pre-1948 to the Present* (Brandeis University Press, Lebanon NH, 2008), p. 44.

99   Ezra Mendelsohn, *The Jews of East Central Europe Between the World Wars* (Indiana University Press, Bloomington IN, 1983), pp. 70–82.

100 For further reading see: Tom Bowden, 'The Politics of the Arab Rebellion in Palestine 1936–1939', *Middle Eastern Studies*, Vol. 11, No. 2 (May 1975), pp. 147–174. Norman Anthony Rose, 'The Arab Rulers and Palestine, 1936: The British Reaction', *The Journal of Modern History*, Vol. 44, No. 2 (June 1972), pp. 213–231.

101 Michael J. Cohen, 'Secret Diplomacy and Rebellion in Palestine, 1936–1939', *International Journal of Middle East Studies*, Vol. 8, No. 3 (July 1977), p. 379.

type of peace was possible, it could only occur if both communities had their own state.

> Manifestly the problem cannot be solved by giving either the Arabs or the Jews all they want. The answer to the question "Which of them in the end will govern Palestine?" must surely be "Neither" ... But, while neither race can justly rule all Palestine, we see no reason why, if it were practicable, each race should not rule part of it.[102]

The Revisionists ideologically rejected the very notion of a partitioned Palestine; of equal and more pressing concern however, was the effective cessation of Jewish immigration.

> In view of the foregoing considerations we advise that there should now be a definite limit to the annual volume of Jewish immigration. We recommend that Your Majesty's government should lay down a "political high level" of Jewish immigration of all categories. This high level should be fixed for the next five years at 12,000 per annum, and in no circumstances during that period should more than that number be allowed into the country in any one year.[103]

Jabotinsky argued that if partition was imposed, it would leave a minority Jewish population, 'facing an elemental calamity, a kind of social earthquake'.[104]

It is clear that this type of rhetoric would have appealed to Briscoe; as well as being Jewish, he had not forgotten the Irish state's own partition tragedy after the Anglo-Irish agreement in 1921. He believed that partition had been a disaster for the Irish state, and concluded almost immediately that if the British proposal was accepted it would also be a disaster for the Jews of Palestine. He was, and remained, a resolute anti-partitionist, and could not help but draw a parallel between the fate of the discriminated minority Catholic-nationalists of the 6 counties, and the potential fate of a minority Jewish population surrounded by an Arab majority in Palestine.[105]

---

102 Royal Commission on Palestine, p. 375.
103 Ibid., p. 306.
104 Ibid., 'Evidence Before the Palestine Royal Commission', p. 130.
105 Briscoe and Hatch, *For the Life of Me*, pp. 223–224. 255–256. 264–268.

Although it was only the start of his Zionist engagement, Briscoe was observing some of the most profound policy decisions of the pre-war Zionist world. He had closely observed Jabotinsky reject the partition proposal, and fully endorsed the revisionist position however, as the commission continued to hear submissions it became clear that even the prospect of a partitioned Palestine was receding, and that 'British policy towards the Mandate', was changing.[106] As the dark clouds of war approached, the British commitment to a two-state solution was deferred, and both the pro and anti-partitionist Zionist factions realized that Arab concerns were increasingly the deciding factor in policy decisions.[107] This was eventually confirmed by the Secretary of State for the Colonies, Malcolm MacDonald, when he informed the Cabinet that if partition gave even partial control of the Mandate to the Yishuv:[108]

> We shall be playing into the hands of those Egyptian and Arab politicians who are our enemies; the situation will be cunningly exploited to our grave disadvantage by the propaganda of those in Europe who are hostile to us.[109]

The Commission had watched with increasing concern at the rise of a pan-Arab nationalism, this concern had only increased when evidence that these groups had looked to Nazi Germany 'for diplomatic and material support', was uncovered.[110] Realpolitik quickly took precedence over any previous commitments, and dictated that now was not the right time to open the borders to mass Jewish immigration, a move that would only

106 T. G. Fraser, 'A Crisis of Leadership: Weizmann and the Zionist Reactions to the Peel Commission's Proposals, 1937–8', *Journal of Contemporary History*, Vol. 23, No. 4 (October 1988), pp. 658–659.
107 Michael J. Cohen, 'Direction of Policy in Palestine, 1936–45', *Middle Eastern Studies*, Vol. 11, No. 3 (October 1975), p. 237.
108 The definitive study of MacDonald remains: Clyde Sanger, *Malcolm MacDonald: Bringing an End to Empire* (McGill-Queen's University Press, Montreal, 1995).
109 TNA CAB/24/282, 18 January 1939. MacDonald to British Cabinet.
110 G. Sheffer, 'British Colonial Policy-Making towards Palestine (1929–1939)', *Middle Eastern Studies*, Vol. 14, No. 3 (October 1978), pp. 308–310.

inflame an already volatile Middle East. British policy quickly became predicated on retaining the status quo, and MacDonald recommended to the Cabinet that 'following the breakdown of the scheme for Partition' the government would resume responsibility for 'the whole of Palestine'.[111] In many respects this suited Jabotinsky; it would allow the Revisionists to argue that 'British policy' was 'anti-Zionist', and as such it would facilitate a more confrontational line of resistance to their continued presence in the Mandate.[112]

The Royal Commission on Palestine had not gone unnoticed in Dublin; this is not altogether surprising, partition was not a theoretical proposition for de Valera, who, unlike Jabotinsky, had been confronting the political and social ramifications of a partitioned country since 1921. This was evident from de Valera's 1937 League of Nations speech; although the focus was on the British plan for a two-state solution to the Palestine problem, he availed of the opportunity to critique the concept of partition itself. In a contentious and wide-ranging debate, de Valera, as the only leader of a partitioned state, opaquely referred to the Irish situation by asserting that 'partition is not the solution. It is the cruelest wrong that could be done to any people'.[113]

De Valera's methodology was as bold as it was ambitious; by using the League of Nations to highlight the fundamental injustice of a divided country, he had embraced a formerly reviled institution in order to reinforce the sovereign rights of smaller nations against the overt aggression of the big powers.[114] This position had made de Valera a recognizable presence on the global political stage, and by the time he assumed the role of President for the second time in 1935 he had become an acknowledged spokesman for the small unaligned nations of the world.[115] By defending the rights of the smaller nations at the world's highest political forum, de Valera hoped to

---

111 TNA CAB/24/282. 18 January 1939. MacDonald to Cabinet.

112 Symon, 'British Policy Toward Jewish Immigration To Palestine, 1933–1939', p. 1

113 *JTA*, 24 September 1937.

114 Patrick Keatinge, 'Ireland and the League of Nations', *Studies: An Irish Quarterly Review*, Vol. 59, No. 234 (Summer 1970), p. 141.

115 Ibid.

focus attention on the fact that Ireland was the perfect example to illustrate how a small nation's sovereignty could be undermined by the geo-political concerns of a global power.[116]

When his role as advocate for smaller nations is acknowledged, de Valera's 1937 statement on the proposed partition of Palestine to the League has to be viewed in a different light. From this perspective it is evident that it was a far more nuanced contribution laden with anti-partitionist conceptual undertones, than an outright pledge of support for the revisionist position.[117] A secret memorandum from Malcolm MacDonald to the British Cabinet supports this proposition. Reflecting on a post-address meeting he had with de Valera, he informed them that the partition of Ireland was the underlying dynamic behind de Valera's Geneva speech. MacDonald expressed the view that when de Valera had informed him of his disappointment 'that the United Kingdom Government accepted partition as the solution' to the Jewish-Arabic conflict in Palestine, it was in fact a veiled reference to the partition of Ireland.[118]

De Valera had got his point across, and it is clear that his oppositional strategy to the proposed partition of Palestine had concentrated British minds on the existing situation in Ireland. His position had also reignited age-old animosities that still existed just below the surface of nascent Anglo-Irish relations. MacDonald explained to de Valera that his critique of the proposed British two-state solution for Palestine 'had caused a great deal of ill-feeling in the United Kingdom', before adding that many of his old enemies believed that he was pursuing the policy of 'England's difficulty is Ireland's opportunity'.[119] MacDonald explained that he understood de

116   Gerard Keown, 'Taking the World Stage: Creating an Irish Foreign Policy in the 1920s', in Michael Kennedy and Joseph Morrison Skelly (eds.), *Irish Foreign Policy 1919–1966 From Independence to Internationalism* (Four Courts Press, Dublin, 2000), p. 25.
117   Colin Shindler, *The Triumph of Military Zionism Nationalism and the Origins of the Israeli Right* (I. B. Tauris, London, 2010), pp. 143–147.
118   TNA CAB/24/271, 14 October 1937.
119   Ibid.

Valera's position on partition, but framed it in the context of a developing Anglo-Irish relationship that had immeasurably improved over recent years.

> I could appreciate that he felt strongly opposed to partition, but I thought that his speech, coming at a moment when we were making a real effort to see whether we could settle some of the disputes between our two countries, had been extremely unfortunate.[120]

MacDonald continued his report to the Cabinet telling them that de Valera denied that this was so:

> He replied that he did not act at all in the spirit of "England's difficulty is Ireland's opportunity." He was opposed to that policy. If he had known that the Palestine question was coming up in the way that it did, he would certainly have let us know first that he intended to oppose partition, and would gladly have had a talk with us. He would always try to work with us in that spirit.[121]

MacDonald acknowledged that de Valera appeared to genuinely desire 'a wholehearted friendship', he was also aware that de Valera 'would rather like to get that friendship on his own terms'.[122] This was undoubtedly true, although de Valera had evolved from an irredentist position to accept that the Irish state's interests were inextricably bound to their powerful near neighbour's, he would still try and extract every conceivable advantage in their developing relationship.[123]

If de Valera was involving the Irish State in the debate on partitioning Palestine into two separate states on the biggest of global political stages, the parochial aspect of Briscoe's dual existence was perfectly illustrated when he was drawn into open warfare with Paddy Belton in a contentious Dáil debate. It had started innocently enough; however, is soon descended

120 Ibid.
121 Ibid.
122 Quoted in Lee, *Politics and Society*, p. 213.
123 Eunan O'Halpin, 'Weird Prophecies: British Intelligence and Anglo-Irish Relations, 1932–3', in Michael Kennedy and Joseph Morrison Skelly (eds.), *Irish Foreign Policy 1919–1966 From Independence to Internationalism* (Four Courts Press, Dublin, 2000), pp. 61–67.

into one with an overtly xenophobic content as Paddy Belton resurrected the anti-Semitic implication that Jews were dominating Irish commerce. Briscoe was reluctantly drawn into it when Belton asked if these profiteers were in fact the owners of 'Jewmen's factories?'.[124] He gamely responded to the slur by suggesting that 'whether the factories are controlled or owned or associated with people of my persuasion' should not be of concern, before tartly adding 'if the Deputy wants to sink to that level, the cross-roads is the place for him, not this House'.[125] So even though Briscoe was on the cusp of becoming a fully engaged Zionist activist, it was clear he still always had to be on guard in the discriminatory atmosphere of parochial Irish political culture.

Briscoe took the final step in a five year Zionist evolution in December 1937 when he was interviewed by the Revisionist Nessuit (Hebrew for Executive Council), who invited into its inner-circle 'to meet our friends and especially the Nassi' (Hebrew for President).[126] The Nessuit was aware of Briscoe and although clearly impressed by his political status, the organization needed to see if he would fit the revisionist template. From Briscoe's perspective it was yet another attempt to find an organization that he was compatible with. It was evident from his previous alliances that he had already interacted with a number of external Jewish agencies that were not philosophically or ideologically attuned to his evolving Zionist worldview. However, when the minutes of the meeting are examined they support the proposition that when he met Jabotinsky he finally believed he had met an individual he could work with.

When assessing his state of mind, this cannot be underestimated; after a fraught and negative experience as an immigration advocate, and a number of false starts, he needed a sense of positivity, and his initial meeting with Jabotinsky appears to have gone some way to fulfilling that need.

---

124   DÉD, Vol. 69, Col. 1199, 24 November 1937.
125   Ibid., Cols. 1199–1200.
126   BFJITA 7/253 0, December 1937.

We have had the pleasure of a visit from Mr Briscoe who spent a couple of days in London. He met the Nassi and I have the feeling that he has gone away with the conviction that he has found a soul-mate.[127]

If Briscoe was excited at the prospect of working with Jabotinsky, the feeling was mutual. Jabotinsky was aware that someone with Briscoe's high-profile status could gain access to senior political actors, a position that was increasingly being denied to the ever more militant revisionists, as the liberal democracies accepted the moderate representatives of the World Zionist Organisation (WZO) as the acceptable spokesmen of Zionism.[128]

It was also clear that Briscoe immediately embraced the radicalism of the revisionist plan for a mass Jewish emigration to Palestine, and his commitment was only reinforced when it became clear that Jabotinsky was also an implacable opponent of the Royal Commission's proposed plan to partition the Mandate into Jewish and Arab sectors.[129] This perfectly reflected Briscoe's own belief that emigration to Palestine was the only hope of saving Polish Jewry, and Jabotinsky's abhorrence of the partition proposal struck a deep chord in his republican psyche, which had been formed during the Irish independence struggle.

Jabotinsky had been developing his thesis for the better part of two decades. He had summarized his vision of a mass Jewish immigration when he gave evidence before the first Royal Commission on Palestine in 1929:

Mr Jabotinsky explained that there is in Eastern Europe a large area extending over several countries which he described as "a zone of incurable anti-Semitism." This zone is overcrowded by Jews, one half of whom, so Mr Jabotinsky states, must be evacuated in the next two generations.[130]

127 Ibid., 23 December 1937.
128 Myron Joel Aronoff, 'Political Polarization: Contradictory Interpretations of Israeli Reality', in Myron Joel Aronoff (ed.), *Cross-Currents in Israeli Culture and Politics* (Transaction Inc, New Brunswick NJ, 1984), pp. 2–6.
129 For further reading see: Yehuda Bauer, 'From cooperation to Resistance: The Haganah 1946', *Middle Eastern Studies*, Vol. 2, No. 3 (April 1966), pp. 182–210. Zouplna, 'Revisionist Zionism', pp. 3–27.
130 TNA CMD/3530. Vol. XVI. 675. *Report of the Commission on the Palestine Disturbances of August, 1929*, p. 109.

He explained to the Commission that his approach to solving the Jewish problem differed from the existing Zionist one. He was attempting 'to revise certain conceptions of the existing 'Zionist policy', a position that earned the organization the Revisionist sobriquet.[131]

The Zionism of the Yishuv (the existing Zionist population of Palestine) was grounded in the principle that before new Jewish migrants to Palestine made Aliyah (Hebrew for 'ascent') they would have to undergo an intensive period of training in their home state to prepare them as agricultural pioneers.[132] This would ensure that when they finally reached Palestine they would immediately and seamlessly fit into the Yishuv template. They were to be the archetypical new Jew, proud, fit and self-sufficient, and above all they would not be a financial burden to the existing community.[133] In some respects this policy complemented the existing British immigration doctrine, which envisaged that any new Jewish settlement would have to be in the context of the Mandate's ability to economically absorb them.[134] This was anathematic to Jabotinsky. His philosophy on immigration was predicated on a new concept he described as 'Humanitarian Zionism', the belief that all Jews, from the 'gifted creators' to 'the downtrodden', should be in Palestine, regardless of any potential financial implication.[135]

Jabotinsky had abandoned the socialist 'Labour movement' and its incremental approach to Jewish statehood, disparagingly labelling it a

---

131   Ibid., p. 108.
132   Michael Berkowitz, *Western Jewry and the Zionist Project 1914–1933* (Cambridge University Press, Cambridge, 1997), pp. 91–124.
133   Donna Robinson Divine, 'Zionism and the Transformation of Jewish Society', *Modern Judaism*, Vol. 20, No. 3 (October 2000), pp. 262–268.
134   Roza I. M. El-Eini, 'The Implementation of British Agricultural Policy in Palestine in the 1930s', *Middle Eastern Studies*, Vol. 32, No. 4 (October 1996), pp. 213–215.
135   Ze'ev Jabotinsky, 'Address at the Physicians and Engineers Club, Warsaw, 1936', in Mordechai Sarig (ed.), *The Political and Social Philosophy of Ze'ev Jabotinsky* (Vallentine Mitchell, London, 1999), p. 9.

process defined by 'small deeds'.[136] To Briscoe, with his history of confrontation with the British, this argument seemed perfectly logical. He had, after, all been part of a small movement that had engaged in a deed of immense magnitude, the Easter Rising, which had brought world attention to a previously insignificant Irish independence movement.

---

136   Eran Kaplan, 'A Rebel with a Cause Hillel Kook, Begin and Jabotinsky's Ideological Legacy', *Israeli Studies*, Vol. 10, No. 3 (Autumn 2005), p. 89.

CHAPTER 7

1938–1939
Political Dichotomy, Parochial Anti-Semitism and Revisionist Apex: Dublin Exclusionism and Missions to Poland, America and South Africa

The fact that Briscoe had apparently found an ideologically compatible Zionist organization should have ensured he did not experience the same frustrations that resulted from his brief alliance with the BDBJ. This certainly appeared to be the case after his first meeting with Jabotinsky, which seemed to have laid the foundations for a perfect working relationship where the Irish republican Jew could channel all his energies into saving his co-religionists through the revisionist template of Jabotinsky's Zionism. Briscoe's complex dual commitment manifested almost immediately when Jabotinsky wasted no time in exploiting Briscoe's personal connection to de Valera to facilitate an introduction.[1]

Securing a meeting with de Valera had been a priority for Jabotinsky since de Valera's anti-partitionist speech in September 1937; he believed that the Irish leader was the perfect man to highlight conceptual objections to partition not just in Ireland, but also the potential plan for co-existing, coterminous Jewish and Arab states in Palestine[2] The plan was abhorrent to Jabotinsky, who believed that if it was implemented it would completely ruin the revisionist plan for a mass Jewish emigration to Palestine.[3] He was

1   BFJITA 7/253 o, 23 December 1937.
2   Penny Sinanoglou, 'British Plans for the Partition of Palestine, 1929–1938', *The Historical Journal*, Vol. 52, No. 1 (March 2009), pp. 131–152.
3   For further reading see: Yehoyada Haim, 'Zionist attitudes toward Partition, 1937–1938', *Jewish Social Studies*, Vol. 40, No. 3–4 (Summer-Autumn 1978), pp. 303–320. Itzhak

desperate to foil the recommendation to terminate 'the present Mandate on the basis of partition', and refocus attention on the creation of a Jewish National Home as defined by the Balfour Declaration.[4]

Jabotinsky was appalled by the prospect of a two-state Palestine and was convinced that if this happened an apocalyptic fate awaited 'the tiny Jewish State', which would then be encircled 'by 10 million people with politically covetous appetites'.[5] In an attempt to appeal to sympathetic members of the British Parliament in 1937, Jabotinsky forcefully argued that self-determination for the indigenous Arab population in a partitioned two-state Palestine would 'openly encourage the proposed Arab State to join the future pan-Arab Federation'.[6] This was a clever tactical move highlighting the threat of a nascent pan-Arab nationalism; Jabotinsky perfectly read the geo-political moment. He was acutely aware that this prospect terrified the British as much as it did the revisionists, albeit for different reasons.[7]

It is therefore clear why Jabotinsky wanted to meet de Valera; he wanted to secure the support of a politician who had already successfully defied the will of the world's most powerful imperial power, Great Britain. It is also clear that Briscoe was fully supportive of Jabotinsky's ambition to meet 'the Chief', a fact that emerges when Jabotinsky's carefully prepared preparatory notes for his meeting with de Valera are examined, they contain information only Briscoe could have provided.

Briscoe introduced Jabotinsky to de Valera on 12 January 1938 in the following manner:

Galnoor, The Zionist Debates on Partition (1919–1947)', *Israeli Studies*, Vol. 14, No. 2 (Summer 2009), pp. 74–87.

4   TNA CAB/24/270. 22 June 1937. Report of the Royal Commission on Palestine, p. 380.

5   Jabotinsky, 'Memorandum to the British Members of Parliament', in Sarig (ed.), *Selected Writings*, p. 99.

6   Jabotinsky, 'Memorandum to the British Members of Parliament', in Sarig (ed.), *Selected Writings*, p. 99.

7   Michael J. Cohen, 'Direction of Policy in Palestine, 1936–1945', *Middle Eastern Studies*, Vol. 11, No. 3 (October 1975), pp. 234–240.

> Many times during these years I have had the pleasure of introducing to you Jewish visitors, but this is the first time that I introduce you to a Jewish leader who speaks also for me.[8]

He then sat back to listen as Jabotinsky made it clear in thirteen concisely articulated points that he would accept nothing less than an independent Jewish state on both sides of the River Jordan.[9] This of course had immense implications for the indigenous Arab population, and it was immediately evident that Jabotinsky had framed the revisionist demand in a way that minimized the negative impact of the anti-partitionist plan on the Arab population. Jabotinsky would have been aware from Briscoe's pre-visit advice that although de Valera despised the concept of partition, his political and social formation under British imperial rule had inculcated an abiding respect and concern for the rights of oppressed minorities.[10]

It was therefore inevitable that the fate of Palestine's Arabs under Jabotinsky's proposed plan would be a central point of discussion/contention. The analogy between the potential plight of the Arab community at the hands of new Jewish immigrants, and the existing plight of the minority Catholic community of Northern Ireland was not merely a symbolic one. When Briscoe had become aware of the British plan for Palestine he had made an immediate comparison between the existing partition of Ireland, and the proposed partition of Palestine.[11] Having the direct experience of being a legislator in a partitioned state, he believed that it was a failed

---

8   Quoted in Katz, *Lone Wolf*, p. 1598.

9   For further reading on Jabotinsky's vision of a future Jewish state see: Rachel Havrelock, *River Jordan the Mythology of a Dividing Line* (The University of Chicago Press, Detroit, 2011), pp. 12–16. Colin Shindler, *The Land Beyond Promise Israel, Likud and the Zionist Dream* (I. B. Tauris & Co Ltd, London, 2002), pp. 10–16. Sasson Sofer, *Zionism and the Foundations of Israeli Diplomacy* (Cambridge University Press, Cambridge, 1998), pp. 215–220.

10   Dermot Keogh, *Ireland And The Vatican The Politics and Diplomacy of Church-state Relations 1922–1960* (Cork University Press, Cork, 1995), 122–127.

11   Briscoe and Hatch, *For the Life of Me*, pp. 264–266.

concept that had effectively disenfranchised the Catholic nationalists of the missing Ulster counties.[12]

It is clear from Jabotinsky's notes that he addressed this potentially divisive issue emphasizing that any negative aspects of the plan for the Arabs of Palestine were minimal, while simultaneously stressing the fact that although a population transfer was inevitable, it would be undertaken with the greatest reluctance:

> Nearly one-half of the actual inhabitants of that "corner" are Arab ... I know ... therefore, the question must arise of "transferring" those Arabs elsewhere so as to make at least some room for Jewish newcomers. Even if it must be hateful for any Jews to think that the re-birth of a Jewish State should ever be twinned with such an odious suggestion of the removal of non-Jewish citizens.[13]

He reinforced the necessity for such a move by emphasizing the devastating effect that partition would have on the fate of Palestine's potential Jewish community. Jabotinsky underscored this point by reiterating the argument he had first made in an address to the 1929 Royal Commission telling de Valera that 'there is a belt of acute and incurable Jewish distress, covering Central and Eastern Europe. It contains more than 8 million Jews, who are facing annihilation unless they can go to Palestine'.[14] It was a clever opening gambit, and was clearly designed to be an emotive appeal to a man who understood the suffering of an oppressed people.

Jabotinsky further justified the potential removal of the Arab community by arguing that the creation of a Jewish state would ultimately impose 'no real hardship for the Arab race'.[15] However, he did not expand on exactly how the revisionists would achieve the whole scale removal of an entire body of people without creating a devastating destabilization of a millennia-old community. According to Briscoe's recollection, de Valera had rigorously interrogated Jabotinsky on this very point, and it appears that in response, he had cleverly drawn an analogy with the Irish population

12   Ibid., pp. 223–224.
13   Jabotinsky Files Jabotinsky Institute Tel Aviv A1-8/52, 12 January 1938. (Hereafter JFJITA).
14   Ibid.
15   Ibid.

surviving under seven centuries of British rule by asking de Valera if only 'fifty thousand' Irish people had remained in Ireland 'would you then have given up the claim of Ireland for the Irish?'[16]

Jabotinsky reinforced this emotive appeal by once again drawing the analogy between the proposed Jewish state as defined by the British two-state plan, and the existing partition of Ireland. He argued that if partition was imposed on Palestine it would leave the Jews with 'less than five per cent' of the available land, thus dealing 'a death blow' to any 'further ... Jewish' immigration'.[17] Jabotinsky was aware that partition was a very real issue for de Valera, and by highlighting the potential injustice for the minority Jewish community he was attempting to deflect attention from the very same injustice that partition would have for the Arab community.

Subsequent events show that Jabotinsky's caution was justified. He had been informed by Briscoe that de Valera had already dispatched Joe Walshe, the Secretary at the Department of External Affairs, to the region on a fact-finding mission.[18] In fact, one of the consequences of Jabotinsky's meeting with de Valera in January was Walshe's second visit to Palestine in the summer of 1938. It is clear that even though de Valera had cordially listened to Jabotinsky's argument, he had not been convinced, and had once again dispatched Walshe to assess the reality of Britain's proposal. Interestingly, when Walshe did submit a report, his recommendation only underpinned Jabotinsky's fears. He concluded that if the proposed British 'ten year' Jewish immigration moratorium was implemented, then this breathing space might allow 'the Arabs and Jews ... to come to some understanding'.[19] This flew in the face of every revisionist aspiration for a mass expansion of Palestine's Jewish population, it is clear they were not interested in reaching a détente with the Arab community.

Although the meeting between de Valera and Jabotinsky would have a number of long-term ramifications for Briscoe, it is clear that in the

16   Briscoe and Hatch, *For the Life of Me*, p. 164.
17   JFJITA A1-8/52, 12 January 1938.
18   Briscoe and Hatch, *For the Life of Me*, p. 263.
19   Crowe et al, *Documents on Irish Foreign Policy 1937–1939*, pp. 308–310.

short term it had been a boost to his flagging morale. He was euphoric after the visit had concluded, and it was clear that the meeting had had a profound effect on him. This is not surprising when the importance of the two men to his political evolution is acknowledged; he described his reaction to Shmuel Katz, a fellow revisionist in the following way: 'That to be present at the meeting between two of the great national leaders of the age, both "absolute in their idealism, their courage, their integrity and their human concern" [as] the most thrilling experience of [my] life'.[20] This was an entirely understandable reaction considering the negativity of his immigration experience over the past number of years. Briscoe's sense of wellbeing would have been reinforced when within a week of Jabotinsky's departure he received a letter of gratitude from the Nessuit in London thanking him for 'his loyal and helpful assistance'.[21]

If Briscoe was ecstatic about the visit, it is also apparent that Jabotinsky concurred, he described the meeting as 'one of the busiest days of' my 'public life' as well as being 'one of the most pleasant and memorable'.[22] His personal notes support the fact that he considered it to have been a highly successful endeavour. It is also clear that both de Valera and the Irish state had made a positive impact on him.

> My impression was one of that broadminded humanity, that chivalrous considera-
> tion for a neighbour's sorrows and ideals, and that innate simple courtesy one almost
> instinctively associates with the very atmosphere of Eire.[23]

The euphoria of Jabotinsky's visit did not last long; the terrible reality of the incremental Jewish persecution took on a personal aspect less than a week after the revisionist leader left Dublin. This time the plea for help came from a much beloved family relative, who had been an integral part of Briscoe's youthful formation in Berlin. And for the first time in his five-year immigration endeavour, Briscoe experienced the horrendous

20   Katz, Lone Wolf, p. 1598.
21   BFJITA 7/253 0, 20 January 1938.
22   JFJITA A1-4/40, 20 January 1938.
23   Ibid.

stresses that many of his fellow Irish Jews had had to contend with as his representations were met with the same callous bureaucratic indifference as the vast majority of German Jewish refugee applications had been.

In late January he received a letter from his aunt Hedwig in Berlin; this was a traumatic experience for Briscoe as his aunt had looked after him and his brother Bert when they had severed their pre-war Berlin apprenticeship with Hecht-Phieffer. It is a terribly sad letter; his aunt and his cousin Tamara were stranded in the German capital, and she was seeking her nephew's help to save their lives. Her precarious position was immediately apparent as his aunt 'urgently' requested Briscoe to obtain an 'aliens … permit' in order that she could flee Nazi Germany with her daughter.[24] This was the first in a stream of letters which became ever more frantic, these were reinforced by letters from Hedwig's sister, Briscoe's aunt Martha who lived in Wicklow after marrying 'a nephew of [his] father's named David Cherrick'.[25] However, no matter how many officials Briscoe approached, he could not gain the necessary entry visa, and with each unsuccessful intervention his aunt Martha became more concerned. This reached a climax when an increasingly agitated Martha informed him that although she used to 'get letters every day asking for help' she does 'not hear anything from Berlin' anymore.[26]

This letter unfortunately coincided with Briscoe's departure to America as Jabotinsky's designated leader of the Revisionist emigration mission, and perhaps not surprisingly given the complexities of that campaign, there is no record of any immediate response. The dialogue did not resume until June 1939 when he made a brief return to Ireland, where his aunt Martha gently admonished him for not responding, saying that despite numerous 'letters' that 'I did not hear from you'.[27] The minutiae of the content is particularly poignant; his aunt continued by saying that she had continued to send '£1' a month to her sister, the letter takes on a tone of melancholy as

24 RBPP, 17 January 1938.
25 Briscoe and Hatch, *For the Life of Me*, p. 8.
26 RBPP, 2 January 1939.
27 RBPP, 16 June 1939.

she suggested to him that by regularly sending money to Berlin, she hoped 'she' would 'be alright'.[28]

That is the last communiqué in the sequence, and in the fullness of time Briscoe would slowly become aware that his aunt Hedwig had been murdered in Auschwitz.[29] The loss of his aunt was reinforced in the postwar period when Briscoe found out that she was not the only member of his extended family to be exterminated by the Nazis. In this respect his personal narrative reflected that of his co-religionists in the global diaspora as it became apparent that more than one hundred and fifty members of his extended family had perished in the Holocaust.[30] It is clear this effort would induce extraordinary psychological stresses, a fact Briscoe acknowledged in 1944 when he admitted to his close friend Paul Bechert, that he was 'in treatment myself' and attending a psychoanalyst.[31]

The schizophrenic nature of Briscoe's reality was once again reinforced when, three days after receiving the first letter from his aunt in Berlin, he received an urgent request from Jabotinsky to exploit his political connections in a desperate attempt to save the life of Yechezkiel Altman a young Betarist who had been sentenced to death by the British Mandatory authorities in Palestine. The Betar was a revisionist youth movement founded by Jabotinsky to instil a sense of élan in Jewish youth; it incorporated educational, political and military aspects to foster an uber nationalism that did not have any association with their downtrodden ancestors of the European ghettos.[32] Over time however the movement had established

---

28   Ibid.
29   Mary Rose Doorly, *Hidden Memories: The Personal Recollections of Survivors and Witnesses to the Holocaust Living in Ireland* (Blackwater Press, Dublin, 1994), pp. 10–12.
30   For further reading see: Peter Novick, *The Holocaust in American life* (Houghton Mifflin Company, New York, 1999), pp. 75–76. Henry L. Feingold, 'Who Shall Bear Guilt for the Holocaust: The Human Dilemma', in Michael R. Marrus (ed.), *The Nazi Holocaust Part 8: Bystanders to the Holocaust* (Meckler Corporation, Westport CT, 1989), pp. 121–143.
31   IMA/G2/X/0040, 21 September 1944.
32   Anita Shapira, *Land and Power: The Zionist Resort to Force, 1881–1948* (Stanford University Press, Stanford CA, 1999), pp. 129–172.

itself in Palestine and evolved to reflect Jabotinsky's emerging belief that a Jewish state could only be achieved if the Jews themselves were capable of militarily forcing the issue.[33]

This progression had seen the Betar become a training organization that would form the core component of armed resistance that would respond to the 1936 Arab riots. The young volunteers assumed a pivotal position defending the unarmed and recently arrived Jewish settlers, a position that in many respects mirrored the activities of the young Irish men and women of 1915–1921.[34] In this context Briscoe became a core actor in the military development of the Betar, although his claim to have almost single-handedly trained them by implementing a structure based on the pre-uprising Sinn Féin formation of a youth wing, the Fianna Éireann, seems slightly exaggerated.[35] The evidence suggests that the Betar had embarked on a militant course long before Briscoe became involved with it; indeed the record shows the organization had become 'openly militaristic' by the mid 30s. This evolution reflected Jabotinsky's ideological progression from theorist to soldier-statesman and was a belated acknowledgement 'that history' could only be ultimately 'determined by force and not by reason.'[36]

Therefore given the openly bellicose credo of the organization, it was perhaps not surprising that when the local Arab population launched a series of attacks on the Jewish community, its young adherents had responded with force.[37] As the intensity of the Arab revolt increased over the latter months of 1937, its members oftentimes mounted a proactive assault on innocent Arab communities; a tactic that was designed to instil a belief that Jews would not simply accept attack without retribution.[38] Yechezkiel

---

33   Yaacov Shavit, *Jabotinsky and the Revisionist Movement 1925–1948* (Frank Cass & Co. Ltd, Abingdon, 1988), pp. 50–58.

34   Ibid.

35   Briscoe and Hatch, *For the Life of Me*, pp. 264–265.

36   Shavit, *Jabotinsky and the Revisionist Movement*, pp. 52–53.

37   Yonathan Shapiro, *The Road to Power Herut Party in Israel* (State University of New York Press, Albany NY, 1991), pp. 48–52.

38   Colin Shindler, *The Triumph of Military Zionism: Nationalism and the Origins of the Israeli Right* (I. B. Tauris & Co Ltd, London, 2006), pp. 200–210.

Altman had taken part in just such an action by shooting at a bus carrying Arabs just outside Tel Aviv and the British authorities had subsequently sentenced him to death under a new, and far stricter interpretation of what was now effectively Martial Law in the Mandate.[39]

When this happened Jabotinsky immediately contacted Briscoe and dispatched him to London in an effort to intercede on Altman's behalf. He had been on friendly terms with John Dulanty the Irish High Commissioner in London, and contacted him to see if he could help. Dulanty was connected to some of the most influential British political figures of the era including de Valera's old adversary Malcolm MacDonald. Dulanty used his connections to introduce Briscoe to William Ormsby-Gore who had just retired as Secretary of State for the Colonies in order to take a seat in the House of Lords.[40] This was the most fortuitous of introductions; Ormsby-Gore turned out to be the quintessential 'Gentile-Zionist', and had been fervently committed to the Balfour Declaration's commitment to a Jewish National Home.[41] Despite his retirement he remained convinced that Britain had a moral obligation to establish a Jewish state, a conviction that had only increased with the Nazi persecution of Germany's Jews.[42] However, as the Nazis had reinforced their vice-like grip on Germany, it was evident that the Colonial Office commitment under Balfour was increasingly overridden by the realpolitik of the Foreign Office.[43]

This was a devastating outcome for a Zionist sympathizer like Ormsby-Gore who felt powerless when confronted by the practical geo-political considerations of the Foreign Office offensive.[44] It was clear that he had been

39   Ibid., p. 203.
40   Cohen, 'Direction of Policy in Palestine', pp. 243–244.
41   Ibid.
42   Aaron S. Klieman, 'The Divisiveness of Palestine: Foreign Office versus Colonial Office on the Issue of Partition, 1937', *The Historical Journal*, Vol. 22, No. 2 (June 1979), p. 426.
43   Aaron S. Klieman, 'In the Public Domain: The Controversy over Partition for Palestine', *Jewish Social Studies*, Vol. 42, No. 2 (Spring 1980), p. 162.
44   Gabriel Sheffer, 'Appeasement and the Problem of Palestine', *International Journal of Middle East Studies*, Vol. 11, No. 3 (May 1980), p. 379.

a true believer in the moral imperative of a Jewish National Home, and in that respect was perfectly primed to help when Briscoe approached him about the Altman case. When the outcome of his intercession is examined, it is evident that even if Ormsby-Gore could no longer influence policy at a macro-level, he was still capable of interceding in issues on an individual basis.[45] He contacted Malcolm MacDonald and mounted a successful intervention resulting in Altman's death sentence being commuted and replaced by a term of imprisonment.[46] Dulanty immediately confirmed this to Briscoe:

> Mr Ormsby-Gore wrote to me saying that he had a telegram from the High Commissioner for Palestine confirming the announcement which you have no doubt already seen in the newspapers that the General Officer Commanding had ... commuted the sentence to one of imprisonment for life.[47]

Briscoe's successful intervention in the Altman case had established his revisionist credentials, it had also earned the gratitude and trust of Jabotinsky who quickly wrote to him asking if he realized that he had 'saved Altman's life?'[48] However, even if that was so, events in Europe and Palestine were evolving at such a rapid pace that Briscoe could only savour Altman's reprieve for the briefest of moments.

This was clear when Briscoe returned to London and was immediately engulfed by prosaic reality of Irish nationalist concerns.[49] This was centred on his role as an aide to de Valera in the on-going negotiations with British officials to conclude the Anglo-Irish Agreement, which would come into effect on the 25th of April 1938.[50] From an Irish perspective the conflict had

---

45   Norman Rose, The Debate on Partition, 1937–38: The Anglo-Zionist Aspect: 1. The Proposal', *Middle Eastern Studies*, Vol. 6, No. 3 (October 1970), p. 297.

46   Shindler, *The Triumph of Military Zionism*, p. 203.

47   BFJITA 7/253 0, 12 February 1938.

48   Ibid., 19 February 1938.

49   McCarthy, 'Robert Briscoe's Relationship with Éamon de Valera', pp. 174–178.

50   Kevin O'Rourke, 'Burn Everything British but Their Coal: The Anglo-Irish Economic War of the 1930s', *The Journal of Economic History*, Vol. 51, No. 2 (June 1991), p. 357–366.

ostensibly been about implementing an independent national policy of self-sufficiency. The six year economic stand-off had included the imposition of tariffs on imported goods by both countries, and the withholding by the Irish state of the land annuities agreed in the 1921 Anglo-Irish-Treaty, which had obliged tenant farmers to repay loans secured pre-independence.[51] Briscoe emotively described the annual annuities of 'five million pounds' as a repayment for land that had been 'stolen ... from its Irish owners after the conquests of Elizabethan and Cromwellian days'.[52] This may have been technically correct; however, the withholding of the annuities was part of a far more modern and prosaic strategy by de Valera to incrementally 'dismantle the 1921 [Anglo-Irish] treaty'.[53]

In the early 1930s this policy was aimed at reinforcing a public perception of Fianna Fáil as the 'defenders of Irish republicanism in the twenty-six counties', and was part of de Valera's strategy to define the organization as the 'national or patriotic party'.[54] However, as the war clouds descended on Europe in the latter part of the decade, he realized that he no longer had the luxury of pandering to populist policies and 'urgently ... sought *rapprochement*' with Britain.[55] This urgency was reinforced by the knowledge that Britain's retention of the three Treaty Ports of Queenstown (Cobh), Berehaven and Lough Swilly would have made any Irish plan to stay neutral in a European war involving Britain, impossible.[56]

On the other hand, the overwhelming imperative for the British was to secure the 'goodwill' and cooperation of the Irish state in the event of a war.[57] If this meant returning the Treaty Ports to Ireland, Neville Chamberlain,

---

51   Kieran A. Kennedy, Thomas Giblin and Deirdre McHugh, *The Economic Development of Ireland in the Twentieth-Century* (Routledge, London, 1988), pp. 48–52.
52   Briscoe and Hatch, *For the Life of Me*, p. 223.
53   Mary E. Daly, *Industrial Development and Irish National Identity* (Syracuse University Press, Syracuse NY, 1992), p. 155.
54   Kelly, *Fianna Fáil, Partition and Northern Ireland*, p. 58.
55   Lee, *Politics and Society*, p. 211.
56   McMahon, *British Spies and Irish Rebels*, p. 242.
57   G. R. Sloan, *The Geopolitics of Anglo-Irish Relations in the 20th Century* (Leicester University Press, London, 1997), pp. 183–184.

the Prime Minister, reluctantly conceded that this was the most pragmatic solution to the problem and 'was convinced that their value to Britain would be negated if Ireland were unfriendly in such a war'.[58] The advice that Chamberlain initially received from his military strategists had conceded this point, but had insisted that if the ports were handed over to the Irish, Britain retained the right to use them in an emergency.[59] De Valera had rejected this proposition, and Malcolm MacDonald the chief negotiator on the British side informed the Cabinet 'I think we must accept it as a fact that he will not, because of his domestic political difficulties, give ... any such assurance'.[60]

De Valera, who had led the Irish negotiation team in London, eventually prevailed; he negotiated a favourable one-off payment of ten million pounds to settle the annuities dispute, and most importantly from an electoral perspective, secured the return of the Treaty Ports.[61] Briscoe had accompanied de Valera as a special courier to ensure that the ministers in Dublin were kept fully appraised of developments. He described the negotiations as 'a complete success' except for the continued injustice of partition, and suggested that although Chamberlain was willing to consider the issue, Lord Craigavon the Northern Ireland Prime Minister, 'obdurately refused to consider any means of ending partition'.[62] On 30 May 1938, de Valera wrote to MacDonald, expressing his satisfaction with every aspect of the agreement, bar one:

> I have no doubt the happy ending of the disputes in question has begotten a new attitude of mind on the part of our people, and if we could only now succeed in solving the problem created by partition, a happy future of mutual understanding and fruitful co-operation in matters of common concern lies ahead before our two peoples.[63]

58   Ibid.
59   Ibid.
60   Ibid., p. 183.
61   Lee, *Politics and Society*, pp. 214–216.
62   Briscoe and Hatch, *For the Life of Me*, p. 256. The absolute rejection of a united Ireland.
63   University College Dublin Archives, Eamon de Valera Papers, P150/2517, 30 May 1938.

It was apparent that de Valera was cognizant of the fact that no matter what economic benefits the ending of the Economic War would bring to the Irish state, ongoing relations with Britain would continue to be defined by partition, and Briscoe concurred absolutely.[64]

In late April, just as the Anglo-Irish negotiations were being concluded, the personal family tragedy of his missing aunt Hedwig in Berlin was contextualized when Briscoe engaged in a confrontational immigration discourse with Paddy Ruttledge, the Fianna Fáil Minister for Justice. The backdrop to this confrontation was Briscoe's unrelenting support of individual applications for entry visas to the state; it appears that Ruttledge was so incensed by his repeated representations that he reinforced in the strongest possible language, the government's determination to maintain the exclusionist status quo. This triggered a hostile correspondence where eventually all of Briscoe's pent-up frustrations poured out as he accused the minister of a discriminatory application of the immigration criteria.[65]

On 11 April 1938, Ruttledge wrote to Briscoe and clarified the position of the Department towards potential Jewish immigrants, the state's existing Jewish community, and Briscoe's own role as an immigration advocate. A clearly frustrated Ruttledge took the opportunity to reinforce the government's position that 'the Jewish community in this country should not be increased by way of immigration'.[66] He justified this statement by using the circular argument that restricting immigration was actually in the best interests of the Irish-Jewish population.[67]

> There has never been in this country any feeling against Jews on the scale whch has shown itself in some other countries but there are anti-Jewish groups ... which would only be too glad to get an excuse to start an anti-Jewish campaign.[68]

64   Kelly, Fianna Fáil, *Partition and Northern Ireland*, pp. 67–70.
65   McCarthy, 'Robert Briscoe's Extraordinary Immigration Initiative', pp. 81–90.
66   RBPP, 11 April 1938.
67   Siobhán O'Connor, '"The Obliviousness of the Fortunate": Policy and Public Opinion towards Refugees 1933–1945'. *German-Speaking Exiles in Ireland 1933–1945*. Gisela Holfter (ed.), (Rodopi B. V. Amsterdam, 2006), pp. 98–102.
68   RBPP, 11 April 1938.

The maintenance of an exclusionist Jewish immigration policy was therefore deemed to be a political imperative if the state was to remain free of the virulent anti-Semitism that had afflicted countries with a large and visible Jewish population. As the Minister for Justice Ruttledge was clearly concerned that a major demographic change could potentially unleash a latent anti-Semitism that would reinforce the anti-Semitic polemic of previously mentioned individuals like George Griffin. He reinforced his position by emphasizing the new reality of closed borders, and informed Briscoe that 'we cannot be certain given the prevailing conditions that if we grant temporary visas, these individuals will not eventually compete with our own citizens' for already scarce employment.[69] This thinking recognized that onward resettlement agreements could no longer be enforced, and Ruttledge was determined that the state would not suffer financially or socially by having to accommodate stranded Jewish refugees.[70]

Ruttledge was clearly determined to reinforce the government position by reminding Briscoe of his duty as a TD. He cautioned him 'to bear' his responsibilities 'in mind when efforts are made to secure your support in facilitating such immigration'.[71] In an effort to underscore his argument, Ruttledge concluded by issuing what can only be interpreted as a veiled warning by suggesting 'that the existing Jewish community ... would be well advised in its own interests not to encourage' any further Jewish immigration' into this country.[72]

It is clear that this did not intimidate Briscoe, who was clearly offended by the implication that he was anything other than a loyal party member.

> I know, and have always known, that I am the bludgeon wit [sic] which any Minister can be berated with and, consequently, I am quite wide awake to what is correct for me to apply for.[73]

---

69 RBPP, 11 April 1938.
70 Siev, 'The Admission of Refugees into Ireland', pp. 109–118.
71 RBPP, 11 April 1938.
72 Ibid.
73 Ibid., 22 April 1938.

Briscoe continued by re-emphasizing his understanding of the situation, and reinforced his position with a well-reasoned and logical counter-argument.

> Nobody is more conscious of the difficulties that the Government would have to face in the event of being generous in the granting of permits to aliens of my persuasion ... Further, I have been more than careful in associating myself with applications by aliens resident in this country for naturalisation requests, and in view of the fact that I am the only member of my persuasion elected to An Dáil I do not think I could be charged with attempting to seek over-indulgence in matters of this kind.[74]

When his caustic response is examined it clearly indicates the high levels of stress that he was experiencing, his anger and frustration were apparent as he challenged Ruttledge to an open debate on the immigration process.

> I am prepared at any time to have brought out, in public if necessary, all cases with which I have been associated, and I am confident that if cases with which I have been associated are set side by side with other cases with which I have no association they could better be stood over than some which the Department has given consent of entry or naturalisation to.[75]

Briscoe supported his accusation by highlighting the numerous German Gentiles who were by then part of the cultural fabric of the state.

> It might interest your Department to know that the National College of Art in Dublin has selected and appointed as its Professor of Design ... a Dutchman; and it's Professor of Sculpture an Austrian as it's Assistant Professor of Sculpture an Englishman. Surely I could equally say that Ireland should be able to produce masters, from the National point of view, from it's own nationals.[76]

He intensified his counter-critique on government immigration policy by suggesting that Ruttledge's argument that Jewish refugees were potential competitors for jobs was hypocritical.

Ruttledge's office was quick to issue a denial and justified its position in the following manner:

74 Ibid.
75 Ibid.
76 Ibid.

> Your statement that a number of non-Jewish foreigners have been appointed to official posts in this country is correct, but the Minister is unable to see its relevancy to the present discussion. When it is found necessary or desirable to appoint a foreigner to a public post ... this office ... is indifferent as to whether the person appointed is or is not a Jew.[77]

Briscoe was having none of it and had pre-empted this line of argument by suggesting that unlike any potential Jewish immigrants who would immediately pledge allegiance to their new home, the Gentile German's 'allegiance is firstly to Mr Hitler'.[78] As to the suggestion that an applicant's religious affiliation did not matter, that was evidently not the case, his immigration advocacy had proved time and again that it was a factor when a potential immigration was being considered. He was merely questioning why this same consideration was not a factor when a state position was on offer.[79]

The confrontation between Briscoe and Ruttledge concluded at this point, and although it was clearly not resolved from the perspective of either man, it is nevertheless one of the most important and informative internal Fianna Fáil discourses on Irish-Jewish affairs. From a government perspective it was evident that a senior minister had made a real attempt to get Briscoe to desist from his immigration endeavours and despite his loyalty to the party, Briscoe had just as clearly rejected the overture. Given his predisposition to conciliation, especially in a Fianna Fáil context, this was an extraordinarily powerful personal statement, which must be acknowledged as an indicator of the dreadful stresses that he was being subjected to. In that context, it also has to be acknowledged that even though the government position had a certain logic, it was predicated on a narrow parochial self-interest, which ultimately abrogated any humanitarian obligation to those unfortunate German citizens who just happened to be Jewish.[80]

77 Ibid., Undated letter May 1938.
78 Ibid., 22 April 1938.
79 Muchitsch, 'Austrian Refugees', pp. 76–80.
80 Birte Schulz, 'Overcoming Boundaries? The Problem of Identity in the Experience of German-Speaking exiles in Ireland 1933–1945, in Gisela Holfter (ed.), *German-Speaking Exiles in Ireland 1933–1945* (Rodopi, Amsterdam and New York, 2006), pp. 119–131.

Briscoe had no sooner disengaged from his bruising confrontation with Ruttledge than the brutal reality of his nascent revisionist engagement became clear. He was once again summoned by Jabotinsky to intervene on behalf of Shlomo Ben Yosef, who, like his young Betar colleague Yechezkiel Altman, had been sentenced to death for a non-lethal response to Arab raiders who had attacked the kibbutz at Rosh Pinah.[81] Ben-Yosef and two young Irgun Zvi Lemui (Hebrew for 'National Military Organisation') colleagues, Avraham Shein and Yehoshua Zurabin, had been sentenced to death for their actions. However, Ben-Yosef unlike his two companions who had been reprieved on the grounds of being under the age of eighteen, was eventually executed.[82]

That was the backdrop to Briscoe's second revisionist intervention, nobody including many members of the British parliament at Westminster, believed that this young man would be executed. The reality of a death sentence actually being carried out in Palestine was so contentious that sympathetic MPs had attempted to save Ben-Yosef by interrogating Malcolm MacDonald in a heated parliamentary debate. They had demanded to know 'whether he' was 'aware that the ages of these youths 'were '13, 18, and 19 years respectively', but MacDonald had denied this was the case and suggested that in fact, 'Ben Joseph [sic] was 23'.[83] Evidently this was not universally accepted as fact, and when he was challenged on humanitarian grounds for refusing 'to postpone the death sentence' so 'that the mother of Ben Joseph (sic) might journey from Poland to Palestine in order to bid farewell to her son', MacDonald turned the tables on his accusers by suggesting that it was all the fault of the revisionists.[84]

> The Jews in Palestine have shown admirable restraint throughout these difficult times, and the vast majority of them continue to show that restraint under their leaders.

81   Katz, *Lone Wolf*, pp. 1608–1610.
82   J. Bowyer Bell, *Out of Zion The Fight for Israeli Independence* (Transaction Publishers, New Brunswick NJ, 2009), pp. 9–60.
83   Hansard, Fifth Series, Vol. 338, Col. 367, 6 July 1938.
84   Ibid., Col. 368.

It is regrettable that in some cases it should have broken down, thus increasing the difficulties of the situation with which the authorities are contending.[85]

It is clear when MacDonald's post-execution speech is examined that the political atmosphere at Westminster had changed considerably since Altman's reprieve barely three months earlier.[86] Moreover, as MacDonald's speech also indicated, they were determined to isolate the revisionists from a moderate Zionist faction, and felt that the sacrifice of a young life was a small price to pay if this was achieved.

This should not have come as that much of a surprise to the Nessuit, the Nazi threat had reinforced a belated belief in Westminster that the Middle East would be a geographically strategic region in any forthcoming conflict. Consequently, the authorities had over the last number of months clearly indicated a determination to restore social stability in the Mandate. Despite signposting their intent to restore the status quo, the British decision to execute Ben-Yosef still stunned the Nessuit who had believed right up to the last minute that the sentence would be commuted. The expectation of Briscoe and his fellow activists was that the same political actors who had interceded on Altman's behalf would react as it had done before, and break 'down under' Revisionist 'pressure'.[87] This was evidently not the case, leaving a stunned Jabotinsky to appeal directly to MacDonald, just as he had with Altman. When he did, he had pointed out that an inadequate British response to Arab terror had alienated young Jews from the legal process.

I urge you to remember that the Arab terror has by now lasted two years ... I beg you to ... try and realise ...... what these "two years" mean in sorrow and humiliation ... Try and visualise what such a collapse of official protection ... means to people ... what a havoc that feeling is bound to work with the people's ideas ... of civic thought ... It is not mere chance that one of these children has been found mad. The whole atmosphere is madness.[88]

85   Ibid.
86   Penkower, *The Campaign for a Jewish Army*, p. 336.
87   JMD, 5 June 1938.
88   BFJITA 1/3/253 0, 3 June 1938.

It is evident from Jabotinsky's letter that even at that late stage of
the appeal he could not believe that the British of all people would hang
a young Jew, who had after all not actually harmed anyone. He stressed
that there were 'no victims' and if the execution was carried out it would
be 'repellent to the very essence of public decency'.[89] On this occasion
MacDonald refused to intercede with the General Officer Commanding
Palestine, arguing that he had complete autonomy in the matter.[90] On
7 July he explained the new reality of martial law to a clearly agitated
House of Commons.

> I received many appeals for a reprieve; but, as has repeatedly been made clear, the deci-
> sion in cases tried by the military courts rests with the General Officer Commanding,
> with whose discretion I am not prepared to interfere.[91]

MacDonald was clearly trying to assuage concerned parliamentarians that
despite a global condemnation of the execution, it had been a military decision based on local conditions, and grounded in the necessity to preserve
the rule of law in the Mandate. This was a new departure for the British,
and despite the fact that Martial Law had been de-facto if not de-jure
policy for two years, this was the first time that the executive in London
had stood back and not interfered.

Evidently Jabotinsky was taken unawares by the new British resolve
to restore stability in Palestine no matter what the cost, and he clearly
could not accept that London would not ultimately intervene. He said as
much to MacDonald when arguing that 'there can be no situations under
British responsibility where central authority is … compelled to abdicate'.[92]
MacDonald however once again refused to intervene, and the following
day Briscoe, who had been stationed in London during the whole process,
sent a telegram to Jabotinsky that read 'Intervention by London impossible',
before adding that 'representations only acceptable Commanding Officer

89   Ibid.
90   Shindler, *The Triumph of Military Zionism*, p. 203.
91   Hansard, Fifth Series, Vol. 338, Col. 588. 7 July 1938.
92   BFJITA 1/3/253 0, 3 June 1938.

Palestine'.[93] Based on this information Jabotinsky dispatched a cable to Colonel Haining, the General Officer Commanding in Palestine, imploring him to 'take into consideration' the 'moral atmosphere in which the Roshpinna incident had occurred.[94] Jabotinsky was evidently still convinced that Ben-Yosef would be reprieved, this proposition is supported by the second part of his plea, as he told Haining 'I refuse to believe British military tradition will disregard this ... factor'. However, as with MacDonald, his plea fell on deaf ears and the execution was carried out on 29 June 1938.

Jabotinsky composed this emotive eulogy to Ben-Yosef less than two weeks after he was executed by the British authorities in Palestine.

> And what of our youth? This youth believes, struggles and sacrifices ... What is the Rosh Pinah unit of Shlomo Ben Yosef? This youth is made up of the poor sons of our Jewish people dedicated to the ideal of service to their nation and homeland. They live and suffer under the most trying of conditions ... In the small town of Lusk in Poland there was a 'Jewboy' who was destined to become a symbol that enveloped the entire world with his radiance. This does not mean that he was the chosen one. On the contrary. He was a simple member of Betar when the Almighty, without looking, took him out from the ranks. My lips are unworthy to speak of him. Only this I will say to you. The entire British world was shocked, and only then began to comprehend.[95]

Although a genuine lament to the murdered young Irgunist, this statement also indicates that Jabotinsky understood the potential propaganda impact the sanctioned execution of an eighteen-year-old by the British Mandate authorities could have on global opinion. From Briscoe's perspective, this was not a new phenomenon; he immediately understood that this was a golden opportunity to pressurize the British. He would undoubtedly have informed Jabotinsky of the highly negative global response to the British decision to execute the leaders of the 1916 Eater rising in his homeland. In many respects, the British response of ignoring the global campaign

93   Ibid., 4 June 1938.
94   JFJITA 1/26/3/11C, 3 June 1938.
95   Jabotinsky, 'Public Address in Warsaw July 1938', in Sarig (ed.), *Selected Writings*, pp. 124–125.

demanding clemency for Ben-Yosef indicated that the world's most successful imperial power had learned nothing from its miscalculation in
1916. The execution of the Rising leaders had generated a wave of societal
support for the independence struggle, which prior to the executions, had
been at best lukewarm. Within months this national support had gained
an unstoppable momentum and allowed de Valera and Collins to mount
a subversive guerrilla campaign that would ultimately force the British to
the negotiating table in 1921, and achieve an independent Irish state the
following year.[96] In many respects, this reaction was replicated in the global
Jewish-diaspora; no other single act could have aroused such a unified
response, and Ben-Yosef's execution had given the Irgun its first martyr.[97]
Briscoe understood the power of political martyrdom better than any of
his revisionist colleagues; he remembered that the execution of the 1916
Rising leaders 'was the worst mistake England ever made, for it aroused
a fire-storm of resentment in Irishmen throughout the world', and was
convinced that this in turn would be replicated in the Jewish diaspora.[98]

The Ben-Yosef execution was carried out on 29 June; the campaign to
save him had consumed the revisionists for that month and would continue
to do so for a considerable period of time. Briscoe had been to the fore of
that campaign, he had visited London on three separate occasions to plead
for clemency and yet, in tandem with this life and death struggle, he had
had to defend his seat in Dublin south in the General Election of 17 June.
De Valera's decision to go to the country after the party's poor showing
only twelve months earlier may have initially appeared to be a high-risk
strategy but was more than justified when Fianna Fáil secured an overall
majority with 51.9 per cent of the popular vote.[99]

96   Lee, *Politics and Society*, pp. 36–40.
97   Joseph Heller, *The Birth of Israel Ben-Gurion and his Critics* (University Press of
     Florida, Gainesville, 2000), p. 258.
98   Briscoe and Hatch, *For the Life of Me*, p. 43.
99   Richard English, 'Green on Red: Two Case Studies in Early Twentieth-Century Irish
     Republican Thought', in D. George Boyce, Robert Eccleshall and Vincent Geoghegan
     (eds.), *Political Thought in Ireland Since the Seventeenth Century* (Routledge, London,
     1993), pp. 169–173.

Although this was a wonderful result for the party, Briscoe's personal performance confirmed a worrying electoral pattern, and while the rest of his colleagues celebrated the victory, he had to face the reality that despite increasing his personal vote from 5.81 per cent to 6.88 per cent, he had only managed to win the seventh and final seat in Dublin South.[100] However, given the parochial nature of constituency politics this is not altogether surprising; his revisionist commitment increasingly required him to spend considerable periods of time away from Dublin. In many respects, this made it virtually impossible to deal with the day to day issues that were an essential component in getting non-ministerial parliamentarians re-elected. The dichotomous nature of Briscoe's revisionist global commitments and parochial nationalist devotion to Fianna Fáil was becoming more apparent as global events led to a fractured Irish society, which reflected in every aspect the disintegration of the fragile post-World War One peace. The Jews of Europe were caught in the contentious crossfire of this disintegration as country after country refused to accept anything other than a token number of refugees from Hitler's determination to eliminate his co-religionists from German society.

These self-centred nationalist concerns were eventually subsumed as American Consular Offices in Europe were besieged by desperate Jews forcing a reaction from President Roosevelt. As the Jewish emigration crisis rapidly took on a global dimension, it could no longer be ignored even by the most disinterested state actor. In part the five-year-long Jewish tragedy reached an apex as a consequence of the Nazi annexation of Austria in the *Anschluss* of March 1938. The leaders of the liberal democracies could no longer ignore the appalling predicament of German-Austrian Jews, and under intense domestic pressure Roosevelt sent a request to thirty-one nations to come together in an effort to solve the crisis.[101]

100 ElectionsIreland.org/?1541
101 For the most comprehensive analysis see: Dennis Ross-Laffer, 'The Jewish Trail of Tears: The Evian Conference of July 1938.' (Unpublished PhD thesis, University of South Florida, 2011).

The Americans asked the invited nations 'to consider what immediate steps' could 'be taken, within the existing immigration laws ... to assist the most urgent cases'.[102] The conference took place in Evian-les-Baines in France where Roosevelt's personal envoy Myron Taylor gave an opening address on 6 July, which finally seemed to acknowledge 'that discrimination and pressure against minority groups and the disregard of elementary human rights were contrary to the principles of civilization.'[103] Although this was a commendable sentiment it evidently did not resonate with many of the other delegate states which were only there under intense US pressure; this was particularly evident in the openly stated belief that America operated one of the most exclusionist Jewish-immigration policies of the era.[104]

In his opening address, the British representative Lord Winterton echoed the parochial concerns of Germany's nearest neighbours. In a statement that almost identically reflected the Irish position, he said his 'Government were stretching their policy as far as they could in view of ... their own problem of unemployment'.[105] He then repeated the immigration principle that Briscoe had heard so often in his many representations to the Department and Industry and Commerce, that only 'refugees' who 'could make a useful contribution to industrial life', would be considered.[106] Sir Neil Malcolm, the League of Nations High Commissionaire for German Refugees reinforced this position by doubting:

> The possibility, at least for some time to come, of any large scale immigrations and settlements because of the present conditions of the labor markets in nearly all the countries in the world. Furthermore, he thought, any large movement of Jews

102   Eric Estorick, 'The Evian Conference and the Intergovernmental Committee', *Annals of the American Academy of Political and Social Science*, Vol. 203. (May 1939), p. 136.
103   *Bulletin of International News*, Vol. 15, No. 14 (16 July 1938), p. 608.
104   Alan M. Kraut, Richard Breitman and Thomas W. Imhoof, 'The State Department, The Labour Department, and German-Jewish Immigration, 1930–1940', *Journal of American Ethnic History* Vol. 3, No. 2 (Spring 1984), pp. 6–10.
105   *Bulletin of International News*, Vol. 15, No. 14 (16 July 1938), p. 608.
106   Ibid.

might result in an increase of anti-semitism in quarters where the sentiment is now negligible.[107]

It soon became clear that whether this fear was grounded in reality or greatly exaggerated to justify exclusionist immigration policies, it framed the response-mechanism of the Christian liberal-democracies at the Evian conference. The majoritarian response was acknowledged in clause three of the conference's concluding recommendations:

> Aware, moreover, that the involuntary emigration of people in large numbers has become so great that it renders racial and religious problems more acute, increases international unrest, and may seriously hinder the processes of appeasement in international relations.[108]

It was apparent that even though the delegates universally condemned without reservation the Nazi persecution of its Jewish citizenry, one by one they abrogated any humanitarian obligation to Europe's most persecuted group of people.[109]

Despite declarations of sympathy for the Jewish plight, the response of the Irish state reflected the majoritarian and exclusionist template imposed on the conference. This was clear in the pre-conference instructions that Frank Cremins, the Irish delegate, received prior to his conference address:

> It is generally agreed that the attitude of our delegation should be one of benevolent helpfulness, except in the case of any attempt being made to impose a quota on Ireland.[110]

Cremins followed his instructions to a tee; his address to the conference on 11 July opened with a fawning platitude:

---

107 As to the Refugees, *World Affairs*, Vol. 101, No. 3 (September 1938), pp. 139–140.

108 www.jewishvirtuallibrary.org/jsource/Holocaust/evian.html [accessed 19 September 2015].

109 For an insightful account of how the nations justified this position see: Theodor S. Hamerow, *Why we Watched: Europe, America and the Holocaust* (W. W. Norton & Co, New York, 2008), pp. 106–118.

110 Quoted in Goldstone, *Benevolent Helpfulness?*, p. 116.

> The Irish Government are deeply grateful to the Governments of the United States
> and France for the opportunity which this meeting affords of expressing their sincere
> sympathy with the objects for which the Committee has been convened.[111]

before quickly emphasizing the state was not in a position to offer any
practical help:

> They have been happy to accept the invitation … even though, for reasons which
> I shall briefly set out, they are not, to their great regret, in a position to make any
> substantial contribution to the solution.

The negative consequences for potential Jewish refugees in the post-Evian
period were clear, and this was borne out as best estimates suggest 'as few
as 60' desperate individuals eventually secured refugee status in the state
between 1938 and the end of the war in 1945.[112]

Professor John M. O'Sullivan shamed the Dáil chamber by voicing
his contempt for the state's stance on the Jewish crisis, showing that at
least one erudite and empathic Irish politician understood the difference
between empty gestures of 'benevolent helpfulness', and true humanity.[113]

> The problem is an extremely grave one. I realise perfectly well that we cannot, or ought
> not, take up the very easy position that a number of people are inclined to take, and
> say "what is it to us?" If we are a nation, claiming to be a nation among other nations,
> then we should have a certain amount of responsibility, just as every other country
> has. We cannot take up the position, taken up on a celebrated occasion before, and
> say that we are not our brothers' keepers. We have obligations to humanity … if we
> are taking part in affairs of that kind.[114]

O'Sullivan's criticism fell on deaf ears, and the state continued to implement a policy of exclusion that reflected the restrictive practices of its
fellow Evian attendees.

111   Catriona Crowe et al, *Documents on Irish Foreign Policy, 1937–1939 Vol. V* (Royal
      Irish Academy, Dublin, 2006), p. 318.
112   Keogh, *Jews in Twentieth-Century Ireland*, p. 191.
113   Professor John M. O'Sullivan's academic and political papers are stored in the UCD
      Archives: Reference Code IE UCDA LA60.
114   DÉD, Vol. 74, Col. 490, 15 February 1939.

The consequences were devastating; Hitler immediately increased the levels of Jewish persecution secure in the knowledge that the West was not going to intervene. He had prefaced the conference with the acerbic comment that:

> I can only hope, and expect that the other world, which has such deep sympathy for these criminals, will at last be generous enough to convert that sympathy into practical aid. We on our part, are ready to put all these criminals at the disposal of these countries, for all I care, even on luxury ships.[115]

When the conference closed, it was clear in the final resolutions that the participating nations were not willing to receive Hitler's 'criminals'. This had emboldened the Nazis, and a series of increasingly vicious assaults eventually culminated in a brutal pogrom on 9 and 10 November 1938.[116]

This terrible event has become universally known by its German name of Kristallnacht, or night of the broken glass. The Nazis used the assassination of Ernst Vom Rath, a middle-ranking official at the German Embassy in Paris, by a disaffected young Polish Jew, Herschel Grynszpan, to bring the simmering assault on Germany's Jews to a vicious climax.[117] It had been the opportunity the Nazis had been waiting for, and they exploited it to the full inflating 'the magnitude of the incident', and investing 'it with a global political significance' that far exceeded Vom Rath's level of importance.[118]

The terror had begun; however, despite the horrific events of Kristallnacht where it was beyond dispute that the Jews of Germany were being brutally assaulted, it is clear that as far as the Irish mission in Berlin

---

115 Cited in, Ervin Birnbaum, 'Evian: The Most Fateful Conference of All Times in Jewish History', *NATIV A Journal of Politics and the Arts*, Vol. 22 (February 2009), p. 1.

116 Longerich, *Holocaust*, pp. 109–113.

117 Will Mara, *Kristallnacht: Nazi Persecution of the Jews in Europe* (Marshall Cavendish Benchmark, White Plains NY, 2010), pp. 51–54.

118 Alan E. Steinweis, *Kristallnacht 1938* (Harvard University Press, Cambridge MA, 2009), p. 19.

was concerned, this was not without justification.[119] The magnitude of the pogrom was downplayed by the Irish state's minister in Berlin, Charles Bewley, who prefaced his report by approvingly explaining to his superiors in Dublin 'the reasons why' he believed the Nazi assault on its Jewish citizens was an appropriate response.[120] He started by espousing the prevailing Nazi worldview that Jews had been the main force behind Germany's defeat in the Great War, and reinforced it by resurrecting the *L'Ami du Peuple* accusation that the American-Jewish bank, Kuhn, Loeb & Co had financed the Bolsheviks in 1917.[121] Bewley continued his anti-Semitic polemic by claiming that:

> A further reason given in Germany ... for introducing discriminating legislation against the Jews is their demoralising influence on the communities among which they live. It is a notorious fact that the international white slave traffic is controlled by Jews. No one who has even a superficial knowledge of Germany can be ignorant that the appalling moral degradation before 1933 was, if not caused, at least exploited by Jews.[122]

The lack of objectivity finally exposed Bewley's rabid anti-Semitism; officials who had ignored the warning signs were forced to act, and he was recalled to Dublin.[123] This decision was underpinned not so much by an empathy with Germany's Jews, but by a belated realization that 'Berlin's destabilising revisionist foreign policy had affected the peace of the continent'.[124] This awareness meant that accurate interpretations of Nazi policy was vital, it was no longer prudent to maintain an individual who 'was neither a faithful executor of official policy nor a trustworthy

---

119   For further reading see: Holfter, 'Some Facts and Figures, pp. 181–192. For a particularly insightful analysis of an evolving bureaucratic understanding of Bewley's rabid anti-Semitism See, Aengus Nolan, *Joseph Walsh Irish Foreign Policy 1922–1946* (Mercier Press, Cork, 2008), pp. 58–108.
120   O'Driscoll, 'The Jewish Question', p. 143.
121   Crowe, et al, *Documents on Irish Foreign Policy 1937–1939*, p. 374.
122   Ibid., p. 376.
123   NAI DFA/217/28, 1 December 1939.
124   O'Driscoll, 'Inter-war Irish-German Diplomacy', pp. 86–87.

chronicler of German developments', as minister.[125] That he was left in Berlin until 1939 despite his superiors becoming increasingly aware of his predilection towards Nazi racial anti-Semitic theories, is an indictment of the uncaring political philosophy of the Irish state towards Jewish refugees. Sadly despite the overwhelming evidence of the next decade, it would not really change.

When the failure of the Evian Conference is underpinned by the tragedy of the Kristallnach*t* pogrom, it puts into perspective how loving parents could almost instantaneously make a decision of heart-breaking dimensions, and send their children to strangers on the *Kindertransports*.[126] In the aftermath of Kristallnacht the remaining ultra-assimilated German-Jewish community finally had to acknowledge that if they stayed, they faced annihilation, and a previously steady process of emigration became a headlong flight of terror.[127] It soon became clear however that Hitler's pre-Evian rant about facilitating Jewish emigration, even if it was on 'luxury ships', was now a much harder proposition than it had been prior to the conference.[128] This devastation Kristallnacht wrought on the German-Jewish psyche was a profound one as their children went into exile, even though they knew it was the only realistic option to ensure their survival, the prospect of not seeing them again prompted a number of suicides and complete mental breakdowns.[129]

125   Ibid.
126   For further reading see: Andrea Hammel and Bea Lewkowicz (eds.), *The Kindertransort to Britain 1938/9: New Perspectives* Rodopi B. V., Amsterdam, 2012).
127   Michael Schabitz, 'The Flight and Expulsion of German Jews', in Beate Meyer, Hermann Simon, and Chana Schutz (eds.), *Jews in Nazi Berlin From Kristallnacht to Liberation* (University of Chicago Press, Chicago IL, 2000), pp. 36–63.
128   Robert Wistrich, *Hitler and the Holocaust* (Weidenfeld and Nicolson, London, 2001), pp. 68–76.
129   For further reading see: Eric J. Sterling, 'Rescue and Trauma: Jewish Children and the Kindertransports during the Holocaust' in James Marten (ed.), *Children and War* (New York University Press, New York, 2002), p. 64. Vera K. Fast, *Children's Exodus a History of the Kindertransport 1938–1939* (I. B. Tauris & Co Ltd, London, 2011), pp. 1–17.

One of the prime facilitators of this process was the Movement for the Care of Children, a non-denominational British charity that began to lobby the government for entry visas for children under the age of seventeen.[130] On 21 November the Prime Minister Neville Chamberlain, in response to a parliamentary question, acknowledged that 'approaches' had been made to Berlin to secure the speedy transfer to Britain of German-Jewish children.[131] However, this was not met with universal approval by the honourable members of the House, and in what had become a highly charged and contentious debate, the main concern of a number of Members was how long they would be allowed to remain in Britain. Three days later on 24 November, the Home Secretary Sir Samuel Hoare was asked to explain the long-term intentions of the government towards these children.

> The duration of time that Jewish refugee children are to be allowed to remain in this country; and whether he will see that steps are taken to keep trace of the children and arrange for their leaving of the country at a fixed age.[132]

Despite these less than generous concerns and to the credit of the British government, the *Kindertransports* proceeded, with the first one arriving on 2 December 1938.[133] In total, approximately 15,000 children escaped from Nazi Germany in the pre-war period. On the eve of the war in September 1939, however, 10,000 children were still listed for evacuation and 'the sad truth is that by far the majority of these children' were eventually murdered in the death-camps.[134]

This endeavour would result in Briscoe's involvement in the most distressing episode of a long and already harrowing refugee advocacy. On 19 November, Briscoe received in his Dáil office a three-person deputation from the Jewish community, who were inquiring into the possibility of

130   www.holocaustresearchproject.org/holoprelude/kindertransport.html
131   Hansard, Fifth Series, Vol. 341. Col. 1317. 21 November 1938.
132   Ibid., Col. 1928. 24 November 1938.
133   Schabitz, 'The Flight and Expulsion of German Jews', p. 43.
134   Michael Geyer, 'A Family History from the Days of the Kindertransports', *History and Memory, Special Issue: Histories and Memories of Twentieth-Century Germany*, Vol. 17, No. 1–2 (Spring-Winter 2005), pp. 323–324.

securing transit visas for 132 German Jewish children. These three ladies presented Briscoe with the list which showed that the oldest had just turned eighteen, the youngest was ten, with the majority of the children aged between thirteen and fourteen. More importantly, from a policy perspective, eighty-two of them had secured the offer of a home with extended family members, friends or concerned co-religionists in Palestine, England or America.[135]

Briscoe received the application to facilitate a Kindertransport three nights after Kristallnacht. The trauma of this request would have been reinforced by the realization that his aunt Hedwig and young cousin Tamara were still unaccounted for. Although it is uncertain if he was as yet aware that one of his aunt's last acts was to place his cousin on one of the last transports that left Berlin, he would clearly have been aware that her position in Berlin was precarious. Yet the fact still remains that despite receiving regular and distressing letters from parents who were pleading for their children's lives, and despite the fact that his own cousin was saved by securing a place on a Kindertransport, there is no evidence to suggest that he made any official request to the Irish government about securing entry visas for the one hundred and thirty two German-Austrian children.

This is difficult to explain, although his fractious encounter with Ruttledge six months earlier must certainly have been a factor. He had been warned in no uncertain terms to be more circumspect about making future representations about potential immigration, and it is possible that even if only at a subliminal level Briscoe accepted that there was no realistic hope of securing even a temporary transit visa for these children. This understanding would have been reinforced by the fact that onward migration plans were becoming increasingly difficult to achieve/enforce. It is therefore clear that by November 1938 Briscoe was aware that an already limited immigration to the Irish state was not going to offer a solution to the Jewish refugee crisis. However, after the Evian Conference, Briscoe was aware that immigration at a macro-level was not possible, and if this was

135   RBPP, 13 November 1938.

the case he also accepted that there was no realistic chance that the transit visas would have been issued

The consequences of Evian and the Kristallnacht pogrom accelerated the revisionist response to the Jewish tragedy; it also drew Briscoe right to the heart of the organization. Less than a month after Kristallnacht, he accepted Jabotinsky's request to lead a mission to Warsaw in order to effect a long-standing plan to secure a mass emigration of Poland's Jews.[136] The organization had been engaged in this endeavour since 1937, oftentimes in cooperation with the Polish Government.[137] This might initially seem strange; however, as a consequence of a 'continuing impoverishment of the Jewish masses', and an increased 'anti-Semitism', the Poles sought to encourage Jewish emigration.[138] Jabotinsky had been promoting the idea of a modern-day Exodus to 'the prime minister of Poland, Slawoy-Skladkowsky, and the foreign minister Colonel Beck', who were by and large supportive of his ambitious plan.[139]

The Polish response to his initiative was simple; if the Jews were willing to go, then the government would facilitate this by every means possible, including, if necessary, financial assistance. However, Jabotinsky needed to convince them that the British would cooperate by accommodating the potential emigrants. However, this proved to be a task too far, and by summer of 1938 it was apparent he had failed to convince the Poles, who clearly did not believe the British would open the borders of Palestine.[140] Consequently Beck had addressed the League of Nations 'demanding that facilities be provided for the annual departure of between 80,000 and 100,000 Jews' from Poland to Madagascar, Kenya or even Australia.[141]

136   Briscoe and Hatch, *For the Life of Me*, p. 265.
137   Howard (Chanoch) Rosenblum, 'Promoting an International Conference to Solve the Jewish Problem: The New Zionist Organization's Alliance with Poland, 1938–1939', *The Slavonic and East European Review*, Vol. 69, No. 3 (July 1991), pp. 478–501.
138   Ibid., p. 482.
139   Laqueur, *The History of Zionism*, pp. 372–373.
140   Rosenblum, 'Promoting an International Conference', pp. 480–486.
141   Hamerow, *Why we Watched*, p. 62.

In an attempt to refocus the emigration plan on Palestine, Jabotinsky had instructed Joseph Schechtman, the resident revisionist envoy in Warsaw, to arrange a meeting with Beck, to effect 'a shift in the Polish position'.[142] For the next six months, the revisionists negotiated with the Poles about where Polish Jews would go, and in December Jabotinsky sent Briscoe to Warsaw. That Briscoe enthusiastically accepted the mission is not really surprising, for although he was a revisionist newcomer, he could see all the necessary precursors for a mass Jewish emigration from Poland seemed to be in place; it had been established that the government were willing to let them go, indeed by the end of 1937, it had become part of the global anti-Semitic narrative:

> Poland has more Jews than any other European country; there, for that reason, is found the core of the Jewish problem ... Ten per cent of Poland's population of 33,500,000 is Jewish ... Two tendencies have come into being as a result ... The Jewish masses of eastern Poland are relapsing into the orthodoxy of the Middle Ages; and on the other hand, Zionism and the emigration movement connected with it have won many followers. In 1934 about half of all Polish emigrants were Jews. And half of the ... Jewish immigration into Palestine was from Poland.[143]

On 24 November 1938, Briscoe informed the Nessuit in London that he had 'a very lengthy conversation with Mr de Valera, and I am very happy at the attitude he is now taking ... I am awaiting news from you as to when it will be expected of me to start for Warsaw'.[144] When he finally arrived in the Polish capital, Schechtman secured him an audience with Beck, the foreign minister, and he set about trying to put into place Jabotinsky's ambitious emigration plan, although it seems clear he was not aware of the increasing reluctance of the Poles to go along with it. Nevertheless, he set about his task with gusto and his account of the meeting with Beck is a dramatic one:

142   Rosenblum, Promoting an International Conference', p. 483.
143   Desider Kiss, 'The Jews of Eastern Europe', *Foreign Affairs*, Vol. 15, No. 2 (January 1937), pp. 331–332.
144   BFJITA 2/253 2, 24 November 1938.

On behalf of the New Zionist Movement, speaking mainly for European Jews, not for those of England or America ... I suggest that you ask Britain to turn over the mandate for Palestine to you and make it in effect a Polish colony. You could then move all your unwanted Polish Jews into Palestine. This would bring great relief to your country, and you would have a rich and growing colony to aid your economy.[145]

Briscoe's plan was based on the revisionist presumption 'that Britain felt itself bound to consult with nations such as Poland before determining immigration schedules for Palestine'.[146] This was not the case as Beck had already found out; Britain merely humoured the Poles by listening to their plans for Palestine, and as the war approached, the Palestine emigration plan for Poland's Jews became inconsequential to British geo-political concerns. Consequently, it is clear the mission was doomed to failure before it ever started, and Briscoe's despair was evident in his concluding remarks about the Warsaw trip. This was summarized not by a meeting with Beck, but by the outcome of his meeting with the Chief Rabbinical authority, which rejected any plan for a mass emigration to Palestine, telling Briscoe 'we must wait for the Messiah to lead us to the Holy Land. All forms of Zionism are to us *traif* (unclean)'.[147]

Given the virulence of the Nazis anti-Semitic project, the eventual murder of more than 90 per cent of Poland's Jews was in all probability inevitable; however, the attitude of Poland's orthodox rabbinate meant that Zionist rescue efforts, however futile they may have been, were met with a resistance from the very people they were aimed at helping. This response devastated Briscoe and perhaps goes some way to explaining the desperation of his actions in the forthcoming revisionist mission to America.

Briscoe was only in Ireland for two weeks after his return from Warsaw before he embarked on a far more complex, but equally futile revisionist mission to America. However, before analysing Briscoe's role as leader of the mission, it is important to contextualize his state of mind as he prepared to accept Jabotinsky's request to be the lead negotiator. It is apparent that after

145   Briscoe and Hatch, *For the Life of Me*, p. 268.
146   Rosenblum, 'Promoting an International Conference. p. 485.
147   Briscoe and Hatch, *For the Life of Me*, p. 270.

a six year involvement with the refugee crisis, Briscoe passionately identified with the suffering of his fellow-Jews, however, it is also clear that he still remained a committed member of Fianna Fáil. In many respects he was experiencing the same identity crisis that had confronted Jews throughout Europe over the previous decade. Like many of Briscoe's co-religionists, who had prior to the success of the Nazi persecution project been secure in their identity, he was highly assimilated. However, the persecution of their German co-religionists had shaken these highly integrated individuals out of a sense of complacency and forced them to acknowledge their heritage.[148]

It was also clear that despite this new allegiance, Briscoe's sense of obligation to de Valera necessitated, just as it had in the recent Warsaw mission, that he secured a formal blessing from 'the Chief' before he accepted Jabotinsky's offer to lead the endeavour.[149] In order to secure this approval, Briscoe informed the Nessuit that he would need a formal letter of explanation to 'secure the permission of my Chief here – Mr de Valera'.[150] This request strongly indicated the level of personal conflict Briscoe was experiencing as the pull of the two dominant, yet contrasting emotional forces of his reality exerted oftentimes dichotomous political and cultural demands.

Although the actual letter of permission is missing from the archive, it is evident that de Valera was once again prepared to facilitate Briscoe, but in yet another example of his political acumen it was not granted without a caveat.[151] De Valera clearly saw Briscoe's involvement in the Revisionist Mission as a unique opportunity to further highlight the continuing injustice of Irish partition. Consequently, Briscoe informed the Nessuit that:

> I may mention that I have already discussed the matter with him and he has indicated that he would have no objection and ... feels that a great deal of good would result for both the Jews and the Irish in America if contact was made on similar lines, that is to

148 David H. Jones, *Moral Responsibility in the Holocaust A Study in the Ethics of Character* (Rowman & Littlefield Publishers. Inc, Lanham MD, 1999), pp. 171–198.
149 Briscoe and Hatch, *For the Life of Me*, p. 272.
150 BFJITA 1/3 253 2, 26 February 1938.
151 McCarthy, 'Éamon de Valera's Relationship with Robert Briscoe', pp. 178–182.

say among the few in connection with its objections to partition and recognizance of independence of National entities.[152]

The London branch of the organization evidently had no issue with de Valera's attempt to synthesize the anti-partition ideology of Fianna Fáil and the revisionists, and informed Briscoe they were thrilled 'that Mr de Valera is in sympathy with your planned trip to the United States'.[153] The Nessuit's relief that Briscoe had secured de Valera's blessing was evident, and it is clear from that relief that in an extraordinarily short revisionist career he had assumed a primacy within the organization which was in many respects second only to Jabotinsky.[154] This is supported by a personal letter from Jabotinsky who was also clearly aware of the profound significance of Briscoe's commitment to the mission. The level of expectation was apparent when Jabotinsky informed him that his responsibility extended beyond simply leading the mission. Indeed he expressed the opinion that unless Briscoe accepted the role, the endeavour would remain nothing more than an aspiration.

> I am still of the opinion that unless you will undertake the task of "creating the delegation", I am very much afraid that it may remain a very good plan, but nothing more, and that is why I requested you not to hesitate to take over the responsibility for this business.[155]

Given Briscoe's relatively new status within the organization, this was a heavy burden to place on his relatively inexperienced shoulders. He was after all, still a revisionist novice, and in the fullness of time, his inexperience would become apparent, however, for now he was simply grateful for de Valera's support.

152 BFJITA 1/3 253 2, 27 February 1938.
153 Ibid. 1 March 1938.
154 Rosenblum, 'The New Zionist organization's American campaign, 1936–1939', pp. 182–184.
155 BFJITA 1/3 253 2, 1 March 1938.

> I need not in this connection tell of urgent necessity of the work to be done, as you
> are fully aware of the horrible situation in which the world, and particularly European
> Jewry finds itself to-day. I cannot conclude this letter without expressing to you my
> very sincere gratefulness for the attitude of mind which is yours in connection with
> this whole business, and I am sure you understand fully the motives which animate
> my undertaking this work.[156]

It is clear from Briscoe's letter to de Valera that organizing the practical
aspects of the mission had taken far longer than originally envisaged. The
timeline shows that Jabotinsky had initially approached him on the matter
soon after he left Dublin in January 1938, and it had taken a full year for
the mission to become a reality. It was not until January 1939 that a conflu-
ence of personal, political and social forces combined to finally make the
mission a viable proposition. Nevertheless, the very fact that diverse forces
had influenced not just events, but also the individual actors, inevitably
meant that personal expectations of and ambitions for the mission itself
would differ even before Briscoe left for America.

Although Briscoe had secured the necessary leave of absence from
his Dáil duties to lead the revisionist delegation, it is patently clear he was
not fully conversant with the subtleties of Jabotinsky's revisionist vision,
moreover, it is equally as clear he did not fully grasp the tightly bound
political parameters of the mission. Jabotinsky's vision of a Jewish state
'hinged on the success of its political efforts', this was essentially focused
on forcing the British to accept 'a broad-based mutual cooperative effort'
with the revisionists and ultimately to 'provide political guarantees' on
statehood.[157] Essentially Jabotinsky's aim for the revisionists was a returned
focus on the political Zionism as defined by Herzl in *Derjudenstaat*. He
articulated this at the onset of the American mission in an interview with
the *Jewish Herald* where he told the correspondent that 'non-political
colonization is not at all possible. We do not claim it is difficult: It is not
possible'.[158] This was brought into sharp focus by the terrible events of

156   Ibid. 17 December 1938.
157   Shavit, 'Jabotinsky and the Revisionist Movement', p. 192.
158   *The Jewish Herald*, 10 February 1939. (Hereafter *JH*).

the *Kristallnacht* pogrom, which reinforced the urgency of Jabotinsky's primary political objective. It was now beyond doubt in his mind that the only possible solution to the escalating Nazi persecution was if Roosevelt personally intervened and applied economic and political pressure on Britain to force open the Mandate's borders.[159]

The objective of Briscoe's undertaking was, at least from Jabotinsky's perspective, the securing of a one-to-one meeting with the American President in order to convince him of the moral imperative underpinning the revisionist plan.[160] In a final communiqué of instruction, Jabotinsky informed Briscoe that it is 'the judgement of the Nesuit, the most essential part of your mission will be that connected with your visit to Washington, [where] its purpose is to gain Mr Roosevelt's support.'[161] However, it is clear that Briscoe believed the political objective could only be achieved if Roosevelt were pressurized by an intense publicity campaign. He recalled that when he asked de Valera for a leave of absence, it was 'to campaign for an aroused American public opinion which might force President Roosevelt to bring pressure to bear on England to allow large scale immigration to Palestine.'[162]

The reality was, however, far more nuanced than either Briscoe or Jabotinsky's somewhat naïve stance allowed for, moreover, if the American performance at Evian had been objectively analysed, it would have been clear that it was in many respects 'a smoke-and-mirrors' presentation designed to 'give the appearance of concern without requiring them or any other country to admit Jewish refugees.'[163] However, it is clear that despite the

---

159 For a complete understanding of the British decision making process behind this decision, see Malcolm MacDonald's draft proposal for the 1939 White Paper TNA CAB/24/282. For one of the best examinations of British policy in Palestine during this fraught period see: Lauren Elise Apter, 'Disorderly Decolonization: The White Paper of 1939 and the End of British Rule in Palestine' (PhD thesis, The University of Texas at Austin, 2008), pp. 61–91.

160 Rosenblum, 'The New Zionist organization's American campaign', pp. 182–186.

161 BPJITA 4/253 2. November 1938.

162 Briscoe and Hatch, *For the Life of Me*, p. 272.

163 Michael Brown, *The Israeli-American Connection: Its Roots in the Yishuv* (Wayne State University Press, Detroit MC, 1996), pp. 59–63.

reality of the American position, Jabotinsky still apparently believed that Roosevelt would see the moral imperative of the Jewish tragedy. It soon became evident however that this was a totally unrealistic expectation, and when it became clear that Roosevelt had no intention of meeting Briscoe, the magnitude of Jabotinsky's political miscalculation also became clear.

This was reinforced by the fact that prior to the Evian Conference the United States of America had at best been a peripheral concern for the revisionists, and if Jabotinsky had prefaced the mission with an objective analysis of the situation, it would have been clear that the movement was only a minority voice in American Zionist circles. Jabotinsky should also have been cognizant that the concept of Zionism itself was not universally popular in the prosperous and detached American-Jewish community.[164] When support was forthcoming, it was usually focused on the incremental, cooperative, and politically acceptable methodology of the World Zionist Organisation led by the Anglophile Chaim Weizmann.[165] This was clear to Briscoe from the moment he arrived in America, when he recalled how 'the Jewish organizations in America looked [on him] as anti-British and believed that [he] was less interested in helping the Jews than in embarrassing England in her hour of need'.[166]

When the profile of the leading American Zionists is examined, it was not surprising that they supported the WZO. They were in many respects a mirror image of their British counterparts, and were oftentimes leading members of the Jewish establishment. For example, two of Weizmann's most ardent supporters were prominent jurist Louis Brandeis, a retired member of the Supreme Court, and Stephen Wise a leading New York

---

164 Michael Brown, 'The New Zionism in the New World: Vladimir Jabotinsky's Relations with the United States in the Pre-Holocaust Years', *Modern Judaism*, Vol. 9, No. 1 (February 1989), pp. 71–72.

165 Rafael Medoff, *Militant Zionism in America the Rise and Impact of the Jabotinsky Movement in the United States, 1926–1948* (The University of Alabama Press, Tuscaloosa AL, 2002), pp. 18–22.

166 Briscoe and Hatch, *For the Life of Me*, p. 272.

rabbi who advised Roosevelt on Jewish matters.[167] In an effort to counteract this negative perception, Briscoe secured a meeting with Brandeis
through the intervention of his replacement on the Supreme Court of
the United States, Justice Felix Frankfurter.[168] Frankfurter was a moderate Zionist who had slowly started to realize that while the conciliatory
attitude of Weizmann was appropriate to peacetime negotiations, a more
urgent approach was now required.[169]

Frankfurter perhaps hoped to persuade Brandeis that a more confrontational, pro-active form of Zionism was now more appropriate; however,
Brandeis was 'very old and frail' when he met Briscoe, and although he
wished him well in his revisionist endeavours, he did not offer the hoped-
for unequivocal support for the revisionist mission. Briscoe could not
convince him that the 'physical force [approach] of the Irgun was justified,
and more importantly could not gain his support for 'the illegal shipping
of human beings to Palestine', a reference to the *Aliyah Bet* campaign[170]
to break the British blockade of the Mandate.[171] Brandeis's reaction is
perhaps not surprising; this type of individual would have been culturally
conditioned to work within the system, and most certainly would not have
been inclined to confront it head on, in a way that was rapidly becoming
the leitmotif of the revisionist political campaign. As Briscoe would soon
find out, this group were and would remain, intrinsically opposed to the
direct methods of Jabotinsky and the revisionists.[172]

More importantly from the mission perspective, this powerful group of
American Jews had direct access to the White House. They used this to their
advantage, and their resistance to Jabotinsky's vision of mass Jewish emigration to the Palestine Mandate would prove an insurmountable obstacle

---

167 Aaron Berman, *Nazism the Jews and American Zionism 1933–1948* (Wayne State
     University Press, Detroit MI, 1990), pp. 22–23.
168 Briscoe and Hatch, *For the Life of Me*, p. 273.
169 Felix Frankfurter and Harlan B. Phillips, *Felix Frankfurter: Reminisces* (Renal &
     Company, New York, 1960), pp. 178–188.
170 The *Aliyah Bet* will be fully expanded on later in chapter.
171 Briscoe and Hatch, *For the Life of Me*, p. 274.
172 Ibid., pp. 272–273.

as Wise and his conservative colleagues counselled an already cautious Roosevelt against meeting Briscoe.[173] This obfuscation was reinforced by the secret support of the British embassy in Washington:

> Do we really wish at this juncture to throw ... "the powerful factor" of the influence of American Jewry into the scales against us? Can we afford to do so? ... Now in the advent of a Presidential election, and when the future is full of measureless uncertainties, I should have thought it was more necessary ... to conciliate American Jewry and enlist their aid in combating isolationist and indeed anti-British tendencies in the United States.[174]

It is clear that officials and perhaps security operatives at the British embassy were not only promoting the interests of this group of Anglophile Jews, but also assisting them with inside information in order to marginalize the revisionists even further.[175]

Briscoe was not disheartened by the obstacles in his path and set about his task with enthusiasm. Jabotinsky was an exponent of the grand gesture, and consequently his pre-mission advice to Briscoe had amounted to not much more than suggesting that he make an emotive appeal to Roosevelt's considerable ego.[176] He told Briscoe that when he had secured access to Roosevelt, he should 'kneel in the middle of the hall', and make it clear that there was 'only one way out' for Germany's Jews'.[177] To emphasize Roosevelt's centrality to the opening of Palestine's borders, Briscoe was instructed to tell the President that he was the only 'man capable of enforcing it'.[178] Briscoe had quickly realized that Jabotinsky's dependence on the emotive nature of the mission cut no ice with the hard-headed Anglophile and isolationist

---

173   Rosenblum, 'The New Zionist organization's American campaign', p. 183.
174   TNA CAB/67/3/51, December 1939. Communiqué from Washington embassy designated Top Secret, and to be kept under lock and key.
175   Medoff, *Militant Zionism in America*, pp. 102–130.
176   James David Barber, *Politics by Humans Research on American Leadership* (Duke University Press, Durham NC, 1988), pp. 177–180.
177   Jabotinsky Institute Tel Aviv Correspondence, Vol. 23.
178   Ibid.

in thought bureaucrats of the State Department.[179] This was underpinned
by the fact that even though Roosevelt was personally sympathetic to the
Jewish plight, he also shared his official's view that Palestine was an internal
concern of the British government, and had no intention of interfering
in the political affairs of America's closest ally.[180] Given the geo-political
moment, it is doubtful that even if Briscoe had presented the most profes-
sionally prepared and well-researched arguments, he would have been given
access to Roosevelt, the fact that these were naïve and emotional meant
that he had no chance at all.[181]

Briscoe's inability to explain the revisionist plan in a pragmatic and
professional manner most definitely hindered him when dealing with
Washington's elite bureaucrats, but despite this ineffective initial approach
it is clear he understood the underlying urgency of the emigration crisis.
His handwritten notes of preparation for the trip reveal a prescience about
the devastating future fate of German Jews if they did not emigrate. He
had hastily scribbled a note expressing the belief that they would face
'extermination', and he had planned to forcefully argue that Palestine was
now the only viable alternative to a Jewish extinction.[182]

> International Governmental support is being sought for the plan to remove 1,000,000
> Jews from affected areas to Palestine within two years. It is proposed that in this
> plan that all German, Austrian, Sudetenland Jewry ... amounting to approximately
> 600,000 souls be included in this number of 1,000,000 ... It is hoped that American
> support for this plan will be forthcoming.[183]

179   For further reading see: Keith Pomakoy, *Helping Humanity American Policy and
      Genocide Rescue* (The Rowman & Littlefield Publishing Group, Lanham ML, 2011),
      pp. 136–142. Monty S. Penkower, 'Jewish Organisations and the Creation of the U.S.
      War Refugees Board', *Annals of the American Academy of Political and Social Science*,
      Vol. 450, Reflections on the Holocaust: Historical, Philosophical, and Educational
      Dimensions (July 1980), pp. 126–128.
180   Richard Breitman and Alan J. Lichtman, *FDR and the Jews* (Cambridge, Harvard
      University Press, 2013), pp. 67–84.
181   Rosenblum, 'The New Zionist organization's American campaign', p. 184.
182   BFJITA 8/253 0, 2 January 1939.
183   Ibid.

In any event, the fact that he had been unable to get past even the lowest layers of American political insulation meant that he never had the opportunity to develop these arguments in any substantive fashion. He poured out his frustrations to Jack Wolff, a prominent American colleague:

> I had a conference today with the State Department, with officials of the Near Eastern Division, and it appears to me that an organisation in America is of paramount importance, because in the discussions it was pointed out to me several times that action could only follow representations of organisations with known large membership.[184]

That was an important statement, it was clear that Briscoe understood the revisionists were not being taken seriously, and he immediately concluded that it was in the movement's best interest to rectify this state of affairs as soon as possible. He would make every effort to fulfil this objective, even though it would mean a drastic falling out with Jabotinsky, his revisionist mentor.

Once Briscoe was denied access to Roosevelt, Jabotinsky regarded the mission as over and expected him to return home; from his refusal to do so, it was just as clear that Briscoe did not concur. In a first, but not last, act of revisionist rebellion he took to heart the State Department admonishment that a small and unimportant organization was not going to be taken seriously. In a unilateral decision, he decided to address this issue by embarking on a one-man revisionist recruitment campaign. This decision would have a far more positive outcome than the failed political initiative, and while Briscoe had been woefully unprepared for the intricacies of Washington power politics, his uniqueness as an Irish-Jewish parliamentarian would charm celebrity followers and ordinary citizens alike.

In making this decision, it was evident that Briscoe exhibited an independent streak that very rarely, if ever, manifested in his Fianna Fáil incarnation; he did not even deem it necessary to consult the Nessuit about his future plans. This had been reinforced by the opaque operational instructions that had emanated from Jabotinsky, who had spoken of the need to court 'non-Jewish ... American circles' to secure public support for

---

184   Ibid., 23 January 1939.

the mission.[185] On the face of it this appeared to give Briscoe a freedom
to pursue extraneous objectives outside of Jabotinsky's strictly defined
political remit, and just as importantly from the perspective of Briscoe's
pre-mission agreement with de Valera, it must have seemed the perfect
opportunity to also highlight the continuing injustice of Irish partition to
the Irish-American community. Consequently a rift in their previously cordial relationship soon developed, and it was only reinforced when Briscoe
continued to remain uncontactable. This breakdown resulted in an immediate personal tension with Jabotinsky which was only exacerbated by
Briscoe's resounding and instant success.

He was soon attracting well-known Jews to the revisionist cause, some
were butterflies like Ernest Hemingway, who seemed to like the notoriety
of the revisionists, rather than being a genuine supporter. Hemmingway
viewed the organization through the same romantic prism that he had
applied to the Spanish Civil War, and on his way to yet another Cuban
sojourn in early 1939 he wrote to Briscoe to express his support, only to be
never heard from again.[186] Like many of the more fleeting expressions of
support, that was the end of his interest, and Jabotinsky was quite reasonably
not attracted to this type of support. However, some celebrity followers
would remain committed and go onto play active roles in the revisionist
movement, for example, Ben Hecht, the Hollywood playwright supported
Briscoe with absolute conviction and proved to be a valuable ally.[187] Hecht,
a gifted writer highlighted the obstacles that Briscoe had confronted from
American Jews who had thwarted his efforts to meet Roosevelt.

> The opposition of Jewish authority won the day. Although we could break the
> conspiracy of silence in large meeting halls and in coast-to-coast newspapers and

185   BFJITA 5/253 o, undated letter, most probably written in the autumn of 1938.
186   BFJITA 8/253 o. Hemingway to Briscoe.
187   For further reading on Hecht, See: Menahem Kaufman, *An Ambiguous Partnership
      Non Zionists and Zionists in America, 1939–1948* (The Magnes Press, Jerusalem, 1991),
      pp. 239–240. Allon Gal, 'Brandeis, Judaism and Zionism', in Nelson L. Dawson
      (ed.), Brandeis and America The University Press of Kentucky, Lexington KY, 1989),
      pp. 92–94.

magazines, we could not grab the ear of government. The slick and respectable Jewish organizations of the United States kept this ear plugged.[188]

As a publicist par excellence, Hecht understood the best way to combat the conservative Jewish establishment was to court public opinion, he was absolutely convinced that this could only benefit the revisionist cause. On the other hand Jabotinsky absolutely subscribed to Herzl's maxim that politics and political solutions were the only true way to achieve a Jewish state.[189] It is therefore perhaps not surprising that he looked askance at Briscoe's courting of individuals like Hecht. This sceptical viewpoint was reinforced by the amount of time and effort that Briscoe was devoting to courting the Irish-American community.[190] Jabotinsky would have been acutely aware after his brief Dublin visit of the awe and respect that Briscoe had invested in de Valera. Moreover, as an astute political mind he was aware that in order to gain de Valera's validation, Briscoe had had to make a commitment to promote the Irish sense of injustice at partition during his time in America.

In fairness to Briscoe, he had made no secret of the dual aspect of his participation, and had informed the Nessuit in London of de Valera's conviction that the Irish state could also benefit from his role as mission leader. To further this goal, Briscoe immediately re-established contact with Irish-American friends from his 1922–1924 exile in New York. He appeared on the same platform as William O'Dwyer, the Brooklyn District Attorney and a future Mayor of New York, who was one of the first Americans to help in 1939.[191] Briscoe was quick to capitalize on his Irish contacts, and in some instances, his dual-mandate synthesized. This was evident when he contacted William Griffin, the Irish-American founder of the *New York*

188   Ben Hecht, *Perfidy* (Milah Press Inc, New London, 1997), p. 189.
189   Ilan Zvi Baron, *Justifying the Obligation to Die: War, Ethics, and Political Obligation with Illustrations from Zionism* (Lexington Books, Lanham MD, 2009), 13–31.
190   BFJITA 5/253 o.
191   Briscoe and Hatch, *For the Life of Me*, p. 273.

CHAPTER 7

Enquirer.[192] Briscoe expressed his gratitude at being afforded the opportunity 'to put before you the plan for the solution of the Jewish problem', before very cleverly appealing to Griffin's Irish roots.[193]

> I have also to tell you that as an Irishman of the Jewish faith Ireland too has to thank you for many things and you are quite right when you say that it is very important that public opinion and especially Irish opinion in America, be kept centred on Ireland until our final goal had been reached, namely the abolition of the border which partitions our land.[194]

It was clear Briscoe's dual commitment did not meet with Jabotinsky's approval, and his focus on furthering an anti-partitionist Irish agenda soon precipitated a confrontation with members of the Nessuit who were increasingly dismayed at his seemingly wayward and erratic behaviour.

The breaking-down of a previously harmonious relationship was initiated when Jabotinsky cabled a stinging rebuke to Briscoe about his unacceptable behaviour. It is important to bear in mind that less than six weeks before he dispatched this censure, Jabotinsky had been singing Briscoe's praises by depicting him as having a quality 'very rare among us Jews, the straight and refreshing ... faith not yet poisoned by' the 'dust of' the 'Ghetto'.[195] That type of rhetoric was part of Jabotinsky's personal charisma, and although the stresses of the last decade had led to a dour public persona, in private he could still exert a magnetism that was difficult to resist. It was however clear that Briscoe was if not immune, then increasingly resistant to Jabotinsky's authority, and the fact that Jabotinsky remained in Europe while Briscoe toured America only reinforced the chasm that was developing between them.[196] It was evident that Briscoe's fluid interpretation of the mission protocols had left Jabotinsky feeling

192   Jack Vitek, *The Godfather of Tabloid: Generoso Pope and the National Enquirer* (The University Press of Kentucky, Lexington, 2008), p. 43.
193   BFJITA 8/253 0, 16 January 1939.
194   Ibid.
195   BFJITA 2/253 2, 2 January 1939.
196   Louis Rapoport, *Shake Heaven and Earth Peter Bergson and the Struggle to Rescue the Jews of Europe* (Gefen Publishing House, Jerusalem, 1999), pp. 30–31.

peripheral to the decision-making process. He was not used to this, and although Briscoe's unilateral action actually reflected the disparate 'political and institutional genesis' of the organization, Jabotinsky clearly did not appreciate his authority being undermined.[197]

This precipitated a contentious two-way exchange where Jabotinsky attempted to reassert his authority and bring Briscoe back under the central control of the Nessuit. Jabotinsky initiated the dialogue by expressing a sense of frustration, by wondering 'what has happened to upset the smooth working of a mission to which great hopes were attached'.[198] He was clearly going to great lengths not to alienate Briscoe, and before launching a carefully crafted yet stinging rebuke, he prefaced his criticism by reaffirming his 'intense regard and affection for' him.[199] Jabotinsky then got straight to the heart of the matter by querying Briscoe's independent decision-making.

> How then did it happen that that instruction had been so deliberately discarded? And without any reference to us here, without explaining why, without asking us if we could suggest some other arrangement?[200]

He was referring to a dispute that Briscoe had with Benjamin Akzin, a colleague who had been part of the resident revisionist delegation, and who had already established connections with some of Washington's political elite.[201] Although it is never entirely clear what Briscoe's problem with Akzin was, it was evidently a personal one that had made it impossible for the two men to constructively engage.[202] On this basis Briscoe pointed out to Jabotinsky that he had been accorded 'definite independence' of 'action here', and that all of his political achievements, such as they were, had been achieved 'without Akzin'.[203] It is evident that if Jabotinsky was determined

197 Judith Tydor Baumel, *The 'Bergson Boys' and the Origins of Contemporary Zionist Militancy* (New York, Syracuse University Press, 2005), p. 1
198 BFJITA 5/253 0, 26 February 1939.
199 Ibid.
200 Ibid.
201 Rosenblum, 'The New Zionist organization's American campaign', pp. 170–180.
202 Ibid.
203 BFJITA 5/253 0, 24 February 1939.

to regain control of a revisionist subordinate, Briscoe was as equally determined to assert what he believed to be a plenipotential authority.

Jabotinsky tried to placate a clearly irritated Briscoe, by once again massaging his ego:

> What an asset your adhesion is not only to the N.Z.O. but to Zionism as a whole. Apart from your personal qualifications which cannot be acquired-from the especial magnetism of an extremely winsome personality to a record as a fighter for liberty unparalleled throughout Jewry today.[204]

That was a clever strategic move; despite Briscoe's many virtues, modesty was not one of them, a membership of the successful Fianna Fáil party had instilled him with a considerable sense of self-confidence. However it is clear Jabotinsky's initial praise was merely sugar-coating to minimize the full impact of his critique.

> This fact of being a newcomer implies that you cannot have at your fingertips all the factual knowledge which an envoy on your present errand <u>must</u> possess. The Zionist business is extremely complicated, our N.Z.O. position doubly so, the Max Nordau plan and all it involves still more so. There are literally <u>thousands</u> of questions one must be ready to answer ... and it is literally impossible to answer them without complete familiarity not only with our theory but especially with all the precedents ... polemics, clashes, names etc.[205]

Evidently Jabotinsky had belatedly realized Briscoe's lack of a revisionist formation had left him woefully underprepared for the mission, and although Briscoe clearly understood the emigration initiative, Jabotinsky now believed his lack of theoretical understanding had exposed the delegation to exploitation by its Zionist opponents. Yet if Jabotinsky was now expressing a concern that Briscoe was theoretically impoverished, it can be justifiably argued that it was more a reflection on his own poor judgment than Briscoe's state of preparation. He had previously expressed this view forcibly to Joseph Schechtman, the Revisionist Envoy in Warsaw

204 Ibid., 26 February 1939.
205 Ibid.

before the American mission had even started.[206] Jabotinsky had cautioned Schechtman when Briscoe had visited Warsaw, the previous December that he needed to 'carefully instruct' him before he undertook any revisionist assignment 'as his preparation is superficial'.[207]

Once again however, any objective examination of Briscoe's limited Zionist formation would have made it manifestly clear that he did not have a theoretical appreciation of the concept. He was evidently a reactive, rather than proactive, Zionist and therefore could not possibly have the conceptual understanding that had taken Jabotinsky three decades to accumulate. This was clearly now Jabotinsky's main concern, and he was making every effort to get Briscoe to accept that he was potentially now a negative asset for the organization.

> I do not for a second admit that a man of your honesty could deny that ... most of this equipment is as yet lacking. A situation doubly dangerous because your mission is bound to be willfully obstructed by the Old Z.O. clique who will do their upmost to inspire skepticism in the minds even of Christian friends, telling them volumes of lies about Zionism and Palestine and the N.Z.O.[208]

Jabotinsky finished his assessment of the situation by suggesting that 'to leave such attacks unanswered ... and to rely just on the fascination of the cause itself, would be fatal'.[209] However, if he thought that this rebuke would bring Briscoe back into the fold then he was very much mistaken, it is clear that he was not in any way intimidated by Jabotinsky's argument, as he continued to tour America addressing both of his constituencies.

Despite the fact Briscoe was engaged in a bitter internal revisionist confrontation with Jabotinsky, it did not mean he was detached from either his Fianna Fáil commitments or developments that affected his co-religionists in Dublin. He was in constant contact with Mary Devoy, his loyal secretary, who informed him that the capitol was unfortunately not

206 Rosenblum, 'The New Zionist Organization's American campaign', p. 179.
207 Review by Joseph B. Schechtman, 'For the Life of Me', *Jewish Social Studies*, Vol. 21, No. 4 (October 1959), pp. 270–271., p. 270.
208 BFJITA 5/253 0, 26 February 1939.
209 Ibid.

immune to the global anti-Semitic tide. In February, Dublin was rocked by the publication of a virulent anti-Semitic manifesto echoing all the racial policies of Nazi Germany. It was issued by the fringe fascist group the Irish-Ireland Research Society (IIRS) and was reprinted in the *Irish Times* of 23 February. The opening paragraph fully enlightened people as to its intent:

> Having fought for our political freedom against England for centuries, we are confronted with a new enemy to-day-the Jew ... Unhappily, the whole question of racial aliens, their special moral code and values, is never widely appreciated until it is too late. When at last a remedy is applied to the evils engendered by leading Jewish propaganda the public is given no opportunity to judge for itself.[210]

The accompanying editorial made it clear that the paper had carried the report to highlight the crude and offensive nature of the document.

> It is difficult to believe that there are people in this country who are prepared to follow the lead of German Jew-baiters; but the notorious Julius Streicher himself could hardly improve upon the methods of the "Irish-Ireland Research Society".[211]

The publication of this distasteful diatribe had ramifications far beyond Ireland however; it was dispatched to Berlin by the German Legation where it was received with glee and republished in the *Völkischer Beobachter*, a Nazi mouthpiece. This was immediately reported to Dublin by William Warnock, who had replaced Charles Bewley as the Irish Plenipotentiary at the Berlin Mission. He supplied a translation of the report, noting the enthusiastic reception.

> There have recently been increasing signs in Ireland of a widespread enmity to Jews, which has been caused not least of all by the "refugee" policy of the Government. Irish Anti-Semitism is still fairly young ... Previous Anti-Semitic feeling was demonstrated merely by occasional attempts to establish a boycott of Jewish shops and firms, but now Irish Anti-Semitism appears to have taken a more definite form, as may be seen from the manifesto of the "Irish-Ireland research Society".[212]

210   NAI DFA, 227/24. 23 February 1939.
211   Ibid.
212   Ibid, 28 February.

The publication of the manifesto set alarm bells off in the security apparatus of the Irish state, the Gárdai Special Branch reported to the Minister for Justice that it had an undercover agent in the IIRS who had reported that the movement was trying to organize 'an anti-Semitic campaign'.[213] When questioned, Thomas Curran, the so-called leader of the IIRS, the agent discovered that the 'work was in better hands' a vital nugget of information that led back to George Griffin, leader of the anti-Semitic Irish Christian Rights Association.[214]

After Griffin was identified, a substantial file was compiled which also included a detailed report on an anti-Semitic attack on Briscoe's relationship with Fianna Fáil and de Valera. In yet another example of Griffin's xenophobic polemic, he vilified some of Fianna Fáil's senior members by insisting that 'the Fianna Fáil selection committee' had 'dropped Briscoe' from the previous year's South Dublin ticket.[215] According to Griffin, they had only relented when 'Mr Lemass had threatened to resign' as the party could not face the sensation of a Ministerial 'resignation'.[216] He developed his thesis by resurrecting the red scare accusations of 1932–1935 and accused de Valera of bowing to the demands of his 'Jewish masters'.[217] In Griffin's distorted worldview it was perfectly natural that de Valera, as the imagined son of 'a Portuguese Jew', would have done so, for after all, they had already 'forced him to protect them by name in the Constitution'.[218] This rant certainly contextualizes the sense of fear that pervaded the Jewish community, who 'for the most part the community depended on Robert Briscoe ... [as] an advocate for the Jewish cause'.[219]

Although disconcerted by events in Dublin, Briscoe was determined to carry on with his efforts to woo Americans to the revisionist cause. This obduracy finally led to Jabotinsky's most overt criticism of Briscoe's

213   IMA/G2/X/0040, 25 May 1939.
214   Ibid.
215   IMA X0040, 31 May 1939.
216   Ibid.
217   Ibid.
218   Ibid.
219   O'Connor, 'Irish Government Policy', p. 194.

behaviour yet, this time in a type of language that left no room for ambiguity. His frustration was clear, as he finally held nothing back, telling Briscoe that his lack of contact was 'unforgivable', and that he was 'deliberately affronted' by his conduct.[220] The tone and content of Jabotinsky's communiqué evidently stung Briscoe who attempted to explain the lack of communication by suggesting that he was under surveillance, and consequently could 'not risk' sending an open 'cable', or any detailed information through the 'post'.[221] Jabotinsky's response was startling, and in a fit of pique he chided Briscoe:

> For goodness' sake, if you had to give up the "courier" idea, why not have cabled to us "courier impracticable" so at least we should know there was nothing to await? And above all: why not have written? Even if there are secrets, surely there is no fear of anybody's interfering with your letters in Dublin.[222]

It is clear from Jabotinsky's comments that he believed Briscoe's reluctance to keep the Nessuit informed was merely another example of his disregard for the organization, rather than a genuine concern he was being observed. Given the controversial nature of the mission, Jabotinsky's response appears naïve in the extreme.[223]

More importantly, from Briscoe's perspective, if Jabotinsky believed, as he clearly did that the Irish state was any less observant when it came to the fact that one of its own elected parliamentarians was involved with an external political organization, then he was gravely mistaken. Although the evidence clearly shows that Jabotinsky was determined to reassert his authority over Briscoe, and clearly did not take his warnings of surveillance seriously, Briscoe's justification for not communicating would prove to be well founded.

His reticence was based on first-hand experience; as an elected member of the Dáil he would have been aware of the state's increasingly rigorous

220 BFJITA 5/253 0, 24 February 1939.
221 Ibid., 24 February 1939.
222 Ibid., 26 February 1939.
223 Ronald W. Davis, 'Jewish Military Recruitment in Palestine, 1940–1943', *Journal of Palestine Studies*, Vol. 8, No. 2 (Winter 1979), pp. 59–60.

censorship policy as the pre-war tension inexorably encroached on an isolationist Irish state.²²⁴ This was particularly relevant when it came to mail to and from Palestine, which was part of a security strategy that had a particular focus on contacts between recently arrived 'Jewish émigrés', and any external Jewish agencies.²²⁵ The fact that this policy was being implemented meant that it would have been implausible to think that the mail of an Irish-Jewish politician who was also a senior revisionist actor, would not have been subjected to the same level of scrutiny by the ruthlessly efficient Irish military intelligence directorate G2, which had, in fact, developed an extensive catalogue of his global Zionist activities.²²⁶

Briscoe's difficulties were not confined to his spat with Jabotinsky and conviction that the security apparatus of the Irish state was monitoring his every move. His wife Lily who had accompanied him on the early part of the Revisionist mission to America, but who as the mother of seven young children had to return home in early March 1939 forcefully pointed out the precarious state of the family's personal finances. When Lily returned to Dublin, she was distraught at her predicament and immediately informed Briscoe about the overwhelming economic difficulties that she had encountered.

> The money you left ... was not sufficient to pay the remaining household bills which makes it awkward to get credit so that I have to pay cash for everything. My very few remaining pounds are gone ... could you manage to let me have some every week just to keep the house going ... I write you all this not to worry you but think it is better you should know as otherwise you might not realise what we are up against.²²⁷

Indeed, Lily Briscoe's needs were so great that she had to start selling some of the family heirlooms, including a piano.

Her concern for Briscoe's well being is clear in the letter, it is an extraordinarily moving, and very intimate communication where in a gesture

---

224 Keogh, 'Irish Refugee Policy', p. 40.
225 Donal Ó Drisceoil, *Censorship in Ireland 1939–1945: Neutrality, Politics and Society* (Cork University Press, Cork, 1996), p. 66.
226 IMA IE/MA/G2/X/0040/P.
227 BFJITA 2/253 2, 28 March 1939.

of love and support she acknowledged what her husband was trying to achieve. She also goes to the trouble of warning him that the people he was encountering might not necessarily be so altruistic.

> I miss you very much my love but realise fully the urgency of the mission you are on and pray you will be successful in your efforts if only you were not so trusting of others I would be still more proud of you but I have hopes that even now at this late hour you will hesitate in giving your remaining crutch away lest you yourself fall and perhaps you will listen to me and realise that friends unfortunately are few and far between.[228]

Lily also included a handwritten note from his young son Joe that puts into perspective Briscoe's involvement in the Revisionist mission. If any one single document summarizes the pressure he was under, then it is this poignant and innocent letter from a son who even at the tender age of eleven, seemed to understand the importance of his father's endeavours.

> Dear Daddy, mammy told me to write to you. I hope you are very well. I am very happy that mammy is back and I am having a great time. Billie is coming back on the 9th of April. I am looking forward to you coming home and hope your mission is a success. I am learning to write in Hebrew and like it very much. We are having a great time with the soldiers. Lots of love Joe.[229]

He clearly understood that Jews were in a perilous position a prescience that would be borne out in barely six months time as Jewish children the same age as Joe would be slaughtered in their hundreds of thousands at the hands of a rapacious Nazi war machine. It is clear from these letters that Briscoe was supported by a loving family who understood the urgency of what he was trying to achieve, and if his revisionist allegiance needed a justification, than it would arguably have been the realization that if his beloved children had had the misfortune to be born in continental Europe, then they would be living under the threat of persecution from an imminent Nazi invasion.

228 Ibid.
229 Ibid.

As the American mission wound down, it was clear Briscoe was a deeply troubled man who was desperately pessimistic about the decreasing survival options available to Europe's Jews. This was clearly expressed in an extended dialogue with Bill Ziff, an American revisionist with whom Briscoe had formed a close bond that would endure throughout the war and beyond. Ziff's revisionist formation reflected Briscoe's own rapid Zionist evolution; it was a reactive response to a crisis situation that was predicated on saving lives.[230] The fact that the two men had instantly connected was not surprising when Ziff's adventurous formative years are compared to Briscoe's. Before he founded a successful publishing business he had participated in South American revolutionary politics, and run for election as a 'United States' Congressman.[231]

Two months after his return from America in August 1939 Briscoe received a letter from Ziff, who, clearly concerned about his friend's well-being, had written in an effort to bolster his moral. Ziff evidently believed he was addressing a colleague who had abandoned the revisionist attempt to convert American Jews to the cause.[232]

> To tell you the truth I have been desperately afraid that the result of your dealings with the people you saw in this country might have definitely soured you on the whole proposition, leading you to believe that further effort was hopeless … I was mortally certain that nothing whatever would come from the promises made by the men you contacted.[233]

Ziff had written this letter to Briscoe on the twenty-sixth of August, only eight days before Britain and France declared war on Nazi Germany, in an effort even at this late stage, to convince him not to give up on the campaign.

The chaotic events of September 1939 meant that it took Briscoe more than a month to respond to Ziff. When he did, his conviction that the WZO had wilfully obstructed the revisionists was evident as the brutal

230 Gal, *David Ben-Gurion and the American Alignment for a Jewish State*, pp. 119–120.
231 Medoff, *Militant Zionism in America*, pp. 39–40.
232 Tydor Baumel, *The 'Bergson Boys'*, p. 126.
233 JMD, 26 August 1939.

reality of war brought home with a terrible certainty the destruction of his co-religionists.

> The Weizmann group are even now living in the clouds; their decisions and pronouncements have been weak and without tact. They apparently have their heads stuck out of one window so far that the only view they have is the view from that window, and all attempts to make them look through any other window to see a different view, is without success.[234]

Briscoe's lament revealed the fragility of his psyche which he confirmed by informing Ziff that he was 'very depressed'.[235] That proposition was reinforced when Briscoe expressed his fears for the future of eastern European Jews.

> It is quite obvious that as far as the Jewish problem is concerned, a lot of it unfortunately has been solved. The population of Jews in Poland will no longer I feel be anything like the 3½ millions, and before this war is over goodness only knows how many more of the people who profess the Jewish faith will be non-existent.[236]

Briscoe's apocalyptic vision of the forthcoming Jewish disaster was frighteningly prescient, he evidently believed that the world was on the cusp of a Jewish Holocaust. This belief was reinforced when he pointed out to Ziff that he had repeatedly cautioned 'American Jews … that the only solution was Palestine', and if this was not achieved, than 'the only alternative' was 'extermination'.[237] It is important to emphasize that Briscoe's insight about the forthcoming Nazi Jewish conflagration pre-dated the Wannsee Conference of 20 January 1942 by almost two and a half years.[238]

One of the major areas of concern for Briscoe in this letter was his precarious financial situation. He clearly believed it was a consequence of his revisionist membership:

234 RBPP, 22 September 1939.
235 Ibid.
236 Ibid.
237 Ibid.
238 www.orte-der-erinnerung.de/en/institutions/list_of_institutions/house_of_the_wannsee_conference_memorial_and_educational_site

> As regards my own personal trouble arising out of my trip to America: I would like very much to hear that a sum of money could be secured to pay off undercharged liabilities ... which I have been unable to clear, and as far as I can see will be unable personally to do for some time if the payments ... are left to me.[239]

However, even though Briscoe was concerned about a difficult personal financial situation, it is clear his distress was reinforced by a realization that the war had ended revisionist aspirations for a mass Jewish emigration to Palestine. The depth of Briscoe's despair was illustrated when he emphasized that any level of debt, no matter how great it was, would have been worth it if the American mission had succeeded.

> I do not claim from anybody one penny for my time, nor do I even claim the expenses ... and if even I were never to recover them if the opportunity arose to do the same again with the slightest hope of success I, without doubt, would risk doing the whole job all over again.[240]

This was evidently not the case, Briscoe's personal assessment was that every aspect of the mission had 'failed completely', and his melancholia came through in every paragraph of a highly personal statement that was elegiac in composition.[241] Briscoe poignantly concluded his dialogue with Ziff with the rejoinder that, 'each 'cause' has to have those who will give their lives and those who will jeopardize their future comforts in a cause'.[242] This somewhat introspective assessment of his role in the American mission has an element of self-pity; however, this is hardly surprising given the level of emotional stress that came from the realization that millions of his co-religionists would now be exposed to the Nazi anti-Semitic project.

One of the most enduring personal legacies of Briscoe's time in America was his initial engagement in the desperate revisionist attempt to save

---

239 RBPP, 22 September 1939.
240 RBPP, 22 September 1939.
241 Briscoe and Hatch, *For the Life of Me*, p. 276.
242 RBPP, 22 September 1939.

German and Austrian Jewish refugees by transporting them to the safety of the only place on earth that was not merely willing, but eager to accept them, the British controlled Palestine Mandate.[243] It is clear from his dialogue with Ziff that Briscoe had been deeply affected by his time in America, and his participation in the *Aliyah Bet* also reveals that he was no longer prepared to limit his contribution to the political or publicity aspects of the Revisionist emigration campaign.[244] The *Aliyah Bet* had been ongoing since 1937, although it only really became a dominant theme within the emigration campaign after the failure of the Evian Conference. This upsurge in so-called illegal attempts to facilitate a mass Jewish emigration to the Palestine Mandate; had originated in the recent the emigration quotas of the MacDonald White Paper of 1939.[245]

All the necessary political and social precursors were now in place, and a divided Zionist movement initiated the *Aliyah Bet*, which like so many aspects of a fractured Zionist reaction to the Nazi inspired emigration crisis, was not a coordinated response. Two operations were simultaneously set in motion; the Yishuv in Palestine established the *L'Aliyah Bet* (Institute for Illegal Immigration) under the direction of the Mossad, and implemented by the soldier volunteers of the Haganah.[246] Contemporaneously, the revisionists established an alternative movement, the *Mercaz Le Aliyah* (Centre

243 Dalia Offer and Hannah Weiner, *Dead-End Journey* (University Press of America, Lanham MD, 1996), pp. 10–20.
244 *Aliyah Bet* (Hebrew for ascend and the letter B) was the chosen codename for the Zionist operation to land as many illegal [as defined by the British] Jewish immigrants on the shores of Palestine as Possible, for further reading see: Murray S. Greenfield and Joseph M. Hochstein, *The Jews' Secret Fleet the Untold Story of North American Volunteers who Smashed the British Blockade of Palestine* (Gefen Publishing House, Jerusalem, 1987), pp. 176–188.
245 For further reading see: Yehuda Bauer, *American Jewry and the Holocaust the American Jewish Joint Distribution Committee, 1939–1945* (Wayne State University Press, Detroit MI, 1982), pp. 129–151. Apter, 'Disorderly Decolonization', pp. 61–91.
246 For further reading see: Tuvia Friling, *Arrows in the Dark David Ben-Gurion, the Yishuv Leadership, and Rescue Attempts during the Holocaust* (The University of Wisconsin Press, Madison WC, 2005), pp. 125–138. Yitzakh Avnery, 'Immigration and Revolt: Ben-Gurion's Response to the 1939 White Paper', in Ronald W. Zwig (ed.),

for Immigration) under the leadership of the Irgun, and implemented by Jabotinsky's young Betarists.[247] The two separate operations may have been united by a desire to rescue Europe's persecuted Jews; however, the very fact that two initiatives were established reinforced the ideological split that had occurred between Jabotinsky and Weizmann.[248] This split would manifest on what was now the biggest political stage of them all, the United States of America, as each faction fought to establish hegemony over the disparate Zionist movement.[249]

The division within Zionism could not have come at a more inopportune moment; even if it had coordinated a unified *Aliyah Bet*, it would have been confronted by an intransigent British policy that was grounded in a geo-political imperative of placating the Arab population. MacDonald had recommended that:

> During the next ten years the principle of the economic absorptive capacity of Palestine to continue to govern the rate of immigration subject to a proviso that in any case the number of immigrants should not exceed a certain level. This level would be such as to ensure that by the end of a ten-year period the Jewish population would not exceed 40 per cent of the total population of Palestine ... I understand that if the figure were 40 per cent., the average Jewish immigration which would be possible per annum during the ten years would amount to 29,840 individuals. If the figure were 35 per cent., it would amount to 15,300.[250]

David Ben-Gurion: Politics and Leadership in Israel (Routledge, London, 1991), pp. 106–112.

247 Dalia Offer, 'The Rescue of European Jewry and Illegal Immigration to Palestine in 1940-Prospects and Reality: Berthold Storfer and the Mossad Le'Aliyah Bet', *Modern Judaism*, Vol. 4, No. 2 (May 1984), pp. 160–162.

248 Goldstein, 'Labour and Likud: Roots of their Ideological-Political Struggle for Hegemony over Zionism', pp. 80–85.

249 For further reading see: Judith Tydor Baumel, 'The IZL Delegation in the USA 1939–1948: Anatomy of an Ethnic Interest/Protest Group', *Jewish History*, Vol. 9, No. 1 (Spring 1995), pp. 80–86. Naomi W. Cohen, *The Americanization of Zionism, 1897–1948* (Brandeis University Press, Lebanon NH, 2003), pp. 135–145. Gal, *David Ben-Gurion and the American Alignment for a Jewish State*, 15–67.

250 TNA CAB/24/282, 18 January 1939.

Initially, Jabotinsky had not believed that the British, whom he held in the highest regard, would desert the Jews in their hour of greatest need; however, once again Jabotinsky's faith in British morality was misplaced.[251] Despite his best hopes, it was clear that just when the borders of Palestine needed to be unrestricted and all-embracing, the British determination to prioritize Christian geo/political concerns over humanitarian Jewish ones effectively reduced the immigration rate to zero.[252]

MacDonald had not recommended the quotas without deep reservations, and he warned the cabinet that the restrictions could possibly be counter-productive as militaristic Zionist factions would undoubtedly exploit them.

> There is one other factor which we cannot ignore. The Jews are naturally in a desperate frame of mind. The events of the last few months have strengthened the extremist Zionist elements as against the moderates like Dr Weizmann.[253]

He explained his statement by referring to the universal Jewish outrage that had resulted from the government's refusal to allow the children of the *Kindertransports* to enter Palestine in their hour of greatest need.

> Jewish feeling inside Palestine is tense and bitter just now; it has been deeply stirred by our refusal to allow the immediate immigration of 10,000 Jewish refugee children from Germany to homes which are awaiting them ... and by our rigid restrictions of many of their own relations ... who owing to our refusal ... must face almost intolerable misery, perhaps in concentration camps in Germany.[254]

MacDonald's concerns were justified; in the final Cabinet meeting before the White Paper was issued he informed it that the Jewish campaign of resistance was no longer confined to the revisionist extremists, but was now equally as strong in the moderate WZO faction. To reinforce

---

251   Shavit, *Jabotinsky and the Revisionist Movement*, pp. 212–215.
252   David Cymet, *History Vs. Apologetics The Holocaust, The Third Reich, And The Catholic Church* (Lexington Books, Lanham MD, 2010), pp. 128–130.
253   TNA CAB/24/282, 18 January 1939.
254   Ibid.

his point, MacDonald quoted at length from a cable he had just received from Chaim Weizmann, the organization's moderate Anglophile President.

> On my return Palestine found Jewish community united resolute determination oppose with all its strength contemplated new policy. Proposed liquidation of mandate and establishment independent Palestine state coupled with reduction Jewish population to one-third total and with restriction area Jewish settlement to small sector ... are viewed as destruction Jewish hopes and surrender Jewish community ... to rule Arab Junta responsible for Terrorist campaign. Adoption these proposals regarded to tantamount to establishment Jewish Ghetto in small corner of country. Jews are determined make supreme sacrifice rather than submit to such regime.[255]

Weizmann's warning to MacDonald proved to be well founded, and although many Jews would resist British policy by joining extreme militaristic organizations like the Stern Gang, the most immediate response to the restrictions of the White Paper was a sustained Zionist campaign of illegal emigration to Palestine.[256]

Although America would be the epicentre of the Aliyah Bet, Briscoe's involvement would take place many thousands of miles away in a South Africa which was home to a strong Zionist community.[257] Despite disagreeing over the American mission, Jabotinsky clearly still believed that Briscoe was a valuable revisionist asset. Consequently on his return from the States he asked him to lead a mission to South Africa. This had a dual purpose; firstly and most importantly it was designed to secure financial support to purchase ships for the Aliyah Bet, a task Briscoe would reinforce by promoting the revisionist emigration plan to Palestine. He left for South Africa in October 1939, and recalled how Jabotinsky had explained the urgency behind the endeavour:

---

255   TNA CAB/24/285, 21 April 1939.
256   For the most comprehensive overview of the internecine politicking that surrounded the Aliyah Bet see: Abraham J. Edelheit, *The Yishuv in the Shadow of the Holocaust Zionist Politics and Rescue Aliya, 1933–1939* (Westview Press, Boulder CO, 1998).
257   Richard Mendelsohn and Milton Shain, 'South Africa' in Danny Ben-Moshe and Zohar Segev (eds.), *Israel, the Diaspora, and Jewish Identity* (Sussex Academic Press, Eastbourne, 2007), pp. 279–285.

He told me that our work must still go on; but money was desperately needed. In South Africa there were ninety thousand Jews; rich Jews and generous. Would I go to South Africa? With one compassionate look at Lily's face, I said "I will".[258]

The revisionists hoped that this group of rich Jews would support its maximalist approach to emigration and understand the necessity of getting as many Jews to Palestine as possible. It was soon clear this strategy had made the organization increasingly vulnerable to exploitation in its desperation, it was oftentimes obliged to take ships that were barely seaworthy.[259] The revisionists hoped that Briscoe's previous contacts in the global shipping community from his time as an IRA gun-runner might lead to them obtaining a better class of ship. However, when he arrived in Durban, he was immediately embroiled in controversy; the conservative Zionists of the WZO had launched a propaganda campaign to undermine the Revisionist Aliyah, and one of their affiliated papers in South Africa had accused him of:

> Squeezing money from the Jewish community for the "coffin ships" bringing immigrants who were "dumped into Palestine without regard for their usefulness for the country; no screening or selection is attempted; some of them are Viennese prostitutes".[260]

This charge infuriated Jabotinsky who demanded Ben-Gurion withdraw it immediately as a slur against both the revisionists and the Jews they brought to Palestine; Ben-Gurion refused.[261] Briscoe was equally outraged, and he explained the revisionist rationale for charging those Jews who could afford it in the following way:

> One of the criticisms was that we charged rich refugees outrageous prices-several thousand pounds for a passage to Palestine. So we did. In the expressive American

258   Briscoe and Hatch, *For the Life of Me*, p. 277.
259   Ofer, 'Illegal Immigration to Palestine', pp. 161–162.
260   Katz, *Lone Wolf*, p. 1712.
261   Dan Nimrod, *Testimony and Warning Reflections on a Pattern of Behaviour* (Dawn Publishing, Nevada City CA, 1980), pp. 22–28.

phrase we soaked the rich. But for every rich man who paid the price of liberty we were able to rescue five or ten impoverished Jews who had no means to pay at all.[262]

This confrontation did not escape the notice of the British who were observing Briscoe's every move; on 20 November the United Kingdom High Commissioner sent the following report to London, with an approving introduction.

> Briscoe … addressed Jewish meeting in Johannesburg and replied at length to attack made on him since his arrival by the "Old Zionist" organisation. He said that Jews throughout the world were anxious for Allied victory, and, as for the Irish people, ninety per cent of them wanted to see victory for the democracies over dictatorship and brutality. He was himself Irish Republican but his country was completely free and he did not want anyone to imagine because he was so strongly pro-Irish and pro-Zionist that he is anti-English, that was an absurd assumption[263]

Having said that, even though Briscoe always emphasized his pro-Allied stance by expressing a personal willingness as a Jew 'to fight alongside of England', he was careful at all times to emphasize this was a personal belief. Likewise when on official business as an Irish politician, he consistently framed this personal viewpoint by stressing that he did 'not permit [his] emotions or [his] loyalty to people of [his] faith to sway [his] judgement', once more emphasizing that he thought 'only of what [was] best for Irishmen.'[264]

However, this was not the case in South Africa, which was very much a personal mission of faith, so he did not hesitate to stress his personal fears for the future survival of European Jewry:

> Some people thought that the Jews should wait until the war was over and the Allies were victorious before the Jewish question could be taken up again. This was all very well but the position was that if the war continued for a long time, say three or four years, the Jewish population of Eastern Europe would be almost completely decimated.[265]

262 Briscoe and Hatch, *For the Life of Me*, p. 272.
263 BFJITA, C. O. 733/406/75872/13. 20 November 1939.
264 Briscoe and Hatch, *For the Life of Me*, pp. 285–286.
265 BFJITA, C. O. 733/406/75872.13. 20 November 1939.

Briscoe once more emphasized his overwhelming and prescient fear first expressed to Bill Ziff earlier that year in America that the Jews of Europe were facing annihilation at the hands of the Nazis. He reinforced this position with a mixture of pathos by declaring that 'he was satisfied that when the war ended the world would give Palestine to the Jews', before caustically chiding his audience that 'the Jews in the meantime ... give their full support to the cause of helping refugees to be re-established in Palestine'.[266] Briscoe concluded his address with a final desperate plea for Zionist unity, stating that 'he was particularly anxious to secure full cooperation amongst the Jews of both organisations, in order to help in the solution of the Jewish problem'.[267]

The Zionist faction fight became so overt that Briscoe was detained by the South African authorities, and was only released through the intervention of a prominent South African revisionist, by the name of Haskell, who used his government contacts to free him.[268] Haskell's intervention was strengthened when de Valera became directly involved in Briscoe's detention, by contacting the South Africans to request that he received 'the same courtesy that members of the South African parliament always received in Ireland'.[269]

When he was released, Briscoe endeavoured to garner support in the South African Zionist community. Shmuel Katz, a revisionist colleague, described him as 'an eloquent man', and his many years of political experience were evident as he replicated the successful publicity component of the American mission. His first task was to make a public rebuttal to the 'coffin ship' accusations; he had spent a considerable part of his incarceration preparing this statement:[270]

> If we were all passengers aboard a sinking vessel and we were ordered to abandon ship; and I was the officer in charge of the gangways, do you think it would be right,

266   Ibid.
267   Ibid.
268   Briscoe and Hatch, *For the Life of Me*, p. 278.
269   Ibid.
270   Katz, *Lone Wolf*, p. 1598.

> if before allowing you into the little boats that would row you to safety, I should ask
> for a confession of your sins or in what profession you make a living? It is none of
> my business what these people are. If they profess Judaism, and because of that their
> lives are at stake, then if I can save them I will, no matter how they have sinned.[271]

Briscoe's impassioned appeal appeared to touch a chord in the Jewish community; he described the South African mission to raise money for the Revisionist Aliyah as 'very successful'.[272]

The money he raised in South Africa substantially contributed to the success of the Revisionist *Mercaz L'Aliyah*, which eventually undertook thirteen voyages between September 1939 and March 1941, bringing 10,628 people to Palestine.[273] It was an operation that had substantive risks for the brave volunteer crews of Briscoe's vessels; there was the constant fear that the ships would sink or that they would be intercepted or fired upon by the Royal Navy warships that were enforcing the blockade.[274] This is evident in the only discoverable Aliyah document in Briscoe's multiple archives, in which he clearly voiced the fear that the revisionists felt, as each so-called 'coffin ship' made its desperate attempt to reach Palestine:

> The N.Z.O. Ship has lost its Captain, and the crew in attempting to bring the ship
> to port have lost the rudder, and the ship is now floundering around ... In the storm
> the ship will sink and all aboard will be lost and with this disaster will come the complete destruction of our Jewish people, and any of the hopes that some of us might
> have had to be able to rescue even a fragment the ship of salvation will be gone.[275]

The melancholia in his reflection illuminated the extraordinary pressure of being involved in the *Mercaz L'Aliyah Bet*; however, it is also clear he did not regret taking part in the operation, despite the terrible losses.

> Conservative Jews in England and America condemned our efforts. They called our
> vessels "coffin ships" because many people died in them. They were right in a way.

---

271 Briscoe and Hatch, *For the Life of Me*, p. 279.
272 Ibid.
273 Bauer, *American Jewry and the Holocaust*, p. 137.
274 Garbarini, et al, *Jewish Responses to Persecution*, pp. 66–74.
275 BFJITA 2/253 2, 4 December 1940.

The conditions in our boats were perhaps more dreadful than those on a Yankee
slaver. But these people were carried out of slavery; and the sum of lives we saved
was infinitely greater than those we lost.[276]

He reinforced this point when he was briefly detained by the British authorities when he returned from South Africa. He told officials that 'I expect
to be arrested any minute, for I have broken all your rules, regulations and
laws. I am responsible to a considerable extent for thousands of Jewish
people smuggled through your blockade into Palestine'.[277] When the arrest
did not materialize, despite admitting that he had no legal 'defense [sic]',
he told the officers that 'I would love to go to jail, for I would be the first
man in the world sent there for saving life instead of taking it'.[278]

Briscoe's decision to accept the mission to South Africa also emphasized the level of scrutiny from his G2 surveillance team who prepared a
comprehensive report for their political masters.

Briscoe visited South Africa in 1939–1940 to secure funds for the New Zionist
Organisation to take Jewish war refugees from Eastern and Central Europe ... The
British press reported in January, 1940 that former members of the I.R.A. were
forming a new Irish Regiment in South Africa. In a letter dated 23/11/1939 from a
woman in Middleburg, South Africa, to a friend in Dublin, the writer stated: "I see
by the papers here ... one of de Valera's men, a Robert Briscoe is in Johannesburg
recruiting for an Irish regiment. He is only here a few days and he already has 800
volunteers, he is only taking Irish and the descendents of Irish parents, he is getting
more than he called for.[279]

This accusation was totally without foundation; Briscoe's sole purpose for
being in South Africa was to facilitate if possible, the revisionist L'Mercaz
Aliyah Bet; of course if this could be furthered by connecting with South
Africa's Irish diaspora, Briscoe would exploit that to the full.[280]

276   Briscoe and Hatch, *For the Life of Me*, p. 271.
277   Ibid., pp. 281–282.
278   Ibid., p. 282.
279   IMA/G2/X/0040, February 1940.
280   McCarthy, 'The Zionist Evolution of Robert Briscoe', pp. 270–274.

1940–1943
Political Retrenchment: Nationalist Reintegration and Zionist Withdrawal

When Briscoe returned from South Africa in the spring of 1940, he had in many respects already reached the apex of his revisionist engagement, and although still fully committed to the organization, he was almost immediately involved in one of the most contentious historical issues of Ireland's wartime neutrality. Despite improved political, social and cultural relations with Britain, the fundamental issue of partition still bedevilled a burgeoning détente between the Irish state and its former colonial master. Indeed in a broader analysis of Briscoe's political evolution, it can be seen that partition had become, in many respects, the defining issue that bound him to de Valera and Jabotinsky in a synthesis that was unbreakable. He had unreservedly supported 'The Chief' when he rejected the partition of the Irish state in the 1920s, and he had offered the same steadfast support to Jabotinsky when the revisionists rejected MacDonald's proposal to Partition Palestine in 1937.

This is clear when Briscoe's schedule for the first six months of 1940 is examined; it was a frenetic mix of revisionist representation that required his presence in London for at least one week a month, and a reintegration into the parochial world of Fianna Fáil politics.[1] A core aspect of these periods in London, which Briscoe dreaded due to the constant bombing of the blitz, was a constant campaign of advocacy with senior members of the British political elite. One of Briscoe's closest contacts was Sir Hugh Seely, the Liberal Chief Whip, who was the Under Secretary of State for

---

1   Briscoe and Hatch, *For the Life of Me*, p. 290.

Air in the wartime coalition.[2] On 27 May Briscoe met Seely, and in a wide-ranging discussion emotively informed him that 'the tragedy of my people grows daily', before imploring him to convey these fears 'to your highest authority'.[3] Briscoe forcefully expressed his support for the allied war effort, insightfully arguing his position by pointing out that 'if defeat comes to you, it comes to us to the extent of extermination. I hope however, that democracy will survive and that little fragment or remnant of my people will also survive'.[4]

This position was certainly noted by his G2 surveillance team, any contact with British politicians outside of a Fianna Fáil remit was a source of concern for the security service. This was reinforced by observations of a more local nature; on 19 June, a report expressed reservations that 'the Jewish section of the population is making a concerted movement towards enrolment in the Local Security Corps'.[5] The report identified Briscoe as the driving force behind this surge of Jewish volunteers, remarking that now that he had returned from South Africa, 'he has called a meeting of the men of his community and instructed them to enrol'.[6] The report further noted that this had precipitated a backlash from some of the Gentile reservists, who 'on finding a large number of young Jews' present, sarcastically remarked 'he thought he had wandered by accident into a synagogue rather than a Garda station'.[7] The G2 operative was careful to couch his remarks in a manner that indicated observation rather then judgement, however, he noted that such a large influx of a minority community was inevitably going to have a deleterious effect on the recruitment of other circles', before recommending a clause necessitating 'a period of residence',

2   Ian Philpott, *The Royal Air Force: An Encyclopedia of the Inter-War Years, Re-Armament, 1930–1939* (Pen and Sword Aviation, Barnsley, 2008), pp. 28–30.
3   BFJITA 2/253 2. 27 May 1940.
4   Ibid.
5   IMA.G2/X/0040, Minute No 2. 19 June 1940.
6   Ibid.
7   Ibid.

which would hopefully exclude 'at least the majority of the persons with ulterior motives and of only 50 percent loyalty'.[8]

Yet despite suspicions about Briscoe's loyalty from certain sectors of Ireland's established ruling mechanism, this view was never shared by Éamon de Valera, the most important man in the state, who never doubted Briscoe's commitment to faithfully represent his vision of a united Ireland. This was evident when he was delegated to represent the government at the 1940 meeting of the Empire Parliamentary Association in London. This personal appointment reinforces the argument that de Valera viewed Briscoe not only as an important member of Fianna Fáil, but also as a trusted confidant who would faithfully reflect his own political worldview. Perhaps the clearest example of this would occur in the rejection of the tentative offer by Britain of a united Ireland in exchange for the abandonment of Irish neutrality in 1940.[9] Despite personal reservations, Briscoe would faithfully endorse de Valera's stance on the issue when he appeared before the Empire Parliamentary Union in London, less than a week after de Valera had rejected the offer.

When Malcolm MacDonald cautiously approached de Valera and made the initial proposal that an end to partition might be possible, it was on the basis that Ireland would enter the war on the side of the allies. For strategic reasons, Britain was frantically trying to regain access to the Treaty-ports it had signed away in the 1938 Anglo-Irish agreement to facilitate the war in the Atlantic.[10] In many respects the offer could be classified as an act of desperation as Westminster was assailed by the awful prospect of invasion and starvation as the U-boats sank its merchant marine with fearful precision.[11] However, it was clear the fear of invasion was not confined to the British; Dublin was equally as concerned as London, and

---

8   Ibid.
9   Thomas E. Hachey, 'The Rhetoric and Reality of Irish Neutrality', *New Hibernia Review*, Vol. 6, No. 4 (Winter 2002), pp. 29–35.
10   Kelly, *Fianna Fáil, Partition and Northern Ireland*, p. 93.
11   Ibid.

only differed by believing that Britain was as likely to invade Ireland as Germany was Britain.[12]

This fear meant that within two weeks of Britain and France declaring war on Germany, the maintenance of neutrality was already a core tenet in the Irish policy-making process.[13] There were a number of reasons for this unyielding position: firstly, there was a determination to implement a foreign policy, independent of Britain. This approach was supported not just parochially, but also by large sections of the Irish diaspora.[14] This was particularly relevant, as Briscoe had found out, to Irish-America where a series of articles 'recounting British brutality ... during the Black and Tan war', argued that British 'materialistic philosophy [guaranteed] that Britain and Eire could never abide in peace under one roof'.[15] Indeed, so ingrained was this worldview that even when evidence of the Nazi Jewish Holocaust entered the public domain in the post-war period, it was oftentimes attributed by this group to 'British Propaganda'.[16]

This intuitive suspicion of Britain was reinforced by a moral argument that rejected the chaos and violence of a global conflict, and was predicated on aligning the national psyche 'to feel compassion for all suffering, regardless of which side the victims were on'.[17] Consequently, the government 'refused to allow the war to be placed in a moral framework', and the conflict was framed and disseminated to an isolated Irish public, as one 'between powers pursuing their own materialistic interests'.[18] However, in order to affect this process in an even-handed way, a policy of strict censorship needed to be enforced that denied the Irish public access to the atrocity stories (particularly about Jews) that were starting to emanate from

---

12   Ibid., p. 94.
13   Ó Drisceoil, *Censorship in Ireland 1939–1945*, pp. 2–6.
14   Lee, *Politics and Society*, p. 263.
15   Robert Cole, *Propaganda, Censorship and Irish Neutrality in the Second World War* (Edinburgh University Press, Edinburgh, 2006), p. 89.
16   Donal Ó Drisceoil, 'Moral Neutrality censorship in Emergency Ireland', *History Ireland*, Vol. 4, No. 2 (Summer 1996), p. 19.
17   Wills, *That Neutral Island*, p. 423.
18   Ó Drisceoil, 'Moral Neutrality', p. 20.

Nazi-occupied Europe.[19] This was deemed essential if 'the desired sense of moral superiority' was to be maintained; it would simply not have been possible to sustain if one of 'the belligerents' was portrayed as outdoing the other in 'the savagery stakes'.[20] Briscoe was the exception, although a loyal member of Fianna Fáil and fervent de Valera loyalist, his revisionist endeavours had endowed a terrible insight into the evolving persecution of his co-religionists. Yet despite this, he accepted de Valera's request to defend a government policy of neutrality he fervently disagreed with.

So it is clear that the spring of 1940 was a particularly volatile social as well as political moment in the evolving wartime position of the Irish state; therefore, it is perhaps not surprising that when the British offer finally came, de Valera reacted with extreme caution, giving it no real 'serious consideration'.[21] In June, de Valera had warned the Dáil of the potential danger of losing what they already had.

> Nobody who does not wilfully blind himself can say that we are well out of the war zone, or that we can be sure it would not suit any of the belligerents to interfere with the liberties which we claim to be ours. ... I am not a prophet. Neither can I try to hide the fact that the whole national territory is not under the control of this Government. That is not the way to look at the problem. Partition did not happen since the war began. It exists, and we have to try and get rid of it, but we are not going to get rid of it by losing the independence we have here.[22]

It is therefore clear that the Irish government, and de Valera in particular, was intent on preserving the status quo and was not tempted by a possible unification. This was clear in his detailed response to the offer on 4 July when he pointed out to Neville Chamberlain that as far as the Irish government was concerned, the offer was 'purely tentative'.[23] He also pointed out that the proposal had 'not been submitted to Lord Craigavon and his

19 Ó Drisceoil, *Censorship in Ireland 1939–1945*, p. 263.
20 Lee, *Politics and Society*, p. 267.
21 Kelly, *Fianna Fáil, Partition and Northern Ireland*, p. 94.
22 DÉD, Vol. 80, Cols. 1665–1666, 6 June 1940.
23 TNA CAB/66/9/31, 4 July 1940.

colleagues', who represented nearly a million recalcitrant Ulster unionists.[24] De Valera told the British that:

> The plan would involve our entry into the war. That is a course for which we could not accept responsibility. Our people would be quite unprepared for it, and Dail Éireann would certainly reject it.[25]

So when Briscoe finally went to London to address the Empire Parliamentary Association in July, it was clear he would be a lone voice advocating a position of neutrality, while every other 'Dominion Parliament' supported Britain in its wartime endeavours.[26] This was despite the fact that on a personal basis he believed that the best hope for Europe's Jews was a British victory, and clearly indicates he was prepared to put his own beliefs to one side when de Valera requested him to.[27] He explained this seemingly contradictory stance in the following way:

> How did I personally feel about Ireland's declaration of neutrality; I who had seen with my own eyes Jewish people hunted and persecuted by the Nazis; who already knew about the plans for the genocide of my race; who had a prevision of that ultimate incredible horror, the crematoria; I who hated Hitler and all he stood for with a fury beyond my power of speech? I thought it was right for Ireland.[28]

As a Fianna Fáil loyalist, he knew as long as partition endured, it would be politically impossible to declare war on the side of England. He explained the rationale behind the Dáil's unanimous decision to adopt a neutral stance in the following way:

> To a considerable extent our action was caused by the cancer of partition. Britain to us was still an aggressor nation with her troops on Irish soil. By her policy of divide and conquer, by deception and economic bribery, she had divided us.[29]

24 Ibid.
25 Ibid.
26 Briscoe and Hatch, *For the Life of Me*, p. 284.
27 Wood, *Britain, Ireland and the Second World War*, p. 203.
28 Briscoe and Hatch, *For the Life of Me*, p. 285.
29 Ibid., p. 284.

Despite an unqualified support for neutrality, it still must have been difficult for Briscoe to reconcile his personal beliefs with his political commitment to de Valera and Fianna Fáil. It is clear that Briscoe was able to support neutrality on the basis of asserting a sovereign independence from Britain, while simultaneously rejecting the moral arguments about impartiality. When viewed from this perspective, perhaps Briscoe's performance at the conference in representing de Valera's position so faithfully, despite personal reservations, is the perfect example of the complex nature of his assimilation.

Addressing the meeting of the Empire Parliamentary Association, Briscoe openly admitted to the forum that he feared a Nazi invasion of the Irish state by stating that 'I am one of those who feel that the danger is more likely to come from your enemy, Germany', than any other source.[30] Although he clearly had no difficulty acknowledging this, Briscoe also emphasized that although he 'had spoken with Mr de Valera' prior to arriving in London, he needed 'to make it perfectly clear' that he was not 'speaking officially on behalf of my Government'.[31] Yet when he addressed the commission on partition/neutrality, his phraseology on the issue was almost identical to de Valera's:

> We desire the unity of Ireland. We do not propose to blackmail you at the present moment into helping to bring about that unity because of the present situation, but we do believe you ought to look at the facts as they are, and forgetting all that has happened in the past realise the present position and your relation to it.[32]

The essence of Briscoe's speech reflected de Valera's 1937 post-Geneva conversation with Malcolm MacDonald, and like de Valera did then, he had to refute suggestions by some of the more aggressive British parliamentary members that the Irish state's position on neutrality was merely a clever tactical ploy designed to secure a favourable resolution to partition.[33]

30 NAI DFA/227/95, 2 July 1940.
31 Ibid.
32 Ibid.
33 Cole, *Propaganda, Censorship and Irish Neutrality in the Second World War*, pp. 5–65.

Briscoe concluded this part of his statement by re-emphasizing the right of the Irish state to determine its own political destiny:

> The main thing is that we are neutral. Some people do not understand why we should be, and why we should not automatically declared war with the rest of the members of the Commonwealth. We have stated our position in relation to that situation.[34]

The fact that Briscoe had spoken to de Valera prior to his departure for London is clearly reflected in his speech, and although he had emphasized that these were his own views it is implausible to think that they did not have de Valera's imprimatur. He told the delegates that his 'views can be taken ... as being the general views of the people of Eire'.[35]

Briscoe's troubles were not confined to addressing a hostile Commonwealth in Westminster, his revisionist engagement was becoming increasingly problematic. This was reinforced by the untimely death of Jabotinsky from a heart attack in New York on 4 August 1940, which had left the revisionists in disarray and unable to appoint a successor due to internal philosophical and political disagreement.[36] If Briscoe felt the loss at a personal level, the members of the Nessuit were stunned; as a member of the ruling executive, Briscoe recalled the immediate aftermath of the organization's devastating loss as a period of chaos as they attempted to put a temporary plan into place.[37]

He recalled the inertia of the moment, and perhaps Briscoe's most telling comment on the post-Jabotinsky period was an explanation that out of a 'respect for his memory', the Nessuit 'did not appoint' a new leader for twelve months.[38] Therefore, although the Nessuit attempted to implement a strategy, it was a fractured response that was bedevilled by infighting and contradiction; initially it appeared to have a dual focus. A diplomatic offensive was mounted to convince 'the governments in exile' of the moral

---

34 NAI DFA/227/95, 2 July 1940.
35 Ibid.
36 Briscoe and Hatch, *For the Life of Me*, p. 290.
37 Ibid., p. 290.
38 Ibid.

necessity for a post-war Jewish state, which was underscored by a campaign to form a 'Jewish Army to fight alongside the Allies'.[39] However, as a member of the Nessuit Briscoe was increasingly aware that the organization was in serious danger of being hijacked by a militant faction set on a direct confrontation with the British in Palestine.[40]

The absence of a dominant and decisive leader had resulted in a political vacuum where ambitious individuals sought to replace Jabotinsky as the revisionist leader. This resulted in an intense internal dispute as the militant wing of the organization mounted a sustained power-grab. This faction was led by Avraham (Yair) Stern, the founder of *Lohamei Herut Israel* (Fighters for the freedom of Israel), a small and virulently anti-English movement which became widely known as the Stern gang.[41] This cadre of ultra-nationalist Jews had embarked on a campaign of bombings and assassinations that targeted the occupying British forces.[42] While Jabotinsky was alive, Stern to a degree had been restrained from asserting sway over the young and increasingly militant revisionists. However, on his death, Stern came to regard himself as 'the legitimate interpreter of the concept of the liberation movement'.[43] The young activists of the Irgun under the charismatic leadership of Stern and Menachem Begin were determined to exert their independence, and the fragile coalition of revisionist activists, which included Briscoe, began to rapidly disintegrate.[44]

It is clear that Briscoe observed the political aftermath of Jabotinsky's death with a mounting sense of horror, and as the internecine split continued, he began to express a disquiet that would ultimately lead to his

---

39 Ibid.
40 Joseph Heller, *The Stern Gang Ideology, Politics and Terror, 1940–1949* (Routledge, London, 1995), pp. 77–92.
41 Patrick Bishop, *The Reckoning: Death and Intrigue in the Promised Land* (Harper Collins, London, 2014), pp. 55–57.
42 Roger Griffin, *Terrorist's Creed Fanatical Violence and the Human Need for Meaning* (Palgrave Macmillan, Basingstoke, 2012), p. 129.
43 Heller, *The Stern Gang*, p. 127.
44 Tydor Baumel, *The 'Bergson Boys'*, pp. 66–67.

resignation from the Nessuit.[45] This process had actually started before Jabotinsky's demise, when in a veiled reference to Jabotinsky's demands for constant contact in the American mission, Briscoe pointedly expressed a lingering dissatisfaction at the way he had been treated.

> I feel I am somewhat reminded of the position into which I was driven by similar requests on another occasion; it is quite true no success resulted on the other occasion, but I am happy to say no damage was done.[46]

The letter had been sent to Eliahu Ben-Horin, a Russian-born revisionist and close personal friend, who had emigrated to Palestine as a teenager before becoming a major figure in the organization.[47] Ben Horin, who was now stationed in New York, acknowledged Briscoe's anger about his treatment in America:

> I tell you in this connection that I ... considered it one of the greatest services rendered by me to the movement, that I was partly instrumental in bringing you into our ranks ....I never told you, and I do not know whether anyone else has told you, the fight which I made in London during your stay in the United States, upholding my great belief in you against severe criticism of you coming from many quarters in our Presidency.[48]

Briscoe's next contact in the ongoing dispute came in December 1940, where he revealed the level of his dissatisfaction with the sequence of events in the aftermath of Jabotinsky's death.[49]

> I regret to have to say at the outset that I am very unhappy about the behaviour of the Delegation in New York. Reading through the Minutes of the meeting ... it is quite clear to me that the views I held all along are the only correct views about these people, and if there is a change at all as a result of their operations, the change of opinion is for the worse.[50]

45   Tydor Baumel, 'The IZL Delegation in the USA 1939–1948', pp. 80–90.
46   BFJITA 2/253 2, 27 May 1940.
47   Medoff, *Militant Zionism in America*, pp. 47–50.
48   BFJITA 2/253 2, 11 September 1940.
49   Medoff, *Militant Zionism in America*, pp. 60–73.
50   BFJITA 2/253 2, 4 December 1940.

As well as being personally disaffected, it is also clear that he was unhappy with the militant direction the New York branch was moving in, and force-fully made his point of view known.[51] His criticism became more personal as he started to question not just the motivation behind the revisionist fracture, but whether in fact the militants were even Jewish patriots.

> It is a tragedy that our people in New York cannot realise their own shortcomings; their own inability to lead ... There is ... absolutely no patriotism whatsoever ... Painful as it is to have to say it, none of them have the requirements to warrant their behaviour as carried on since their attempt to take control ... I have no objections to your transferring to New York a copy of these my views. There is in New York absolutely no patriotism whatsoever.[52]

His appraisal of the situation turned into a lament for what might have been, and it is soon evident that despite the ideological differences that had manifested in America, he had revered Jabotinsky and the prin-ciples he stood for.

> I look back over the last few years and I feel that the foundation stones of human lives, toil, hardship and privations will now be abandoned without even the semblance of an edifice. All we can do I suppose now is to mourn for Jabotinsky, to mourn for Jewry because Jabotinsky has come and gone, and to pray to God for a miracle; as for me I cannot even find solace in regarding the behaviour of the custodians of the N.Z.O. Movement with the slightest suggestion of dignity.[53]

Briscoe's active revisionist involvement continued to wind down in the most distressing manner as he forlornly lamented the passing of Jabotinsky and the hijacking of the revisionists by the militants.

> All the utterings of unswerving loyalty to the policy and teachings of the Nassi, were either not sincere or have been soon forgotten. For myself I feel I will be left where

---

51   Walter Laqueur, *The New Terrorism Fanaticism and the Arms of Mass Destruction* (Oxford University Press, Oxford, 1999), pp. 22–26.

52   BFJITA 2/253 2, 4 December 1940.

53   Ibid.

I was before 1935. Acceptance of N.Z.O. policy and abandonment of N.Z.O. ideals discards Herzl, Nordau, Jabotinsky and Jewry.[54]

The level of Briscoe's frustration at a disintegrating revisionism was reinforced by the apparent lethargy of his Irish co-religionists to the evolving Jewish tragedy. His anger was clear in a withering critique of his fellow Irish-Jews in April 1941.

> Our local co-religionists still live in the land of dreams of the security of wealth. I cannot understand how it is that the love of money has had such a terrible effect on people as to make them selfish, harsh and lacking in consideration to the most elementary requirements of humanity.[55]

Briscoe was evidently struggling to maintain an equilibrium between his own personal knowledge of the impending extermination of Europe's Jews, the revisionist fracture, and the seeming indifference of his fellow Jews to a rapidly escalating tragedy. His sense of loss was apparent in a eulogy given on the first Yahrzeit (anniversary) of Jabotinsky's death. It is clear that at a twelve-month remove Briscoe was emoting not just a sense of respect and loss over the death of a man who had awakened in him an awareness of his Judaic roots, but also the loss Jabotinsky was to the Zionist movement itself.

> To appreciate any man's worth one has to know his qualities. To appreciate the worth of a really great man one has to have respect for his qualities. Vladimir Jabotinsky had, however, so many qualities that it is impossible to single out any special one and to say; in this he was great .... On Vladimir Jabotinsky fell all the abuse vileness could produce. A man good, and true, maligned every hour of every day. Had he served any other people his value would have been honoured and esteemed, and he would have been brought up to the level of ordinary man's highest regard and love.[56]

He was clearly speaking from the heart, and the lament is all the more forceful because of this awareness; it has an air of authenticity that was missing from the more lyrical reminiscing in his memoir where he wondered

---

54   Ibid.
55   BFJITA 2/253 2, 22 April 1941.
56   *Jewish Standard*, 18 July 1941. (Hereafter *JS*).

if Jabotinsky had died from a 'broken' heart.[57] Briscoe's eulogy was also an important example of his multi-layered political reality during this extraordinary era, as he adroitly synthesized the disparate narratives of the two most important political influences of his career, with an almost religious fervour.

> Only once did he, in my opinion, ever meet a man equally imbued with the love of his people-Eamon de Valera. I had the honour of arranging the meeting between them. These men understood each other immediately. Each realised in the other burned that unquenchable fire of service in the cause of people ... Two men equally contemptuous of things material. Two men who knew the value of idealism.[58]

Briscoe's despair is palpable, and it is clear in all of his written statements of the period, that he had finally given up on any realistic expectation of a revisionist rapprochement.

That being said, Briscoe's links with senior and controversial revisionist actors endured long beyond his official resignation from the executive council. This was exemplified by his ongoing relationship with Bill Ziff who once again entered Briscoe's political orbit in the winter of 1941 with devastating local repercussions. Briscoe's previously detached and discreet Zionist activities came to the attention of fellow Fianna Fáil TD Dan Breen, when he learned that he was exploring the possibility of introducing Ziff to de Valera in Dublin. Breen, an obsessive Anglophobe and irredentist republican, represented a republican militancy that had never entirely dissipated within the Fianna Fáil ranks, and looked for every opportunity for to attack de Valera's accommodation with the British.[59] This had been a decades-long concern for de Valera who was concerned that if Breen and his fellow irredentists were given the opportunity, they could reignite a latent violence that lay just below the surface of an Irish society only two decades removed from an internecine Civil War.[60]

---

57 Briscoe and Hatch, *For the Life of Me*, p. 282.
58 Ibid.
59 Wood, *Britain, Ireland and the Second World War*, pp. 68–69.
60 Sean Kinsella, 'The Cult of Violence and the Revolutionary Tradition in Ireland, *Studies: An Irish Quarterly Review*, Vol 83, No. 329 (Spring 1994), p. 22.

When Ziff had arrived in London on the first leg of his trip to Dublin, only to be immediately arrested (which was not at all surprising given his militant revisionist activities), he immediately cabled Briscoe to intervene on his behalf. This Briscoe duly did by contacting his friend Wilfred Roberts, the Chief Whip of the Liberal Party, asking him to 'secure [an] exit permit to visit me here [Dublin], he is a first class leading American'.[61] Roberts used his prominent position to facilitate the release of Ziff who was granted an exit visa, an act that somehow came to Breen's attention and released his visceral hatred of England. He immediately dispatched an angry letter to Briscoe, demanding to know 'why the hell have you [brought] pro-American and pro-British agents over here ... You can meet them in England'.[62]

On 17 November, Briscoe responded to Breen, by telling him that 'my friend-Mr Ziff-is not a pro-British agent; he is certainly anti-German ... he is pro-American and hopes Germany will be beaten'.[63] Then, clearly angered by Breen's intervention, Briscoe caustically continued 'that it is a matter for your own conscience that you are friendly and on visiting terms with the German and Italian Legations'.[64] Moreover, Briscoe emphasized that he had de Valera's full support, telling Breen that he 'is fully aware of my activities in every direction and until he finds fault I will continue to do what I judge as in the best interests of the country'.[65]

This initiated a vitriolic response from Breen who had been one of the IRA's most feared operatives in the War of Independence. He was still able to reignite a latent violence in like-minded individuals, bearing in mind that the nascent Irish state was only two decades removed from a bitter conflict with Britain.[66] He explained his position thus:

61   IMA, G2/X/0040/P. November 1941.
62   NAI DFA P/40, 14 November 1941.
63   Ibid., 17 November 1941.
64   Ibid.
65   Ibid.
66   Sean Kinsella, 'The Cult of Violence and the Revolutionary Tradition in Ireland',
      Studies: An Irish Quarterly Review, Vol. 83, No. 329 (Spring 1994), p. 22.

> I hold the old Irish view and that one is very plain and simple and has not changed with time. Some Irish men may like to twist it for their own ends, but the words are "you can't serve Ireland well without a hatred for England" this is old but is as true today as when it was first spoken.[67]

Breen continued in this vein and justified his relationship with German and Italian representatives to Briscoe in the following manner:

> I visit both the German and Italian delegations why not? The Germans and Italians are not the people's [sic] that murdered and robbed my people for 700 years. It took your good English friends to do that and they continue to do that now.[68]

This type of rhetoric was not merely an attack on Briscoe, but was also an indirect attack on de Valera; this concerned the G2 operatives who were monitoring the position of irredentists like Breen, who could not comprehend de Valera's sophisticated long-term approach to ending partition.[69] So Briscoe was once more to the fore of security concerns regarding de Valera's vulnerability from within his own ranks, a position that would remain throughout the Emergency years.

Nevertheless despite creating difficulties for de Valera, Briscoe's reintegration into mainstream parochial politics continued apace accompanied by a reengagement with his 1930s Irish immigration initiative. In 1941, Gerry Boland, Ruttledge's replacement as the Minister for Justice, responded to yet another of Briscoe's applications in the following way.

> With reference to your representations on behalf of Mr and Mrs Rose, British subjects, I desire to inform you that, after careful consideration of the case, I cannot agree to Mr and Mrs Rose continuing their residence in this country, and, accordingly, they should arrange for their departure without delay.[70]

---

67 NAI DFA/P 40, 18 November 1941.
68 Ibid.
69 Neal G. Jesse, 'Choosing to Go It Alone: Irish Neutrality in Theoretical and Comparative Perspective', *International Political Science Review*, Vol. 27, No. 1 (January 2006), pp. 9–11.
70 RBPP, 16 September 1941.

Briscoe was not prepared to accept this decision, and an extended dialogue with Stanley Rose shows that the couple were still in the state six months later. In March, Rose wrote to Briscoe outlining how he and his wife proposed to be financially self-sufficient if they were allowed stay.

> The funds we have together with the cash we hope to realise from the sale of our goods, will meet our absolute needs. May we hope that in a world of tears there is still a corner where human feeling still prevails.[71]

However, despite Briscoe's efforts on behalf of the Roses, it is clear that Boland remained unconvinced and in December they were served with a final expulsion order by the Minister.

> I have given careful consideration to the case of Mr and Mrs Rose against whom Deportation Orders were issued in April, 1940, but I cannot agree to permit Mr and Mrs Rose to pay any further visits to Dublin. I return herewith the letter from Mrs Rose which was forwarded with Miss Devoy's letter of the 19th ultimo.[72]

In many respects, Stanley Rose's poignant lament about finding a small corner of humanity in a world of tears summarizes the terrible predicament of not being wanted anywhere. It is evident that he was a frightened, elderly man whose options were running out, and perhaps this is what motivated Briscoe not to give up on the case. In an extended and at times fractious exchange with Boland he persevered and ultimately secured one of his few wartime successes. In June 1943, Boland eventually relented and with a number of impositions reluctantly conceded that the Roses could stay.

> With reference to your representations relating to the case of Mr and Mrs Rose, I am now prepared to Revoke the Deportation Order against these persons provided they submit to this Department written undertakings that while they remain in this country they will not engage in any trade, profession or occupation other than the business of disposing of their stocks of goods, and that they will make arrangements to emigrate from this country at the earliest possible date.[73]

71   Ibid., 3 March 1942.
72   Ibid., 5 December 1942.
73   Ibid., 30 June 1943.

This immigration dialogue was conducted, as were many others, against a constant undercurrent of Irish anti-Semitism. Perhaps the perfect example of Official Irish antipathy towards Jewish refugees was when another member of Briscoe's extended family was refused an entry visa in the autumn of 1942. This followed the protracted 1939 effort to unsuccessfully secure a visa for his much loved aunt Hedwig from Berlin, who would eventually be murdered in Auschwitz. On 2 November, Dan Costigan from the Department of Justice, who wrote to Colonel Dan Bryan, head of G2, to query whether there was any reason why he should not submit (Briscoe's brother) Wolfe Tone's request 'for the grant of visas [for] his mother-in-law and his two sisters-in-law to enable them to come to this country'.[74]

Bryan replied at great length on 6 November, firstly making it clear that 'we are opposed on general security grounds to the granting of visas to aliens residing in the continent of Europe'.[75] He then acknowledged that 'from time to time', exceptional cases that did not meet the strict criteria imposed by the state for successful immigration, could under special circumstances be viewed favourably. Bryan then admitted that Wolfe Tone Briscoe had 'not come under unfavourable notice from [a] security standpoint' but echoing the 1922 concern at his involvement in supplying arms to the Provisional Government, expressed a concern 'that people who are willing to rush into the armament business ... can be a source of trouble for us'.[76]

Bryan then brought Briscoe into the dialogue, telling Costigan that he 'is high up in the councils of international Jewry which in present circumstances has aligned itself on the side of one group of belligerent powers in the present war'.[77] Based on the above, Bryan then concluded that 'the relationship between Mr B. Briscoe and Mr W. Briscoe cannot be ignored in considering these visa applications', before making his final recommended to Costigan, that 'in the light of the foregoing observations I feel that the balance of the argument is against granting of visas to the three ladies'.[78]

74   IMA/G2/X/0040, 2 November 1942.
75   Ibid., 6 November.
76   Ibid.
77   Ibid.
78   Ibid.

Despite Briscoe's standing as a TD and personal friend of de Valera's, he could not get entry visas to the Irish state for his brother's extended family members.

Throughout this stressful period, Briscoe was being subjected to an ever-increasing level of G2 scrutiny. This was clear in a report that had taken more than three years to collate. The agent in charge delivered the following analysis of Briscoe's external commitments.

> Briscoe is in constant contact with international Jewry in England, America, New York, and is apparently an important figure in the New Zionist Organisation whose objects appear to vary from time to time. One of its objects is a separate Jewish Army to enable Jews to fight as an entity and be present at the Peace Conference as a Jewish Body.[79]

Having established his revisionist status, the officer then focused on Briscoe's relationship with Bill Ziff:

> In June, 1942, Mr Briscoe contacted by wire a Jewish publisher in New York to write a thesis on "Post war emancipation and status of nations and humans as a prelude to real world order based on my Irish and Jewish background and experience and international contacts.[80]

Although that observation was informative, it was soon apparent that what really concerned the officer was Ziff's request that Briscoe use his personal connection with de Valera to facilitate the writing of an introduction for the article.

> Ziff asked him to undertake an article ... with an introduction by De Valera, but naturally Briscoe could not commit the Taoiseach to an introduction before the article was written.[81]

This level of scrutiny was perfectly understandable; the security services were tasked with protecting the best interests of the state and therefore

79 IMA/G2/X/0040, 3 November 1942.
80 Ibid.
81 Ibid.

any mention of Briscoe involving de Valera in a project that might make him vulnerable, would have been a top priority. The report broadened to include concerns about his on-going revisionist commitment, which although diminishing was clearly still of interest:

> The latest development is that the New Zionist Organisation and others have begun an intensive campaign for recognition of Jewish people as members of United Nations and a great rally in New York is planned ... Briscoe has been cabled to this effect and told-it is important your coming to New York to address meeting and other functions ... These cables suggest that Briscoe is regarded as a very important figure in international Jewry.[82]

Given the precarious global situation in late 1942, this report was fulfilling the primary function of a security service by recording the external activities of an elected TD. It needs to be stressed that Briscoe was, and remained, an elected member of Dáil Éireann for the duration of his revisionist allegiance; however, if his external activities were a legitimate cause for surveillance, a note of caution has to be attached to the officer's concluding, and pejorative comment.

> Mr Briscoe is a frequent visitor to London. He interests himself in visas for Jews on the Continent and is, as is to be expected of one of his race, an internationalist indulging in any and every line of business that will bring financial benefit.[83]

The intuitive prejudice exhibited by the security operative, although distasteful, was representative of a civil society in thrall to Catholic dogma about Jews as the killers of Christ, a position contextualized by a censored report from the *Irish Times*.

> They [Jews] were guilty of every dirty trick allowable within the law to establish themselves, and then like parasites, they pull down the tree which gives them succour.[84]

---

82   Ibid.
83   Ibid.
84   IMA/G2/X/0040, 15 March 1943.

Although Briscoe's reengagement with the Irish immigration had revealed a baser side to his fellow countrymen's attitude towards Jews, it was also punctuated by the more prosaic demands of parochial politics, as the country held two elections in June 1943 and May 1944. The fact that he had only secured the seventh and final seat in Dublin South in the 1938 election meant that even in the most stable electoral environment, it would have been an uphill battle to be re-elected; however, Emergency Ireland was anything but stable. His precarious foothold in Dublin South was all the more tenuous because of his extended absence from constituency politics on Zionist business, a position of electoral vulnerability that Briscoe had recognized in 1941.

> I myself have been having a rather difficult time, as my own personal affairs suffer very much in my absence and people become very impatient when I cannot meet obligations on their due dates and they really feel that I have no right to rush away to foreign parts and neglect thrie [sic] interests or overlook attention to little matters concerning them.[85]

This statement essentially explains Briscoe's electoral difficulty. He readily acknowledged his absences from the state had not been well received by his constituents. Moreover, Briscoe's electoral difficulties were underscored by constant financial concerns, which prior to the 1943 election had apparently 'reached the lowest possible level'.[86] This combination of personal and political complications prompted Briscoe to make two profound decisions; firstly he finally severed his official link with the revisionists by submitting his resignation to the Nessuit on 1 April 1943, which was reluctantly accepted.[87] Simultaneously he offered his resignation as a TD to de Valera who refused the request, and telling Briscoe to put aside his personal problems telling him that he was one of the few remaining individuals 'with whom I can work in perfect confidence and trust'.[88] Briscoe's reverence for 'The Chief' was so great that he immediately acquiesced and secured the fifth seat in

85   BFJITA 2/252 2, 22 April 1941.
86   Briscoe and Hatch, *For the Life of Me*, p. 288.
87   IMA IE/MA/G2/X/0040/P, 1 April 1943.
88   Ibid., p. 289.

Dublin South, even though his vote decreased from 3,791 in 1938, to 3,127 in 1943.[89] When de Valera called an election less than twelve months later, in May 1944, Briscoe's vote decreased again to its lowest ever point of 2,852, but he did secure the seventh and final seat and could now at least in part, refocus his energies on addressing the appalling consequences of the Holocaust for Europe's Jews; however, this would not be straightforward as personal issues and age-old accusations resurfaced.

89   ElectionsIreland.org/?1541

CHAPTER 9

1944–1953
Irreconcilable Differences: Financial Difficulties, the Holocaust and the Birth of Israel

Even though Briscoe had survived as a Fianna Fáil TD, his electoral difficulties had included unsavoury insinuations alluding to the precarious state of his personal financial situation. Much of this could be ascribed to his revisionist engagement, Jabotinsky was notorious for making financial demands on his subordinates and the Briscoe Files in the Jabotinsky Institute are full of requests for an immediate £50, £100 or even £200 donation.[1] This aspect of Briscoe's Zionism certainly contributed to his money issues; however, when a 1944 G2 intelligence report is examined, it leads to the inescapable conclusion that there was a far more prosaic contributory factor. The report indicates that he had a considerable gambling problem.

> During an interview between Briscoe and Mr T. W. Justice, Briscoe stated that he had lost £6,000 in the last five years, playing poker and racing. Mr Justice gathered from Briscoe's conversation that he is not in a strong financial position at the moment.[2]

Briscoe's admission is indicative of the depth of his debt; £6,000 was an extraordinary sum in 1944 and would translate to a present-day debt of more than £186,000. He had always enjoyed a flutter on the horses; this was widely known and accepted in an Irish political culture where casual gambling was commonplace.[3] This was reinforced by a love of poker, and Briscoe was a member of one of political Ireland's most infamous card schools run

---

1   Brown 'The New Zionism in the New World', pp. 72–74.
2   IMA G2/X/0826, 11 January 1944.
3   Noël Browne, *Against the Tide* (Gill and Macmillan, Dublin, 1986), p. 203.

by his constituency colleague Seán Lemass, who was also Minister for Industry and Commerce.[4] However, it is clear Briscoe's predilection for games of chance was not simply an out-of-control gambling addiction; the timeline of increasing debt strongly indicates he was gambling as a destressor. Although an unprovable supposition, it is probable rather than possible, that Briscoe's increased level of gambling was a consequence of having to contend with the realization that Hitler's extermination project was slaughtering millions of his co-religionists.

This contention is borne out by his silent observation of the government's callous response to Isaac Herzog's heartbreaking pleas to his good friend Éamon de Valera to intervene in the Jewish tragedy.[5] These requests were not new; Herzog had been sending this type of emotive missive to de Valera since late 1942, warning about Jewish extermination. On 12 December, he implored 'revered friend, pray leave no stone unturned to save tormented remnant of Israel, doomed alas to utter annihilation in Nazi Europe'.[6] Initially Herzog's concern was on the increasingly precarious plight of Italy's Jews, who were facing evermore draconian acts of persecution.[7] He had been contacted in early December by members of the besieged community, who had been interred by the fascists and who were now increasingly aware of their potential fate.[8]

On 10 July 1943, Herzog cabled Briscoe asking him to request 'if Catholic authorities [in] Dublin could use influence through [the] Vatican [to] prevent [the] last minute deportation over 3000 Jews interned in Ferromonti. Possible also please petition there ... His Holiness the Pope'.[9] Herzog's telegram to Briscoe was dispatched immediately after one to de Valera where he had warned that '8,000 Jews in Italy, native and refugees

4   Horgan, *Seán Lemass the Enigmatic Patriot*, pp. 102–104.
5   Eliash, *The Harp and the Shield of David*, pp. 64–66.
6   NAI DFA/419/44. 12 December 1942. Herzog to de Valera.
7   Clair Wills, *That Neutral Island: A Cultural History of Ireland During the Second World War* (Faber and Faber Limited, London, 2007), p. 395.
8   Michele Sarfatti, *The Jews in Mussolini's Italy: From Equality to Persecution* (The University of Wisconsin Press, Madison WI, 2006), p. 282.
9   NAI DFA/419/44/ 10 July 1943. Herzog to Briscoe.

[are] threatened with deportation to Poland which, means their certain death', he was clearly attempting to reinforce the sense of urgency in the hope that Briscoe could influence de Valera.[10] There was a precedent for this type of representation, contacts had been established between the Irish government and the Vatican on Jewish refugees as early as the late 1930s.[11] However, it is clear that Herzog, in his desperation, had overestimated the strength of de Valera's influence with the Vatican. Moreover, Pius XII was charting a neutral course through the turbulent waters of a fascist regime and at best made 'very limited protests' at Jewish persecution.[12] Therefore, when a coded cable was dispatched to the Irish mission in Rome asking 'if there is any truth in report that 80,000 Jews in Italy are threatened with deportation to Poland', it was more from a sense of humanitarian duty rather than any realistic hope that the Irish government could do anything to help, even if the answer was in the affirmative.[13]

This dialogue came to a head between December 1943 and April 1944 when Herzog mounted a sustained campaign to secure asylum for more then 200 Polish Jews who were interred by the authorities at Vittel in Vichy France.[14] On 15 December 1943, he cabled de Valera that 'two hundred respectable Jewish families, Polish refugees in Vittel France holding South American states passports in extreme danger. Threatened with deportation, pray grant them visas to enter'.[15] On 30 January, Herzog once more contacted de Valera directly to report that 'two million European Jews perished, five million threatened with extermination. Deportations from Germany, Holland, Belgium, France, Norway to Polish ghettoes, thence continues mass execution'.[16]

10   Ibid.
11   Keogh, *Ireland and the Vatican*, p. 188.
12   Rebecca Clifford, *Commemorating the Holocaust: The Dilemmas of Remembrance in France and Italy* (Oxford University Press, oxford, 2013), 75.
13   NAI DFA/419/44. 15 July 1943.
14   Emmanuel Ringelblum, *Polish-Jewish Relations During the Second World War* (Northwestern University Press, Evanston Il, 1974), p. 127.
15   NAI DFA/419/44, 15 December 1942. Herzog to de Valera.
16   Ibid. 30 January. Herzog to de Valera.

The intensity of the representation forced the Irish authorities into action, and contact was initiated by the Irish missions in Paris and Berlin with the German authorities to inquire about the possibility of the Vittel Jews being granted 'temporary relocation to Ireland'.[17] In March, Con Cremin, who was the minister in Vichy, approached the German Foreign Office to see if there was any realistic possibility of the Vittel Jews gaining exit visas.[18] In a detailed report, Cremin recounted the meeting with an official he believed to be an SS officer, who obliquely informed him 'that exit-visas will not be granted in these cases, not even to those families which may have relatives in Ireland'.[19] Cremin followed this up on 27 March by expounding on the technical difficulties imposed by the Nazis on visa applications. He cabled Walsh with the following update after a detailed conversation with his Swiss counterpart, outlining how the Nazis would not grant the visa if the applicant did not have a valid passport, before pointing out the obvious 'it is doubtful whether a Jew … would now be granted a passport by the German authorities'.[20]

However, even that proved to be a fabrication, as many of the Jewish families in Vittel were originally from Warsaw, and had managed to purchase at exorbitant rates, the nebulous protection of South American passports by paying enormous bribes to Gestapo thugs out to profit from Jewish misery.[21] Sadly however, as with most dealings with the Gestapo, the protection of these neutral passports had merely been an illusion, and on 18 April 1944 the first deportation from Vittel to the transit camp at Drancy started.[22] This continued on 16 May and 2 August when the

---

17   Shulamit Eliash, *The Harp and the Shield of David; Ireland, Zionism and the State of Israel* (Routledge, Abingdon, 2007), p. 65.
18   Niall Keogh, *Con Cremin: Ireland's Wartime Diplomat* (Mercier Press, Cork, 2006), p. 76.
19   NAI DFA/419/44. 24 March 1943.
20   Ibid., 27 March 1943.
21   David Engel, *Facing a Holocaust: The Polish Government-in-Exile and the Jews, 1943–1945* (The University of North Carolina Press, Chapel Hill NC, 1993), pp. 160–166.
22   Renée Poznanski, *Jews in France during the Second World War* (University Press of New England, Hanover NH, 2001), p. 443.

remaining sixty Jews began the tragic journey back to Poland, not to Warsaw, but to Auschwitz where the entire Vittel compliment of Polish Jews was eventually exterminated.[23]

The trauma of this extended tragedy was clear from Herzog's cable of 24 July stating that 'terrible scenes took place ... we fear that ... they have already been sent to death camps in Poland'.[24] In a final desperate plea Herzog implores Walsh 'on behalf House of Israel [that] you make [a] final call to German Government [to] halt deportation [of] these tragic people'.[25] This was clearly more in desperation then expectation, as Herzog continued to outline the 'cruel tragedy which will shock history till [the] end of days [where] the voice of any civilisation calls to whole [of] humanity not to rest [but] save what can be saved [and to] snatch precious branch from [the] fire'.[26]

The Vittel tragedy contextualizes the desperation of Herzog's representations as it was once more confirmed that even if a state wanted to help save European Jews, it was far too late as the Nazi genocide increased in ferocity. Nevertheless, Herzog was not about to give up, and in February 1944, he contacted Briscoe and requested him to revive his shipping contacts in an attempt to save a small number of Budapest's Jews from Eichmann's *Aktion*.[27] Herzog had become part of a loose federation of Zionists and concerned Christians in Istanbul who were engaged in a desperate attempt to save as many of these individuals as possible.[28] This group of refugees had fled from Budapest, and Zionist agents from the Yishuv were desperately

---

23   Leni Yahil, *The Holocaust: The Fate of European Jewry, 1932–1945* (Oxford University Press, Oxford, 1991), p. 433.
24   NAI DFA/419/44. 27 July 1944. Herzog to Walsh.
25   Ibid.
26   Ibid.
27   Yaacov Lozowick, *Hitler's Bureaucrats The Nazi Security Police and the Banality of Evil* (Continuum, London and New York, 2000), pp. 238–268.
28   Yitzhak Ben-Ami, 'The Irgun and the Destruction of European Jewry', in Randolph L. Braham (ed.), *Perspectives on the Holocaust* (Springer-Science+Business Media, B. V., Dordrecht, 1983), pp. 80–82.

attempting to get them to the relative safety of neutral Turkey.[29] Briscoe responded immediately after receiving Herzog's frantic cable and attempted to revive his contacts from the *Aliyah Bet* and source a number of ships to effect Herzog's daring rescue plan.[30]

Given Briscoe's revisionist experience, he instantly understood the urgency of Herzog's plea. After arriving in Ankara on 8 February, Herzog realized the rapid escalation of Eichmann's *Aktion* against Hungary's 725,000 Jews, meant extermination for the entire community.[31] Consequently, he cabled Briscoe with the following information:

> Arrived here ascertain possibilities rescue. Only hope expeditious transport refugees stranded in Roumania appears maritime. Crucial question provision neutral vessel to proceed Constanza thence Istanbul possibly continuing Haifa or handing over at Istanbul to allied ship from Mediterranean. Redcross safe conduct can be secured. If securing Irish vessel feasible please approach Premier grant permission such vessel undertake mission mercy have remnants otherwise faced imminent danger. Financial outlay fully guaranteed.[32]

Herzog had previously contacted de Valera concerning the plight of Hungary's Jewish refugees, and it is clear from the telegram that he was now asking Briscoe to reinforce this approach by seeing if he would sanction a rescue ship that sailed under the Irish flag.[33] Briscoe responded to Herzog's request telling him he would 'make every immediate effort', and would cable 'continually reporting progress'.[34] However, despite strenuous efforts, Briscoe could not source a ship of any description, never mind an Irish one, which, given the wartime demands of an island nation on its merchant navy, was not surprising. However, he had received permission

29 Tony Kushner, 'The Meaning of Auschwitz: Anglo-American Responses to the Hungarian Jewish-Tragedy', in David Cesarani (ed.), *Genocide and Rescue the Holocaust in Hungary 1944* (Berg, Oxford, 1997), pp. 160–168.

30 Moisés Orfali Levi, *Leadership in Times of Crisis* (Bar Ilan University Press, Tel Aviv, 2007), pp. 90–94. See sections 5.3, and 5.3.1.

31 Lozowick, *Hitler's Bureaucrats*, pp. 238–242.

32 IMA G2/X/0826, 8 February 1944.

33 Eliash, *The Harp and the Shield of David*, p. 67.

34 IMA G2/X/0826, 8 February 1944.

from de Valera to sail a vessel under the Irish flag of neutrality if one could be located.

> No passenger or other suitable ship available here. If suitable ship could be obtained feel that question of flag and crew will be favourably considered subject your securing safe conduct. Am exploring possibility chartering ship and will advise you of progress. Meanwhile advise number of refugees to be moved.[35]

It was however as equally apparent that Herzog was experiencing the same difficulties in Istanbul. The German navy had been instructed to locate and sink any refugee ships, and consequently neutral ship owners were reluctant to lease any of their vessels to the Yishuv agents.[36] This was reinforced by the still negative influence of British agents in the region, who were warning the regional actors that Britain was still unwilling 'to deal with the' issue.[37] It was not until March 1944 that the full reality of the situation dawned on the British and American governments, an they finally informed the Turkish government that any Jews who safely reached Istanbul would be allowed to enter Palestine.[38]

This clearly meant that it was impracticable to move the refugees, especially given the numbers, and Herzog made this clear in his response to Briscoe.

> Ship must be originally of neutral origin. Please continue efforts charter one. Refugees number over five thousand. Returning Palestine. Continue communications ... Many thanks.[39]

That is the end of the Herzog-Briscoe dialogue and the fate of that particular group of refugees remains undetermined. However, it is clear that

---

35 Ibid., 18 February 1944.
36 Dina Porat, 'The Transnistria Affair and the Rescue Policy of the Zionist leadership in Palestine, 1942–1943', in Michael Marrus (ed.), *The Nazi Holocaust Part 9: The End of the Holocaust* (Merkler Corporation, Westport CT, 1989), p. 246.
37 Ibid.
38 Ibid., 247–248.
39 IMA G2/X/0826, 28 February 1944.

this loose federation of concerned individuals did succeed in rescuing as many as seven thousand refugees.[40]

This belated acknowledgement of the horrors of what was happening in Auschwitz ultimately meant that only a pitifully small number of Jews were saved. It took only eight months following the Herzog-Briscoe initiative for Eichmann to oversee the murder of 450,000 of Hungary's 650,000 Jews, a kill-ratio of 70%.[41] It was clear that Briscoe's failure to successfully intervene in the rescue had a profound personal effect, and he was in no doubt about the level of success that Eichmann was achieving. On 25 October he had written to Walshe, in External Affairs, to inform him of his commitment to the World Jewish Congress (WJC) that he would 'do [his] utmost' to secure Irish diplomatic support.[42] Briscoe expressed the belief that the full extent of the Jewish slaughter 'may be quite new to you' and that your response might 'require some thought'.[43] The WJC in New York had supplied Briscoe with a detailed account of the Jewish extermination in the hope that he could persuade the Irish government to make an official intervention with the Nazis. A hope that Leon Kubowitzki, the founder and General Secretary of the WJC, who was also the head of its Rescue Department, had shared with Briscoe on a number of occasions. On 23 December, Kubowitzki evoked the Swedish rescue mission under Raoul Wallenberg as a template Briscoe might present to the Irish government.[44]

> View tragic developments of Jewish situation Hungary urge you suggest your government send special diplomatic or Redcross mission to Budapest purpose extending Jewish groups protection along lines Swedish Wallenberg mission ... Also request urgent intervention against German plans wipe out inmates Oswiecim Birkenau Buhenwalde [sic] other camps.[45]

---

40   David Engel, 'The Holocaust', in Gordon Martel (ed.), *A Companion to Europe 1900–1945* (Blackwell Publishing, Chichester, 2011), pp. 480–484.
41   www.jewishvirtuallibrary.org/jsource/Holocaust/killtable.html
42   NAI DFA/419/44, 25 October 1944.
43   Ibid.
44   www.pbs.org/wgbh/amex/holocaust/filmmore/reference/primary/bombworld. html [accessed 19 September 2015].
45   NAI DFA/419/44, 23 December 1944. Leon Kubowitzki to Briscoe.

However, it is evident that even though the Irish government did make representations to the Hungarian government, it was only in support of a half-hearted protest from the Vatican.[46] Dermot Keogh, has suggested that even though the government did inquire as to the fate of Hungary's Jews, it 'could have taken a more vigorously independent line', but 'chose not to do so'.[47] This suggestion is reinforced when Walshe's response to Briscoe is examined, it appears to indicate a governmental acceptance of Nazi reassurances that nothing untoward was happening in the extermination centres.

> We have now received a reply from the German authorities to our enquiries about the Oswiecim Hoss and Birkenau camps. They say that the rumour that it is their intention to exterminate the Jews is pure invention and devoid of all foundation, and that, if the camps were to be abandoned, the inmates would be evacuated.[48]

If the Irish government actually accepted the Nazi guarantee, it represented a position of stunning naiveté, and it is far more likely that this assurance was forwarded to Briscoe to placate him, rather than as a true reflection of the government's knowledge of what was happening.[49] It is clear that the government had been aware of German atrocities from early 1941, and that it was in receipt of 'daily reports' of ever more violent acts of Jewish persecution.[50] The fact that Walshe would have had access to this type of information makes his response to Briscoe seem all the more dismissive, and perhaps indicates that the authorities did not differentiate between the Nazi extermination of six million Jews, and the more general atrocities that inevitably occurred in wartime. This seeming indifference was part of a strict censorship regime designed to reinforce the state's neutrality, the 'authorities refused to allow the war to be placed in a moral framework', and sanitized any atrocity information emanating from 'Allied sources'.[51] On this basis Walshe's response to Briscoe supports Siobhán O'Connor's

46 Keogh, *Ireland and the Vatican*, p. 191.
47 Ibid.
48 RBPP, 27 November 1944.
49 Sompolinsky, *Britain and the Holocaust*, pp. 194–198.
50 Ó Drisceoil, 'Moral Neutrality', p. 20.
51 Ibid.

recent research on the remaining Irish Jewish community, which indicates a belief that the authorities 'never took Briscoe's appeals seriously'.[52]

On 28 December barely a month after Walshe had reassured Briscoe that the Germans were not murdering Jews, Isaac Herzog made one last despairing plea to de Valera to intervene. He begged him to make a 'supreme effort' to save 'Budapest Jews' who were facing 'imminent extermination' - a fate Herzog described to his friend as a 'heartrending tragedy'.[53] De Valera did not personally respond to Herzog, and Walshe dispatched the following reply, 'your telegram received have been doing everything possible behalf of Hungarian Jews'.[54] On 28 January 1945, Rabbi Stephen Wise, who had blocked Briscoe at every possible opportunity in the 1939 revisionist mission to America but was now fully involved in the Jewish tragedy, sent the following cable to Dáil Éireann as de Valera was about to visit America: 'The World Jewish Congress respectfully urges you to put on [your] agenda ... problem of rescuing about six hundred thousand Jews remaining in Nazi occupied territories. Threatened anew with extermination in view [of] tragic annihilation of more than five million Jews ... That the German government again be solemnly warned in the spirit of your previous statements that all perpetrators of such crimes will be held accountable'.[55] Paula Wylie has described this response mechanism as part of a smokescreen to convince Herzog that the Irish authorities were 'doing everything possible', whereas the reality was clearly 'no action is fine'.[56]

Although Briscoe had resigned from the Nessuit in 1943, his involvement in the attempted rescue of Budapest's Jews emphasized this was a reaction to an increasingly powerful militancy rather than a rejection of the core Zionist principle of a Jewish state. This ongoing Zionist commitment did not escape the attentions of one of the Irish state's most notorious

---

52   O'Connor, 'Irish Government Policy', p. 195.
53   NAI DFA/419/44, 28 December 1944.
54   Ibid., 17 January 1945.
55   NAI DFA/419/44. 28 January 1945. Stephen S. Wise to Dáil Éireann.
56   Paula Wylie, *Ireland and the Cold War: Diplomacy and Recognition 1949–63* (Irish Academic Press, Dublin, 2006), p. 205.

anti-Semites, Oliver J. Flanagan, who claimed in an infamous 1943 Dáil speech that:[57]

> There is one thing that Germany did, and that was to rout the Jews out of their country. Until we rout the Jews out of this country it does not matter a hair's breath what orders you make. Where the bees are there is the honey, and where the Jews are there is the money.[58]

In February 1946, Flanagan launched an attack on Briscoe by claiming he had played a pivotal role in negotiations between Britain and America in an attempt to facilitate Jewish emigration to Palestine.[59] He asked de Valera if he was 'aware that Deputy Briscoe had travelled to Washington', and told authorities there 'that he was in favour of 100,000 Jews being allowed into Palestine'.[60] De Valera had to staunchly refute Flanagan's allegation, by informing him 'if the Deputy will look up the journals of the House he will see that Deputy Briscoe was here during 1946'.[61] Despite being consistently depicted as a Zionist agent in the Dáil, Briscoe was clearly not discouraged and continued to give his full support to the idea of a Jewish state. He supported the resumption of the *Aliyah Bet*, and although he played no active role in this phase of the endeavour, he gave the 'regular Zionist organization' his full support as it sought to bring as many camp survivors to Palestine as possible.[62]

Briscoe's Zionist activism in this period focused on the Irgun which was waging a vicious guerrilla war against the British. It revived memories of the IRA's campaign in the Irish War of Independence, and Briscoe immediately saw the parallel.[63] He was not the only one. Yitzak Shamir, the future Israeli Prime Minister had adopted the '*nom-de-guerre* ... Michael' in

---

57   Richard B. Finnegan and Edward McCarron, *Ireland: Historical Echoes, Contemporary Politics* (The University of Michigan Press, Ann Arbour MI, 2000), pp. 156–160.
58   DÉD, Vol. 91, Col. 572. 9 July 1943.
59   Wylie, *Ireland and the Cold War*, pp. 204–205.
60   DÉD, Vol. 104, Col. 1473. 27 February 1946.
61   Ibid.
62   Briscoe and Hatch, *For the Life of Me*, p. 293.
63   Ibid., p. 295.

his incarnation as a member of the Stern Gang, in deference to the tactical genius displayed by Michael Collins three decades earlier.[64] In the autumn of 1947, Briscoe went to Palestine 'to confer with the leaders of the Irgun'.[65] Briscoe did not expand on why he met the leadership of the Irgun, but it is reasonable, given his reasons for resigning from the Nessuit, that it was in an attempt to persuade them that their military campaign was misguided.

The duality of Briscoe's political reality was underscored in February 1948 when a General Election was held. When the results emerged, it became clear Fianna Fáil had lost power for the first time in sixteen years, a scenario Briscoe wistfully described as a natural reaction to familiarity musing that 'perhaps the people were just tired of voting for de Valera'.[66] Although still the largest single party, Fianna Fáil were outvoted by an unlikely alliance led by Fine Gael, the Labour Party and Clan na Poblachta; a new republican party led by Briscoe's old adversary Seán MacBride.[67] Although de Valera had been confident of forming a minority government, the various parties put aside their ideological differences to form the First Inter-Party Government, and Briscoe along with his colleagues, had, as he admitted, 'a little time on our hands'.[68]

After getting over the shock of being in opposition, Briscoe must have taken great satisfaction from the extraordinary turnaround in his personal electoral fortunes. In less than four years, he had more than doubled his vote from 2,852 in 1944, to 5,961 in 1948, which in terms of a share of the popular vote translated into a phenomenal increase of nearly 200 per cent.[69] His political renaissance can perhaps be ascribed to two distinct factors. Firstly, and perhaps most importantly, he had been able to devote himself to the minutia of constituency politics, a facet of his political life that had been side-lined during his active revisionist engagement. Secondly, although less certain, is the possibility that as the horrors of the Holocaust

64   Wylie, *Ireland and the Cold War*, p. 204.
65   Briscoe and Hatch, *For the Life of Me*, p. 295.
66   Ibid., p. 302.
67   Lee, *Politics and Society*, pp. 296–300. See sections 1.3, and 1.8.
68   Briscoe and Hatch, *For the Life of Me*, p. 302.
69   ElectionsIreland.org/?1541

had slowly filtered through the barriers of a relaxed post-war censorship, a public realization of Jewish persecution had manifested in an increased vote for the state's only Jewish TD. Whatever the reason, it was clear that he was no longer vulnerable electorally, and this was a situation that would remain for the rest of his political career.

The fact that he was now clearly safe in a parochial electoral setting, meant that Briscoe could, at least in part, devote some of his time and energy to the problems facing the new state of Israel. As the full horrors of the Holocaust had become apparent, there had been a groundswell of support for a Jewish National Home, and the state of Israel had been declared on 14 May 1948 after a tense vote in the United Nations where America had used its new-found economic power to pressurize states to vote in favour of the 'UN plan'.[70] The new state immediately sought diplomatic recognition from countries around the world, including Ireland. However, the first inter-party government was reluctant to grant this, and instead afforded Israel 'the virtual minimum of recognition ... that it was possible to concede'.[71] This effectively recognized the reality of Israel without acknowledging the new state in a formal sense, and this policy remained in place until 1963. Although it was not overtly anti-Semitic, it was predicated on a line of 'reasoning which viewed Israel as anti-Christian [and] endured as a policy in deference to the diplomatic wishes of the Holy See'.[72]

Pope Pius XII had issued an encyclical on Jerusalem (*In multiplicibus*) in October 1948, which called for Jerusalem to be an international city with 'a judicial status'.[73] The 'problem of the Holy Places' had been recognized by

---

70   Tom Lansford, 'Pragmatic Idealism: Truman's Broader Middle East policy', in Michael J. Divine, Robert P. Watson and Robert J. Wolz (eds.), *Israel and the Legacy of Harry S. Truman* (Truman State University Press, Kirksville MO, 2008), p. 37.

71   Paula S. Wylie, 'The Virtual Minimum: Ireland's Decision for De Facto Recognition of Israel, 1947–9', in Michael Kennedy and Joseph Morrison Skelly (eds.), *Irish Foreign Policy 1919–1966: From Independence to Internationalism* (Four Courts Press, Dublin, 1999), p. 137.

72   Ibid., p. 138.

73   Rory Miller, 'Public Tensions, Private Ties: Ireland, Israel and the Politics of Mutual Misunderstanding', in Clive Jones and Tore T. Petersen (eds.), *Israel's Clandestine Diplomacies* (Oxford University Press, Oxford, 2013), p. 193.

Briscoe's Zionist mentor Jabotinsky, who in an effort to secure the support of de Valera on his 1938 visit to Dublin, had pledged to the Papal Nuncio that 'a system of concordats with all creeds concerned shall guarantee the status of the Holy Places' if the revisionists were in power in a Jewish state.[74] Whether this was merely part of Jabotinsky's strategy to secure de Valera's support is open to debate; however, even if it was, it was an astute tactic as Briscoe knew that de Valera had a genuine reverence for Christianity's most venerated shrines.[75]

The Vatican's policy on Jerusalem was enthusiastically supported by the new Inter-Party Government, with the Taoiseach John A. Costello firmly of the belief 'that a Christian policy was in Ireland's best interests'.[76] Paula Wylie has pointed out that when 'the diplomatic recognition files' are examined, an alternative interpretation is possible, one which suggests that the refusal to recognize Israel was possibly 'motivated by a fear of [a] rising "Jewish influence" in Ireland'.[77] This argument is reinforced by Wylie, who cites a 1946 letter from Joe Walshe, the former secretary at the Department of External Affairs, who was now the ambassador to the Holy See. Walshe stated that:

> Something ought to be done to prevent the jews [sic] buying property and starting or acquiring businesses in Ireland. There was a general conviction that the jewish [sic] influence is, in the last analysis, anti-Christian and anti-national and, consequently, detrimental to the revival of an Irish cultural and religious civilisation.[78]

Considering his condescending 1944 letter to Briscoe, which offered a clearly false reassurance about the fate of Hungary's Jews, Walshe's musings from Rome were perhaps not entirely unexpected. There is one important aspect of Walshe's letter that needs to be emphasized; he had addressed it for the personal attention of de Valera as Taoiseach. However, it was intercepted

---

74   BFJITA 2/253 2, 24 February 1938.
75   Briscoe and Hatch, *For the Life of Me*, p. 304.
76   Miller, 'Public Tensions', p. 193.
77   Wylie, 'The Virtual Minimum', p. 138.
78   NAI DFA 313/6, 17 October 1946. Cited by Wylie, 'The Virtual Minimum', p. 140.

by his successor at External Affairs, Frederick H. Boland, who was clearly of the view that de Valera did not share Walshe's prejudicial worldview.[79]

This is borne out by de Valera's intervention in an on-going post-war humanitarian crisis affecting the Jewish child survivors of the Holocaust. From an Irish perspective, it is clear that even when the full horrors of the Hitler's exterminationist project had entered the public domain that there was still an intuitive resistance to allowing Jewish refugees into a homogeneous Christian Irish state. In stark contrast however, Ireland not only provided £12 million in aid to a devastated Germany, but also took in 500 traumatized Christian child refugees. The first children arrived on the 27 July 1946 and by the end of June 1947, almost 500 children had been hosted in Ireland. Most of them returned to their families two or three years later, however, more than 50 stayed in Ireland after being adopted by Irish families. In order to receive governmental permission, a strict denominational ratio of four Catholic to every one Protestant child had to be adhered to; there was not so much as single mention of Jewish children during the initial debate

This was clear when the state only begrudgingly allowed 100 Jewish child survivors of the camps entry visas for a maximum 12-month period after Éamon de Valera was contacted by his old friend Isaac Herzog from Palestine who begged him to intervene and overrule Gerry Boland the Minister for Justice who reluctantly agreed to a limited admittance of Jewish orphans:

> On the understanding that they would be removed to some other country as soon as arrangements could be made, and that the Chief Rabbi's Religious Emergency Council would take full responsibility for the proper care and maintenance of the children while they remained in the country.[80]

These children were permitted to spend one year in Clonyn Castle in County Westmeath, it was only a brief hiatus, but even this would not

79   Ibid.
80   NAI TAOIS S11007B/1, 28 April 1948.

have happened if de Valera had not at Briscoe and Herzog's request over-
ruled Boland.[81]

Briscoe's intervention with de Valera on the issue of Jewish child refugees was coterminous with the life and death struggle that accompanied
the birth of an independent Jewish state in the former British mandate
of Palestine. It is widely known that Israel had faced an external threat of
extinction from the Arab World when it achieved statehood. However,
what is perhaps not so widely appreciated is how close the new state came
to repeating the tragic Irish Civil War which followed the successful War
of Independence against the British. Indeed the terrifying scenario of Jew
fighting Jew in the aftermath of the Holocaust is reinforced by Briscoe's
account of a 1949 meeting with Menachem Begin in Paris. It occurred
after Israel had successfully defended itself from the combined might of
the Arab nations, which had attacked the new state immediately after its
foundation on 14 May 1948. The first Arab-Israeli war had united the disparate Zionist factions in a desperate attempt to save the fledgling state.
This was an almost direct replication of Irish republicanism in 1922, and
it was evident that once the external threat had ceased, the Zionists were
now on the cusp of a civil war. Briscoe feared this above all else, he was
aware that the Irgun, like the anti-Treaty republicans in 1922, were being
marginalized, and that Menachem Begin was seriously considering a direct
attack on the legitimate armed force of Israel, the *Haganah*.

When he met Begin, he told him that:

> At the touch of a match you could have civil war in Israel ... A war such as we had
> in Ireland. Though I was ardent on the Republican side of that war, I bitterly regret
> the sorrow and misery and death it caused; for no good came of it. You are in the
> same position that we were. For god's sake benefit by my knowledge of the disaster
> which overtook us.[82]

Briscoe's evolution from physical-force republican to constitutional nationalist is clear in this single statement. He was apparently not sure whether

---

81   Rivlin, *Jewish Ireland*, pp. 42–44.
82   Briscoe and Hatch, *For the Life of Me*, p. 300.

his argument convinced Begin; however, the Irgun did disband and its ideological leadership founded the Herut Party, which eventually evolved into the present-day Likud Party.[83]

As Briscoe had previously remarked, many members of the Fianna Fáil party had time on their hands; this apparently included de Valera, who approached him and proposed that they undertake a trip to Israel. He described how de Valera had on many occasions expressed an interest in a visit 'to the Holy Land', and now that he was no longer Taoiseach, the opportunity was there to fulfil this ambition. He told Briscoe:

> You know how interested I am in your people; and how long I have wanted to make a pilgrimage to the Holy Land. I'll go now if you'll go with me. You can show me the ropes and bring me to the right people. On the spot we can judge for ourselves of many things.[84]

Briscoe's response was instantaneous, and he joyfully responded to de Valera's request by telling him 'this is the thing I've dreamed about, Chief'.[85]

That was the political backdrop to de Valera and Briscoe's visit to Israel in 1950. It was not a state visit, and given the circumstances, it is highly unlikely that de Valera would have been able to undertake it if he had still been Taoiseach. It appears to have been a trip that he greatly enjoyed, and he was received by his old friend Isaac Herzog who hosted a private dinner that was attended by the new Israeli Prime minister, David Ben-Gurion. This was a moving experience for Briscoe. Briscoe, de Valera and Herzog had enjoyed a complex relationship for over two decades, and this meeting in Jerusalem must have stirred deep emotions in the three men. Chaim Herzog, the Chief Rabbi's son and future President of Israel, recalled the context of the visit:

---

83   For further reading see: Amir Goldstein, '"We Have a Rendezvous With Destiny": The Rise and Fall of the Liberal Alternative', *Israeli Studies*, Vol. 16, No. 1 (Spring 2011), pp. 26–52.
84   Briscoe and Hatch, *For the Life of Me*, p. 302.
85   Ibid.

My father was an open partisan of the Irish cause. ... The Jewish community as a whole gave a lot of help to the Irish. After the establishment of the Irish Free State, when Eamon de Valera was in opposition, he would come to visit, usually with Robert Briscoe, and un burden his heart to my father. He obviously never forgot these sessions, because in 1950 ... de Valera was one of the first foreign statesmen to visit. He dined with Ben-Gurion and Bobby Briscoe at my parents' home in Jerusalem.[86]

It is apparent in Chaim Herzog's recollection that Briscoe, de Valera and Herzog enjoyed a close and long-standing personal relationship. It is also clear that the Chief Rabbi had a deep respect and affection towards de Valera that it had endured despite de Valera's failure to positively respond to repeated pleas to allow Jewish refugees access to Emergency Ireland.[87] Briscoe described the visit to Herzog's home in a somewhat superficial manner, and insisted that when Ben-Gurion engaged de Valera in a post-dinner conversation, neither man 'discussed anything in the nature of their respective experiences, or the expectations for the future of their own countries'.[88] However, given the ambition of the new state to secure global recognition,[89] this statement has to be regarded as suspect, and it is surely implausible to suggest, as Briscoe did, that Ben-Gurion would not have availed of Herzog's relationship with de Valera to at least raise the issue of recognition.[90]

Despite certain reservations about Briscoe's recollection of de Valera's meeting with Ben-Gurion, it is still an important account of a significant event in a complex post-war political reality. Based on the above recollections, it is reasonable to suggest that the trip to Israel reinforced a friendship that had begun in the white-hot atmosphere of the Irish War of Independence; certainly Briscoe believed this to be the case. He finished

86   Cited by, Wylie, *Ireland and the Cold War*, p. 205.
87   For further reading see: Rivlin, *Shalom Ireland*, pp. 42–44. Wills, *That Neutral Island*, pp. 395–397. Orfali Levi, *Leadership in Times of Crisis*, 90–94.
88   Briscoe and Hatch, *For the Life of Me*, p. 305.
89   Stefan Talmon, *Recognition of Governments in International law: With particular reference to governments in exile* (Oxford University Press, Oxford, 1998), pp. 72–73.
90   Miller, 'Public Tensions, Private Ties', pp. 193–194.

his account of the trip to Israel by drawing an analogy between the Irish and Israeli people.

> There are far more bonds between Ireland and Israel than differences. We have both fought for and won our freedom. We have both sought to revive an ancient language and an ancient culture. And we have both faced the economic difficulties of a poor small nation in a world overshadowed by industrial giants ... In the case of Israel the spiritual inspiration came from the age-old desire of the Jews to find sanctuary in their historic homeland, and the religious fervour of our ancient faith. The Irish were inspired by the love of their dear green island; and their unbreakable desire to be free.[91]

Fianna Fáil returned to power in the 1951 General Election, and one of de Valera's first acts was to appoint Briscoe as the designated government spokesman at the 40th Inter-Parliamentary Conference (IPC), which was due to be held in Istanbul that September. This global forum was founded in 1889 as a 'focal point for worldwide parliamentary dialogue [that work] for peace and co-operation among peoples'.[92] The IPC had over the decades debated many issues; its priority in the post-war period had been the terrible plight of displaced peoples, and Briscoe's address to the conference needs to be framed against this theme as well as the still contentious relationship between the new state of Israel and a re-emerging Germany still grappling with the enormity of its murder of 6,000,000 Jews less than a decade earlier. In the summer of 1949, the new Federal Government of Germany had made the decision to offer 'material compensation for the mass killings and confiscation of Jewish property', this outraged Israel which initially rejected the offer 'as blood money which after what had occurred no self-respecting nation could accept'.[93] On this basis, the government of Israel had refused previous invitations, including the one in Dublin in 1950. Their attendance in an invitation to the Istanbul conference was a contentious one internally as the statement by one dissenting politician illustrates:

---

91   Briscoe and Hatch, *For the Life of Me*, p. 308.
92   http://www.ipu.org/english/home.htm [accessed 19 September 2014].
93   George Lavy, *Germany and Israel: Moral Debt and National Interest* (Routledge, Abingdon, 2013), p. 56.

Insult to any honest and decent human being to have to negotiate with Germans as if the Germans were free of all that had been done in their name and especially to the Jewish people.[94]

Although he was representing Ireland at the conference, Briscoe was determined to emphasize the combined Irish-Israeli abhorrence of partition, just as he had done on the 1939 Revisionist Mission to America. He emphasized that his government fundamentally disagreed with the conclusion that this problem was solely a consequence of World War Two, and availed of the opportunity to once more reinforce de Valera's rejection of partition as a solution to national issues:

Some refugee problems are the result of war as we understand it; some are due to religious difficulties, others again arise from new political developments, and in particular a great number of our refugee problems arise from what was thought to be, in the recent past, a cure for certain ills, namely, the application of the medicine called partition.[95]

This was a vitally important point; not merely from an Irish perspective but also from the perspective of an Israeli one, Briscoe continued by critique by highlighting how the solution of partition was essentially a Western concept for the supposed ills of the East:

Partition, in my opinion, is one of the most recent causes of refugee problems in the eastern part of the world as distinct from new political developments and war in the western part ... The [debate], in my opinion, is concerned with the political and national outlook as distinct from the humanitarian aspect, and as I understand it, it should be our effort to bring goodwill to bear upon those who are already suffering from this problem.[96]

As well as reflecting de Valera's wishes, Briscoe's speech was a response to the earlier one by the delegate who had tried to shift the emphasis from a global refugee context into an intense concentration 'the Arab refugees

94   Ibid.
95   BPNLI, Ms, 26456. Undated copy of Briscoe's speech September 1951.
96   Ibid.

from Palestine'.[97] Then in a comment that echoes down through the decades to the present moment, Briscoe turned the spotlight back on the Arab nations of the Middle East by opining that:

> I would suggest that the Palestinian Arabs who are refugees from the present Israeli Government might easily find help by being rehabilitated and absorbed in the Arab world around them, particularly in what is now known as Transjordan.[98]

Briscoe was at pains to point out the exceptional nature of Israel's position:

> One has to remember and take into account [...] the remnant of European Jewry who were able to flee abroad to some place, to Israel in particular ... I think it is logical for the Israeli Government to recognise a responsibility to the balance of refugee Jews in different parts of the world not likely to be absorbed other than in Israel, and to feel that they must provide accommodation for these people.

However, his statement was far more than a simple apologia for Israel; it was also a prescient commentary on a future progression that we know in 2015, to have been tragically prophetic:

> I appeal to the delegates from the Middle East and Israel to try to remember that they are going to have possibly something worse than a refugee problem in the immediate future; the problem might resolve itself into an attempt by one group to extinguish the other entirely. I would rather see them try to come together, and regard this problem of the refugees from Palestine as a joint problem, and that they should seek without outside interference, but with outside help, to bring about a speedy settlement. The Jewish people themselves are the most experienced refugees of all the ages. They know the insecurity and inhumanity of the situation which confronts the refugees.[99]

Briscoe's speech had the full backing of de Valera, it could not have been given otherwise, and once more offers a rebuttal to those who simplistically depict the Irish leader as either anti-Semitic or anti-Israel.

97   Ibid.
98   Ibid.
99   Ibid.

His empathy towards Briscoe and his Jewish endeavour was perfectly summarized when Chaim Weizmann, Briscoe's old nemesis from the pre-war Zionist split and first President of Israel, died in November 1952. The President of Ireland Seán T. Ó Ceallaigh, Briscoe's old friend from his early days as a member of Dublin Corporation, had requested permission to send an official letter of condolence to the Israeli state when Weizmann died. This request had been denied by officials in the Department of External Affairs who took 'the view that, since we have not given de jure recognition to the state of Israel, it would be inappropriate for the President to send such a message'.[100] Protocol might have dictated that the Irish state offer no official sympathy; however, the depth of de Valera's friendship and respect for Isaac Herzog was evident when he sent him a personal note of condolence, which importantly also included a request that this be conveyed to the Israeli government.

> Dear Dr Herzog, Will you please accept yourself, and convey to your government my sympathy on the death of President Weisman [sic.] He was a great leader of his people. With all good wishes to you and your family. Sincerely, Eamon de Valera.[101]

This was greatly appreciated by Herzog, who responded to de Valera in the following manner:

> My Dear Mr de Valera, I duly acknowledge the receipt of your kind letter expressing your sincere regret at the great loss the State of Israel and the Jewish people generally have sustained through the death of our distinguished leader, Dr Weitzman [sic.][102]

The depth of Herzog's affection for de Valera became clear once he had conveyed his official gratitude.

> Knowing you so well as a deeply religious man and at the same time as a great humanitarian and a sincere friend of the afflicted state of Israel, I fervently pray to

100   NAI TAOIS S/15392 A, 10 November 1952.
101   Ibid., 11 November 1952.
102   Ibid., 30 November 1952.

the Almighty for your speedy recovery and hope to hear about the improvement of your eyesight before long. With the blessings of Zion to you and your dear family.[103]

De Valera had contacted Herzog from Utrecht in Holland where he had been receiving treatment for an eye condition, a fact that Herzog was clearly aware of and seemed all the more grateful for the time de Valera had taken to express his sympathies. Weizmann's death was marked by an official service of remembrance at the Adelaide synagogue on 16 November 1952. The Minister for External Affairs was represented by Bob Briscoe, the only Jewish member of the Dáil.[104]

It was clear Briscoe was once more a core member of Fianna Fáil; the party had returned to power in the 1951 General Election, although it remained short of an elusive and much desired overall majority. On a personal level, Briscoe's remarkable political renaissance continued when he topped the poll for the first time in Dublin South West with 8,417 votes.[105] It was an extraordinary increase of nearly 300 per cent since his disastrous performance in 1944; however, if he thought this new-found electoral popularity would manifest in an ability to influence policy at any level, he was sadly mistaken.

This was borne out in the spring of 1953 when Briscoe once again attempted to secure asylum for ten Jewish families as part of a humanitarian endeavour by the Paris-based Joint Distribution Committee which cared for Jewish refugees. On 12 February he met Gerry Boland, the Minister for Justice, along with a small deputation from Dublin's Jewish community, he told Boland that the proposed refugees were part of a:

> Hundred orthodox Jewish families who have escaped from behind the Iron Curtain into Austria. They are mostly Hungarian or Czechoslovakian origin. Their position is very dangerous and the Joint Distribution Committee which maintains the people, are fearful of the consequences which would flow to these people if by any chance or act they should again come under the power of the Communist authorities.[106]

103 Ibid.
104 Ibid.
105 ElectionsIreland.org/?1541
106 JMD, Box 29, Category 32.01. 12 February 1953.

Briscoe continued to reinforce the potential danger these families were facing before asking the minister 'if the Government would agree to permit approximately ten such families to enter Ireland as refugees for a maximum period of two years'.[107] Then in a reference to the rigid criteria imposed on the Jewish child refugees at Clonyn Castle in 1949, Briscoe told Boland:

> Their maintenance would be covered by the Joint Distribution Committee, and housing would be found for them as was the case of the hundred children who were allowed in, all of whom have since left the country.[108]

It took the Department of Justice more than a month to respond to Briscoe's plea despite the urgency of his request. When he received it; it was once more laden down with a rigid entry criteria regarding 'character, health, maintenance, length of stay, etc'.[109] Moreover, even then the final decision of the department did not meet Briscoe's humble request to offer sanctuary to just ten families, instead and only if all of the above requirements were met, he was told 'the Minister will be prepared to approve the admission of five ... refugee families'.[110] It had still managed to exclude fifty per cent of the original applicants despite Briscoe's efforts. It is also important to emphasize that this decision was made when these officials were fully aware of the extermination of six million Jews and could no longer claim to have been unaware of Jewish suffering.

Sadly this response would not have surprised Briscoe, he was well aware that the Irish state was not prepared to welcome refugees, particularly those of the Jewish faith. This had become apparent over the course of a fractious interaction with conservative officials in the Department's of Justice and Industry and Commerce in the pre-war years.[111] It was clear Irish officials who were responsible for overseeing immigration to the state had implemented a conservative interpretation of an already restrictive policy.

107   Ibid.
108   Ibid.
109   Ibid, 14 March 1953.
110   Ibid.
111   Ferriter, *The Transformation of Ireland*, p. 387.

This resistance to Jewish immigration is contextualized by a post-war file in the Department of the Taoiseach which admitted there had been a long-standing anti-Jewish discrimination in terms of refugee policy.

> In the administration of the alien laws it has always been recognised in the departments of Justice, Industry & Commerce and External Affairs that the question of the admission of aliens of Jewish blood present a special problem and the alien laws have been administered less liberally in their case.[112]

After acknowledging that potential Jewish refugees had been discriminated against, the file attempted to offer a justification for this position by admitting that it reflected a wide-spread cultural anti-Semitism that was grounded in a traditional Catholic dogma depicting Jews in a less than favourable light.

> Although the Jewish community in Ireland is only 3,907 persons according to the 1946 census, there is a fairly strong anti-Semitic feeling throughout the country based perhaps on historical reasons, the fact that Jews have remained a separate community and have not permitted themselves to be assimilated and that of their numbers they appear to have disproportionate wealth.[113]

This was the culmination of Briscoe's two decade long immigration initiative, it succinctly explains why his efforts were for the most part singularly unsuccessful and is a caustic indictment of the Irish state's response to one of the twentieth-century's greatest humanitarian crimes.

112   NAI TAOIS S11007A28. February 1953.
113   Ibid.

CHAPTER 10

1954–1969
Epilogue: A Political and Personal Swansong

In many respects, Briscoe's partially successful representation on behalf of Jewish families in the spring of 1953 marked the end of his active engagement with the Jewish tragedy. He would of course always be more than a passive observer when it came to the welfare of the Jewish diaspora and the new the Israeli state, however, from now on, he would increasingly re-engage with the Fianna Fáil national project. This was primarily focused on an unrelenting personal devotion to Éamon de Valera, who Briscoe believed without reservation had facilitated his immigration and Zionist endeavours. He understood that as a Jewish TD, it was difficult, if not impossible to achieve ministerial rank in twentieth-century Catholic nationalist Ireland. He never blamed de Valera for this and had always supported 'The Chief' in every political decision, even when he did not personally agree with it. This was evident in Briscoe's speech to commemorate the Silver Jubilee of the founding of Fianna Fáil in 1951, he spoke almost lovingly about de Valera:

> An organisation founded by the greatest of our people who emerged from the war against the British and our unfortunate Civil War. It is also a wonderful happy thing to be able to say that most of those who were prominent in the founding of this Organisation are still with us, with the same understanding and acceptance of the fundamentals and principles, together with the same affection and trust in the leaders of this movement, under that inspired man Éamon de Valera, who, fortunately, has been spared to us and the people of this country, and who we hope will be with us for many years to come.[1]

1   BPNLI, Ms, 26460, 3 February 1951.

Having accepted that a ministerial rank was unobtainable, Briscoe focused much of the early 1950s on re-establishing his position on Dublin City Council of which he had been a member of nearly a quarter of a century. In the late 1940s, de Valera had sounded him out about whether he would put his name forward for Lord Mayor of Dublin, a request Briscoe initially declined due to his concerns 'of the problems which might arise should a Jew, a member of a minute minority, become the First Citizen of a predominantly Catholic city'.[2] However, as time passed, Briscoe built a high profile n the council, which was predicated in many respects on an overt defence and advocacy for its Catholic ethos. For example, in 1950, a Catholic Holy Year, Briscoe had added the following personal motion to a council resolution pledging filial devotion to the Pope:

> That as a non-Catholic member of the corporation, I heartily endorse the motive behind the sending of the message. Ireland ... [is] a Catholic country and the more Catholic the people become, the more I like it.[3]

This was a clever strategy, and by 1955, Briscoe felt secure enough to allow his name to go forward for election to this historic and exalted position, however, he faced a daunting task as Denis Larkin, son of Jim, the great Trade Union leader who had led the 1913 general strike which became infamous as the 'Dublin Lockout', opposed him for the position.[4] Discretion proved the better part of valour, and Briscoe offered to step aside in return for Larkin's support in 1956. However, although Larkin agreed, he had gotten to like the position of Lord Mayor and reneged on his agreement with Briscoe and decided to stand once more in 1956.[5]

This precipitated one of the most contentious and exciting mayoral elections of the modern era, Briscoe and Larkin finished with 19 votes apiece as the Fine Gael block voted for Larkin in order to stop a Fianna Fáil

2   Briscoe and Hatch, *For the Life of Me*, p. 309.
3   Keogh, *Ireland and the Vatican*, p. 315.
4   For further reading see: Donal Nevin (ed.), *James Larkin: Lion of the Fold* (Gill and Macmillan, Dublin, 1998) and Pádraig Yeates, *Lockout: Dublin 1913* (Gill and Macmillan, Dublin, 2001).
5   Briscoe and Hatch, *For the Life of Me*, pp. 310–311.

candidate winning. Then, in an ancient act, Briscoe and Larkin's names were put into a hat where after a tense wait, Briscoe's name was drawn out and he became Lord Mayor. His recollection of the event is an amusing one:

> You could not have heard a pin drop as he fumbled under the handkerchief, because everyone was breathing so hard, including myself. The Little piece of paper was handed to Lord Mayor Larkin who studied it for a terrible minute. Then he said one word "Briscoe!" And lo and behold! I was now Lord Mayor of Dublin.[6]

Briscoe's mayoralty was filled with great joys; such as being presented to his old friend Seán T. O'Kelly now President of Ireland, and the designing of a mayoral crest which incorporated the Star of David, great confusions; such as how to conduct himself at the great Catholic ceremonies of 1950s Dublin, and great personal conflict; such as having to receive the representative of the Federal Republic of Germany. His recollection of this meeting is anything but amusing, it is filled with a poignancy for his murdered co-religionists of the Holocaust:

> He Said. "It is quite obvious from your crest where your feelings lie in regard to the Hitler Government. I hope, however, that the present Germany and the future German citizens will be able to show by their acts and their consideration for your people that those dark days of humanity are gone forever". It was to this man that I said, "as far as I am concerned, I forgive. I cannot, however, forget, and I hope my crest will be a reminder to my children of what happened, and what can happen".[7]

Such was Briscoe's popularity that he was invited to tour America for two months, the highlight being a contested battle of wills between the Mayor of New York, Robert Wagner, and John B. Hynes, the Irish-American Mayor of Boston, to review the 1957 St Patrick's Day parade.[8] Briscoe had already pledged to review the New York parade, so had to refuse Hyne's offer, however, Hyne's was not going to accept no for an answer and made the extraordinary offer to postpone the Boston parade until 18 March.[9]

6   Ibid., p. 312.
7   Ibid., p. 319.
8   *JTA*, 18 July 1956
9   *Haaretz*, 18 March 2014.

Briscoe's New York visit was a stunning success, with reports of it having almost reached mythical levels, with following oft-quoted, but surely apocryphal exchange between two Jews reaching near legendary status, "'did you know that Robert Briscoe is Jewish?". "Amazing! Only in America" said his companion'.[10]

Although that sounds wonderful, and even though there is no mention of negativity in Briscoe's description of his trip, it was not by any means without, anti-Semitic content. When he did get to Boston for the postponed parade, he was met with a tirade of abuse from conservative Catholics in the city, who were outraged that their parade had been put-back for a Jew. This was articulated by Fr. Leonard Feeney, of the Saint Benedict Center, who edited the reactionary *Point Magazine*. The following extract is taken from the March 1957 edition:

> The city of Boston is not planning a Saint Patrick's Day Parade for March 17, this year. The reason is not merely that the day is a Sunday. It seems there is a Jew headed for Boston who cannot conveniently get here until the day after Saint Patrick's Day, and this has been proposed by certain Boston Jews as a fine reason for delaying the March 17 festivities. Some highly-placed Hibernians have been found to agree. Thus, the Catholics of Boston have been instructed to hold off on their tributes to Saint Patrick until said anticipated Jew arrives to witness the proceedings. The advent of this visitor was disclosed on the front page of the *Boston Herald*: "The Lord Mayor of Dublin, Robert Briscoe, will arrive in Boston, March 18, be welcomed by a band of Irish pipers and be seen by all of South Boston, which postponed its annual Saint Patrick's Day parade one day so he could be in it."[11]

Briscoe's summation of the trip is an uncritical one; he makes the most of the slightly cloying faux Irish-Americana that undoubtedly accompanied much of his visit.

> One of the newspapers in Boston greeted me with a great green headline saying "ERIN GO BRAGH" (Ireland Forever) in both English and Yiddish characters. The

10   The Ballad of Robert Briscoe: https://www.youtube.com/watch?v=-AXgbBgGXTE [accessed 19 September 2015].
11   https://archive.org/stream/ThePoint1957/ThePoint1957_djvu.txt [accessed 19 September 2015].

supposedly proper Bostonians gave me such a welcome as almost made me weep ...
Mayor Hynes gave a wonderfully simple and touching introduction of me. He said,
"we have here with us two fine fellows-an Irishman and a Jew. I give him to you now,
Lord Mayor Robert Briscoe".[12]

Still despite not touching on the level of personal vitriol, Briscoe's trip
to America has to be considered an extraordinary success which brought
extensive publicity to Dublin in particular, and Ireland in general.[13] He
also achieved something quite extraordinary on this visit, despite not being
a government minister, he received a personal invitation from the sitting
American President, Dwight D. Eisenhower, to visit him in the White
House. This was an opportunity to good to miss, and in a humorous reference to his failed attempt to meet Roosevelt in 1939, Briscoe finally aired
the Irish state's grievance about partition when presenting Eisenhower
with a hand-loomed rug depicting the four Irish provinces, telling him
'Mr President, may I call your attention to how it unbalances the design
when one of the four provinces is taken away'.[14]

There was of course with Briscoe, as there always was, a sub-plot to
his American visit. Before he left Dublin, Briscoe had been approached by
representatives of the United Jewish Appeal to help fundraise for Jewish
causes on his visit as mayor. He wryly pointed out that these individuals
had been the very people who had thwarted the political aim of his 1939
revisionist mission; however, he like they had clearly moved on from pre-
war intransigencies and responded positively when it was explained that:

"This is not just a Zionist activity, it is a humanitarian effort by the United Jewish
Appeal which raises money not only to help the Zionist cause, but for our charities
in America. The old disputes will not impair your usefullness. We believe that you
can help us and the need is very great". Then they told me what was happening to our
people even now, in Poland and Hungary; and what was happening in Egypt and

12   Briscoe and Hatch, *For the Life of Me*, p. 325.
13   The full chronology of Briscoe's visit can be tracked through the following catalogue
     in the National Library of Ireland: http://catalogue.nli.ie/Record/vtls000649417/
     HierarchyTree [accessed 19 September 2015].
14   Briscoe and Hatch, *For the Life of Me*, p. 326.

the Arab nations of the Near and Middle east. "We are trying to raise one hundred million dollars to bring one hundred thousand refugees from those places to Israel".[15]

With his extensive knowledge of the previous twenty years, Briscoe certainly did not need any of this explaining to him, indeed he had made these very same arguments at the 1951 Inter-Parliamentary Union Conference in Istanbul. Nevertheless, he agreed to help, and over the two month duration of his trip, claimed to have personally raised thirty million dollars through public appearances on game shows like *What's my Line?*[16]

Briscoe returned to Ireland towards the end of May 1957, although the trip to America had been a personal triumph, it had left Briscoe exhausted and the remainder of his mayoral year was a relatively low-key one that extended in the main to becoming the visible face of an Ireland thousands of Americans had been enticed to come and visit after seeing Briscoe on his successful tour. As it drew to a close, he was looking forward to returning to the government backbenches, however, this was not going to be as easy as he had previously had thought. His high profile in America as the public face of Dublin was now a real financial asset, and there was a genuine concern that if he was not mayor then American tourists would not visit. On this basis, de Valera summoned him to a meeting and asked if he would consider standing again, saying that 'we may not reap all the fruits of your great American success if you retire. I ask you to do it for the good of Ireland'.[17]

Briscoe's response, 'when you ask it, I have to do it Chief' was the perfect example of his veneration for de Valera and somewhat reluctantly allowed his name to go forward to stay on as mayor for another year.[18] The election was once again a contentious one, and in an extraordinary twist, Briscoe once again received the same number of votes as his opponent. This time however, he was not as lucky as twelve months earlier when

15   Ibid., pp. 321–322.
16   Briscoe appears on *What's my Line?* as part of UJA fundraising appeal: https://www.youtube.com/watch?v=QgTbrLcN_C8 [accessed 19 September 2015].
17   Briscoe and Hatch, *For the Life of Me*, p. 333.
18   Ibid.

his name had been drawn out of the hat, this time his opponent James Carroll's name was drawn bringing an end to his highly successful stint as lord mayor of Dublin.[19]

However, this was not the end of Briscoe's mayoral duties, he was elected to this highest of offices once again in 1962. Briscoe immediately set off for America, where he outdid his 1957 meeting with President Eisenhower, by being received in the Oval Office by the first Irish-American Catholic president, John Fitzgerald Kennedy.[20] He also received a Doctorate of Humane Letters from the New York Medical College, in recognition of his unstinting efforts on behalf of Jewish refugees through the decades.[21] However, despite these personal milestones this trip was far more low-key than the 1957 one, he attended receptions across the country from Texas, to Colorado to Chicago and California. This was as much a consequence of age rather than a lack of zeal, Briscoe was edging ever closer to the end of half a century of involvement in Irish politics at the highest level.

He retired at the end of the 17th Dáil in 1965 after successfully defending his seat in Dublin South-West 12 times, He was succeeded by his son Ben, who held the seat for a further 37 years, giving father and son a combined and unbroken Dáil service of 75 years. Briscoe lived just four more years after retiring; he died on 11 March 1969 surrounded by his family. According to his son Ben, an extraordinary incident exemplifying his devotion to de Valera occurred at this point. In his final few days, Briscoe was essentially uncommunicative; however, when de Valera (who was almost 87 years old and in his second term as President of the Irish State) visited him to say goodbye, he opened his eyes and said, 'Is that you, Chief?'.

19   Briscoe and Hatch, *For the Life of Me*, p. 333.
20   Briscoe meets President John F. Kennedy in the Oval Office: https://www.youtube. com/watch?v=mGCNMwb7e5I [accessed 19 September 2015].
21   http://sources.nli.ie/Record/MS_UR_087016 [accessed 19 September 2015].

Conclusion

Unlike many of his revolutionary colleagues, Briscoe never achieved ministerial rank; in many respects, however, his global fame exceeded every surviving member of this generation except Éamon de Valera. He was fêted in America as the Jewish Lord Mayor of Dublin and twice received in the Oval Office by Presidents Eisenhower and Kennedy. Not surprisingly therefore, Briscoe like many of his contemporaries in the revolutionary generation had a considerable ego. This was reinforced on a personal basis, by the absolute uniqueness of participating in two armed and ultimately insurrections against Britain, the world's dominant imperial power. Such was his appeal to New York's Jewish residents, that an annual awards ceremony was dedicated to his memory honouring the contribution of an individual for his/her efforts on behalf of immigrants.[1] He was responsible for attracting the first wave of American tourists to the state, who drawn by his personal charisma, and uniqueness as an Irish-Jewish politician, visited Ireland in the first wave of mass tourism bringing much needed dollars to a depressed economy.

Briscoe embraced his fame, and could be found holding court in Dublin's Gresham Hotel over morning coffee, where he regaled his companions with tales from his globetrotting. He played up to this stereotype, happily extolling the virtues of an Irish state that cherished its Jewish community, and loyally supported the Fianna Fáil line that 'the anti-Semitic movement was so insignificant that the Government did not deem it worthy of notice'.[2] However, all of this window dressing pales into insignificance when the extent of his contribution to Éamon de Valera's nationalist project, the immigration initiative of the pre-war era and the global Zionist rescue effort of the thirties and forties is examined. Although these contributions

1   http://eiic.org/blog/annual-robert-briscoe-awards [accessed 19 September 2015].
2   *JTA*, 5 January 1938.

have at various times been touched upon, the contemporary narrative essentially focuses on Briscoe's crude post-war caricature as the happy-go-lucky Jewish Lord Mayor of Dublin. However, very much like an iceberg, this self-cultivated position reflects barely a tenth of Briscoe's contribution to a parochial nationalist project and global Zionist movement.

The incremental process of Briscoe's Zionist awakening was underpinned by a five year long Jewish immigration advocacy, which had been an almost universally negative experience. His initial hesitant involvement in the immigration initiative had been at the behest of Isaac Herzog in 1933, and was defined by a contentious discourse with conservative officials in the departments of Justice and Industry and Commerce, who were intent on implementing a rigid interpretation of an already exclusionist immigration criterion. All that being said, it is important to emphasize that Briscoe's high level of assimilation meant that even when he experienced a negative reaction to his advocacy, he still could not abandon the dominant imperative of his complex political evolution, a lifelong allegiance to the Irish nationalist project.

He had been brought up by a loving father to always believe that he was first and foremost an Irishman, who just so happened to be Jewish by religion. This had manifested in an active republican participation, and an unswerving allegiance to de Valera and the nascent Irish state. This fidelity did not waver even when Briscoe had developed a strong Zionist consciousness after meeting the charismatic leader of the New Zionist Organisation, Ze'ev Jabotinsky, an event that reinforced a determination to participate in the Zionist rescue effort. However, this was conducted in an atmosphere where a disparaging attitude towards Jews framed the worldview of the Dáil's Gentile actors; however, it is important to also acknowledge the temporal context of these incidents. They occurred in the 1930s, a decade that witnessed a titanic struggle for supremacy between the two great totalitarian ideologies of the era, Communism and National Socialism. The foundational principle of the Nazi anti-communist project was a concerted propaganda offensive depicting Jews as the prime motivational force of a Moscow-inspired conspiracy to secure global domination. It is therefore reasonable to argue that the anti-communist ideology of Nazism influenced a number of otherwise reasonable individuals to ignore the anti-Semitism which underpinned National Socialism.

The anti-communist agenda of the 1930s found a receptive audience in the Irish state; it was reinforced by the Catholic Church which viewed socialism of any description as a threat to its very existence. This synthesis precipitated a 'Red Scare', which quickly pervaded every strata of an Irish society which was already one of the most observant and deferential Catholic congregations in Europe. These were the social and political imperatives that formed the backdrop to Briscoe's immigration endeavours, and were indicative of the extent to which a global anti-Semitic ethos had pervaded 1930s Ireland. All these incidents, political and civil, would have framed Briscoe's response-mechanism until he could no longer avoid the realization that only by helping themselves could the Jews be saved. This was reinforced by the Evian Conference in 1938 where despite emoting about the plight of Germany's Jews, it was clear that the Christian liberal-democracies did not care, and that their support, such as it was, would be confined to issuing moral platitudes condemning the Nazi's persecution of its Jewish population.

It was also clear that Briscoe's high level of assimilation meant that his commitment could not be absolute, and would have to be balanced by his loyalty to de Valera and the Irish state. This dual obligation would result in a revisionist engagement that had a number of caveats. Firstly, although it would be grounded in an absolute commitment to saving Jewish lives, it would have to run in tandem with his fidelity as an Irishman. This stance was reinforced by the fact that Briscoe's involvement with the revisionist movement only occurred after he secured de Valera's permission. When this was achieved, a synthesis emerged that exhibited both aspects of his dual loyalties, and was focused on the question of partition. This was an issue that united Briscoe, de Valera and Jabotinsky. Briscoe and de Valera had been dealing with a partitioned Irish state since 1922, while Jabotinsky had vehemently rejected the British proposal to partition Palestine into Jewish and Arab sectors under the 1937 MacDonald White Paper. This shared abhorrence of partition resulted in Jabotinsky's visit to Dublin in 1938, although it soon became clear that even though de Valera was sympathetic to the Revisionist position, he was far too shrewd a political operator to risk annoying the British with an overt commitment, and confined himself to a moral condemnation of partition in any manifestation.

Although Briscoe was determined to help secure an independent Jewish state, it is necessary to posit the question of how far this belief extended; in other words, did Briscoe ever consider making Aliyah on a personal basis? The answer appears to be a resounding No. He was, like most Jews, especially those who had been directly involved in the Holocaust, faced with the choice of remaining where he was or emigrating to a pre-Israel Palestine. The evidence suggests that this was never a serious proposition; his identity was, and at all times remained, that of a proud Irishman who just happened through a quirk of birth to have been born a Jew. It is evident that he never envisaged living in 'the Promised Land', and his reason for supporting the concept of a Jewish state was that as long as one existed as a place of refuge, another Holocaust could never happen. Like many of his contemporary co-religionists, he had responded to the Nazi persecution out of an empathy with his fellow Jews rather than any desire to live in a potential Jewish state. He was, and remained, Jabotinsky's worst nightmare, a fully assimilated Jew who was committed to his host nation.

Bibliography

Primary Sources

Archives

Briscoe Files Jabotinsky Institute Tel Aviv
Briscoe Papers National Library of Ireland
Eoin O'Duffy Papers National Library of Ireland
Irish Military Archives G2 Files
Irish Military Archives MA Files
Jabotinsky Files Jabotinsky Institute Tel Aviv
Jabotinsky Institute Tel Aviv Correspondence
Jewish Museum Dublin (These archives are partially un-catalogued.)
National Archives of Ireland
The National Archives (United Kingdom)

Private Papers

Robert Briscoe Private Papers (This archive remains the private property of Mr Ben
Briscoe.)

Memoir

Briscoe, Robert and Alden Hatch. *For the Life of Me*. Boston and Toronto: Little,
Brown and Company, 1958.
Browne, Noel. *Against the Tide*. Dublin: Gill and Macmillan, 1986.
Frankfurter, Felix and Harlan B. Phillips. *Felix Frankfurter Reminisces*. New York:
Renal & Company, 1960.

Parliamentary debates

Dáil Éireann Debates (Available at: www.oireachtas-debates.gov.ie/)
House of Commons Hansard
(Available at: o-parlipapers.chadwyck.co.uk.library.ucc.ie/home.do)

Newspapers

An Phoblacht
Haaretz
Irish Independent
Irish Press
Irish Times
Jewish Chronicle (UK)
Jewish Herald (South Africa)
Jewish Standard (UK)
Jewish Telegraphic Agency
New York Magazine
New York Times

Web Sites

Aliens Act 1935
www.irishstatutebook.ie/eli/1935/act/14/enacted/en/html

The Ballard of Robert Briscoe
https://www.youtube.com/watch?v=-AXgbBgGXTE

Briscoe's Electoral Record
www.ElectionsIreland.org/?1541

Briscoe Meets JFK
https://www.youtube.com/watch?v=mGCNMwb7e5I

Briscoe Appears on What's my Line?
https://www.youtube.com/watch?v=QgTbrLcN_C8

Briscoe's Doctorate of Humane Letters
http://sources.nli.ie/Record/MS_UR_087016

Bunreacht Na hÉireann 1937
www.taoiseach.gov.ie/attached_files/html%20files/Constitution%

Bunreacht Na hÉireann Constitutional Referendum 1937
www.environ.ie/en.LocalGovernment/Voting/Referenda/PublicationDocuments/
    Ref.FileDownloads.1894,en

Control of Manufactures Act 1932
http://www.irishstatutebook.ie/eli/1932/act/21/enacted/en/html

Dublin South Electoral Results
www.electionsireland.org/result.cfm?election+1932=102

Evian Conference Recommendations
www.jewishvirtuallibrary.org/jsource/Holocaust/evian.html

Evian Conference Participants
www.jewishvirtuallibrary.org/jsource/Holocaust/killtable.html

Kindertransports
www.holocaustresearchproject.org/holoprelude/kindertransport.html

Moneylending Bill 1929
https://acts.oireachtas.ie/zza36y1933.1.html

Full Text of Fr. Leonard Feeney's Anti-Semitic Attack on Briscoe, 1957.
https://archive.org/stream/ThePoint1957/ThePoint1957_djvu.txt

Wannsee Conference
www.orte-der-erinnerung.de/en/institutions/list_of_institutions/house_of_the_
    wannsee_conference_memorial_and_educational_site

Documents

Adler, Cyrus and Henrietta Szold. (eds.), *American Jewish Year Book*, Vol. 40. Miami:
    American Jewish Committee, 1938.

Coates, Tim. (ed.), *The Irish Uprising, 1914–1921: Papers from the British Parliamentary Archive*. London: The Stationary Office, 2000.

Crowe, Catriona, Michael Kennedy, Dermot Keogh and Eunan O'Halpin. (eds.), *Documents on Irish Foreign Policy 1937–1939*. Vol. V. Dublin: Royal Irish Academy, 2006.

Crowe, Catriona, Ronan Fanning, Michael Kennedy, Dermot Keogh and Eunan O'Halpin. (eds.), *Documents on Irish Foreign Policy 1932–1936*. Vol. IV. Dublin: Royal Irish Academy, 2004.

———. (eds.), *Documents on Irish Foreign Policy 1939–1941*. Vol. VI. Dublin: Royal Irish Academy, 2008.

Estorick, Eric. The Evian Conference and the Intergovernmental Committee. *Annals of the American Academy of Political and Social Science* 203. 1939.

Fanning, Ronan, Michael Kennedy, Dermot Keogh and Eunan O'Halpin. (eds.), *Documents on Irish Foreign Policy 1919–1922*. Vol. I. Dublin: Royal Irish Academy, 1998.

Jabotinsky, Ze'ev. *The Political and Social Philosophy of Ze'ev Jabotinsky: Selected Writings*. Ed. Mordechai Sarig. London and Portland: Vallentine Mitchell, 1999.

Noakes, Jeremy and Geoffrey Pridham. (eds.), *Documents on Nazism*. New York: Viking Press, 1975.

Rabinovich, Itmar and Jehuda Reinharz. (eds.), *Israel in the Middle East: Documents and Readings on Society, Politics and Foreign Relations, Pre-1948 to the Present*. Lebanon NH: Brandeis University Press, 2008.

Sarig, Mordechai. (ed.), *The Political and Social Philosophy of Ze'ev Jabotinsky: Selected Writings*. London: Valentine Mitchell, 1999.

Secondary Sources

Allen, Kieran. *Fianna Fáil and Irish Labour: 1926 to the Present*. London: Pluto Press, 1997.

Apter, Lauren Elise. 'Disorderly Decolonization: The White Paper of 1939 and the End of British Rule in Palestine'. PhD. The University of Texas at Austin, 2008.

Aronoff, Myron Joel. 'Political Polarrization: Contradictory Interpretations of Israeli Reality'. *Cross-Currents in Israeli Culture and Politics*. (ed.) Myron Joel Aronoff. New Brunswick: Transaction Inc, 1984. 1–27.

Ashby Turner, Henry. *Hitler's Thirty Days to Power: January 1933*. New York: Basic Books, 1997.

Avnery, Yitzhak. 'Immigration and Revolt: Ben-Gurion's Response to the 1939 White Paper'. *David Ben-Gurion: Politics and Leadership in Israel.* (ed.) Ronald W. Zweig. London: Routledge, 1991. 99–114.

Barber, James David. *Politics by Humans: Research on American Leadership*. Durham: Duke University Press, 1988.

Barron, Ilan Zvi. *Justifying the Obligation to Die: War, Ethics, and Political Obligation with Illustrations from Zionism*. Lanham: Lexington Books, 2009.

Bauer, Yehuda. *American Jewry and the Holocaust: The American Joint Distribution Committee, 1939–1945*. Detroit: Wayne State University Press, 1982.

——. 'From Cooperation to Resistance: The Haganah 1938–1946'. *Middle Eastern Studies* 2. 3 (1966): 182–210.

Baumel, Judith Tydor. *The 'Bergson Boys' and the Origins of Contemporary Zionist Militancy*. Syracuse: Syracuse University Press, 2005.

——. 'The IZL Delegation in the USA 1939–1948: Anatomy of an Ethnic Interest Protest/Group'. *Jewish History* 9. 1 (1995): 79–89.

Ben-Ami, Yitshak. 'The Irgun and the Destruction of European Jewry'. *Perspectives on the Holocaust*. Ed. Randolph L. Braham. Dordrecht: Springer-Science+Business Media, B. V., 1983. 71–93.

Berkowitz, Michael. *Western Jewry and the Zionist Project, 1914–1933*. Cambridge: Cambridge University Press, 1997.

Berman, Aaron. *Nazism the Jews and American Zionism, 1933–1948*. Detroit: Wayne State University Press, 1990.

Binchy, Daniel. 'Adolph Hitler'. *Studies: An Irish Quarterly* 22. 85 (1933), 29–47.

Bishop, Patrick. *The Reckoning: Death and Intrigue in the Promised Land*. London: Harper Collins, 2014.

Birnbaum, Ervin. 'Evian: The Most Fateful Conference of All Times in Jewish History'. *NATIV A Journal of Politics and the Arts* 22 (2009): 1–4.

Bowden, Tom. 'The Politics of Arab Rebellion in Palestine, 1936–39'. *Middle Eastern Studies* 11. 2 (1975): 147–174.

Bowyer-Bell, J. *The Gun in Politics: An Analysis of Irish Political Conflict, 1916–1986*. New Brunswick: Transaction Publishing, 2009.

——. *The Secret Army: The IRA*. Vol. 3. New Brunswick: Transaction Publications, 2008.

——. *Out of Zion: The Fight for Israeli Independence*. New Brunswick: Transaction Publishers, 2009.

Brannigan, John. *Race in Modern Irish Literature and Culture*. Edinburgh: Edinburgh University Press, 2009.

Brasier, Andrew. and Kelly, John. *Harry Boland: A Man Divided*. Dublin: New Century Publishing, 2000.

Braustein, William I. *Roots of Hate: Anti-Semitism in Europe before the Holocaust.* Cambridge: Cambridge University Press, 2003.

Breitman, Richard and Alan J. Lichtman. *FDR and the Jews.* Cambridge: Harvard University Press, 2013.

Brest, Anne Lapedus. 'The Yodakiens: Migrations and Re-Migrations of a Jewish Family'. *Jewish Affairs* (2008): 23–27.

Brockmann, Stephen. *Nuremberg: The Imaginary Capital.* Woodbridge: Boydell & Brewer Ltd, 2006.

Broderick, Eugene. 'The Corporate Labour Policy of Fine Gael, 1934'. *Irish Historical Studies* 29. 113 (1994), 88–99.

Brown, Michael. *The Israeli-American Connection: Its Roots in the Yishuv, 1914–1945.* Detroit: Wayne State University Press, 1996.

——. 'The New Zionism in the New World: Vladimir Jabotinsky's Relations with the United States in the Pre-Holocaust years'. *Modern Judaism* 9. 1 (1989): 71–99.

Butler, Katherine. 'Centenary of a Synagogue: Adelaide Road 1892–1992'. *Dublin Historical Record* 47. 1 (1994): 46–55.

Byrne, Elaine. *Political Corruption in Ireland 1922–2012: A Crooked Harp?* Manchester: Manchester University Press, 2012.

Carroll, Francis M. *Money for Ireland: Finance, Diplomacy, Politics and the First Dáil Éireann.* Westport: Praeger Publishers, 2002.

Cesarani, David. *Eichmann: His Life and Crimes.* London: William Heinemann, 2004.

——. 'The Politics of Anglo-Jewry Between the Wars'. *Authority, Power and Leadership in the Jewish Polity: Cases and Issues.* (ed.) Daniel J. Elazar. Lanham: University Press of America, 1991. 141–165.

Clark, Gemma. *Everyday Violence in the Irish Civil War.* Cambridge: Cambridge University Press, 2014.

Clifford, Rebecca. *Commemorating the Holocaust: The Dilemmas of Remembrance in France and Italy.* Oxford: Oxford University Press, 2013.

Cohen, Michael J. 'Direction of Policy in Palestine, 1936–45'. *Middle Eastern Studies* 11. 3 (1975): 237–261.

——. 'Secret Diplomacy and Rebellion in Palestine, 1936–1939'. *International Journal of Middle Eastern Studies* 8. 3 (1977). 371–393.

Cohen, Naomi W. *The Americanization of Zionism, 1897–1945.* Lebanon: Brandeis University Press, 2003.

Cohen, Stuart A. 'Anglo-Jewish Response to Antisemitism'. *Living with Antisemitism: Modern Jewish Responses.* Ed. Jehuda Reinharz. Dartmouth: Brandeis University Press, 1987. 84–103.

Cole, Robert. *Propaganda, Censorship and Irish Neutrality in the Second World War.* Edinburgh: Edinburgh University Press, 2006.

Coogan, Tim Pat. *Ireland in the Twentieth Century*. London: Hutchinson, 2003.

——. *Michael Collins the Man Who Made Ireland: The Life and Times of Michael Collins*. New York: Palgrave, 2002.

Cooney, John. *John Charles McQuaid: Ruler of Catholic Ireland*. Syracuse New York: Syracuse University Press, 2000.

Cotter, Colette Mary. "Anti-Smitism and Irish Political Culture, 1932–1945." *M. Phil.* University College Cork, 1996.

Cronin, Mike. *The Blueshirts and Irish Politics*. Dublin: Four Courts Press, 1997.

——. 'Catholicising Fascism, Fascistising Catholicism? The Blueshirts and the Jesuits in 1930s Ireland'. *Totalitarian Movements and Political Religions* 8. 2 (2007): 401–411.

Cymet, David. *History Vs. Apologetics: The Holocaust, the Third Reich, and the Catholic Church*. Lanham: Lexington Books, 2010.

Daly, Mary E. 'An Irish-Ireland for Business?: The Control of Manufactures Acts, 1932 and 1934'. *Irish Historical Studies* 24. 94 (1984): 246–272.

——. 'Cultural and Economic Protection And Xenophobia In Independent Ireland, 1920s–1970s'. *Facing the Other*. (ed.) Borbála Faragó and Moynagh Sullivan. Newcastle: Cambridge Scholars Publishing, 2008. 6–19.

——. *Industrial Development and Irish National Identity, 1922–1939*. New York: Syracuse University Press, 1992.

——. 'Irish Nationality and Citizenship since 1922'. *Irish Historical Studies* 32. 127 (2001): 377–407.

Davis, Ronald W. 'Jewish Military Recruitment in Palestine, 1940–1943'. *Journal of Palestine Studies* 8. 2 (1979): 55–76.

Davison, Neil R. *James Joyce, Ulysses, and the Construction of Jewish Identity: Culture, Biography, and 'the Jew' in Modernist Europe*. Cambridge: Cambridge University Press, 1998.

Derrida, Jacques and Eric Prenowitz. 'Archive Fever': A Freudian Impression'. *Diacritics* 25. 2 (1995): 4–24.

Dháibhéid, Caoimhe Nic. *Seán MacBride: A Republican Life*. Liverpool: Liverpool University Press, 2011.

Dolan, Anne. *Commemorating the Irish Civil War: History and Memory, 1923–2000*. Cambridge: Cambridge University Press, 2003.

Doorly, Mary Rose. *Hidden Memories: The Personal Recollections of Survivors and Witnesses to the Holocaust Living in Ireland*. Dublin: Blackwater Press, 1994.

Douglas, R. M. *Architects of the Resurrection: Ailtirí na hAiséirghe and the Fascist 'New Order' in Ireland*. Manchester: Manchester University Press, 2009.

Duggan, J. P. 'An Undiplomatic Diplomat: C. H. Bewley (1888–1969)'. *Studies: An Irish Quarterly Review* 90. 358 (2001): 207–214.

Dunphy, Richard. *The Making of Fianna Fáil in Power in Ireland, 1923–1948*. Oxford: The Clarendon Press, 1995.

Edelheit, Abraham J. *The Yishuv in the Shadow of the Holocaust: Zionist Politics and Rescue Aliya, 1933–1939*. Boulder: Westview Press, 1998.

El-Eini, Roza I. M. 'The Implementation of British Agricultural Policy in Palestine in the 1930s'. *Middle Eastern Studies* 32. 4 (1996): 211–250.

Eliash, Shulamit. *The Harp and the Shield of David: Ireland, Zionism and the State of Israel*. Oxford: Routledge, 2007.

Engel, David. *Facing a Holocaust: The Polish-Government in Exile and the Jews, 1943–1945*. Chapel Hill: The University of North Carolina Press, 1993.

——. 'The Holocaust'. *A Compannion to Europe 1900–1945*. (ed.) Gordon Martel. Cichester: Blackwell Publishing, 2011. 472–486.

English, Richard. *Armed Struggle: The History of the IRA*. Oxford: Oxford University Press, 2003.

——. *Ernie O'Malley: IRA Intellectual*. Oxford: Oxford University Press, 1998.

——. 'Green on Red: Two Case Studies in Early Twentieth-Century Irish Republican Thought'. *Political Thought in Ireland Since the Seventeenth Century*. Ed. Robert Eccleshall, Vincent Geoghegan and David G. Boyce. London: Routledge, 1993. 169–189.

——. *Irish Freedom: The History Of Nationalism In Ireland*. London: Macmillan, 2006.

Enright, Seán. *Easter Rising 1916: The Trials*. Kildare: Merrion, 2014.

Epstein, Catherine. *Nazi Germany: Confronting the Myths*. Winchester: John Wiley & Sons, 2015.

Evans, Bryce. *Seán Lemass: Democratic Dictator*. Cork: The Collins Press, 2011.

Falter, Jürgen W. 'How Likely Were Workers to Vote for the NSDAP?' *The Rise of National Socialism and the Working Classes in Weimar Germany*. Ed. Conan Fischer. Providence: Berghahn Books, 1996.

Fanning, Bryan. *Racism and Social Change in the Republic of Ireland*. Manchester: Manchester University Press, 2012.

Fast, Vera K. *Children's Exodus: A History of the Kindertransport, 1938–1939*. London: I. B. Tauris & Co Ltd, 2011.

Feingold, Henry L. 'Who Shall Bear Guilt for the Holocaust: The Human Dilemma'. *The Nazi Holocaust Part 8: Bystanders to the Holocaust*. (ed.) Michael R. Marrus. Vol. 8. Westport: Meckler Corporation, 1989. 121–143.

Ferriter, Diarmaid. *The Transformation Of Ireland, 1900–2000*. London: Profile Books, 2005.

Finnegan, Richard B. and Edward McCarron. *Ireland: Historical Echoes, Contemporary Politics*. Ann Arbour: The University of Michigain Press, 2000.

Foster, Gavin. 'Class Dismissed? The Debate over a Social Basis to the Treaty Split and Irish Civil War'. *Saothar* 33 (2008): 73–88.

Foy, Michael T. and Barton, Brian. *The Easter Rising*. Stroud: The History Press, 2011.

Fraser, T. G. 'A Crisis of Leadership: Weizmann and the Zionist Reactions to the Peel Commission's Proposals, 1937–38'. *Journal of Contemporary History* 23. 4 (1988): 653–671.

Friling, Tuvia. *Arrows in the Dark: David Ben-Gurion, the Yishuv Leadeship, and Rescue Attempts During the Holocaust*. Madison: The University Press of Wisconsin, 2005.

Fuller, Louise. *Irish Catholicism Since 1950: The Undoing of a Culture*. Dublin: Gill and Macmillan, 2004.

Gal, Allon. *David Ben-Gurion and the American Alignment for a Jewish State*. Jerusalem: The Hebrew University Press, 1991.

———. 'Brandeis, Judaism, and Zionism'. *Brandeis and America*. (ed.) Nellson L. Dawson. Lexington: The University Press of Kentucky, 1989. 65–95.

Gallagher, Michael. *Political Parties in the Republic of Ireland*. Manchester: Manchester University Press, 1985.

Galnoor, Itzhak. 'The Zionist Debates on Partition (1919–1947)'. *Israeli Studies* 14. 2 (2009): 74–87.

Gardner, Hall. *The Failure to Prevent World War One: The Unexpected Armageddon*. Farnham: Ashgate Publishing Ltd, 2015.

Gellately, Robert. *The Gestapo and German Society: Enforcing Racial Policy 1933–1945*. Oxford: Clarendon Press, 1991.

Gerrits, André. *The Myth of Jewish Communism: A Historical Interpretation*. Brussels: P. I. E. Peter Lang S. A. Éditions Scientifiques Internationales, 2009.

Geyer, Michael. 'A Family History from the Days of the Kindertransports'. *History and Memory* 17. 1–2 (2005): 323–365.

Girvin, Brian. *Between Two Worlds: Politics and Economy in Independent Ireland*. Savage: Barnes and Noble, 1989.

Goldberg, Chad Alan. 'Introduction to Emile Durkheim's "Anti-Semitism and Social Crisis"'. *Sociological Theory* 26. 4 (2008): 299–323.

Goldstein, Amir. '"We Have a Rendezvous With Destiny": The Rise and Fall of the Liberal Alternative'. *Israeli Studies* 16. 1 (2011): 26–52.

Goldstein, Jan. 'The Wandering Jew and the Problem of Psychiatric Anti-Semitism in Fin-de-Siecle France'. *Journal of Contemporary History* 20. 4 (1985): 521–552.

Goldstein, Yaacov N. 'Labour and Likud: Roots of their Ideological-Political Struggle for Hegemony over Zionism, 1925–35'. *Israel: The First Hundred Years: Politics and Society since 1948 Problems of Collective Identity*. Ed. Efraim Karsh. Vol. III. London: Routledge, 2002. 80–91.

Goldstone, Katrina. '"Benevolent Helpfulness"? Ireland and the International Reaction to Jewish Refugees, 1933–39'. *Irish Foreign Policy 1919–1966: From Independence to Internationalism*. Ed. Michael Kennedy and Joseph Morrison Skelly. Dublin: Four Courts Press, 2000. 116–136.

——. 'Christianity, conversion and the tricky business of names: Images of Jews and Blacks in the nationalist Irish Catholic discourse'. *Racism and Anti-Racism*. Ed. Ronnit Lentin and Robbie McVeigh. Belfast: Beyond the Pale Publications Ltd, 2002. 167–176.

Golway, Terry *Irish Rebel: John Devoy and America's Fight for Ireland's Freedom*. New York: St Martin's Press, 1999.

Gordon, Sarah. *Hitler, Germans, and the Jewish Question*. Princeton: Princeton University Press, 1984.

Greaves, C. Desmond. *Liam Mellows and the Irish Revolution*. London: Lawrence & Wishart, 1971.

Greenfield, Murray S. and Joseph M. Hochstein. *The Jews' Secret Fleet: The Untold Story of North American Volunteers who Smashed the British Blockade of Palestine*. Jerusalem: Gefen Publishing House, 1987.

Griffin, Roger. *Terrorist's Creed: Fanatical Violence and the Human Need for Meaning*. Basingstoke: Palgrave Macmillan, 2012.

Hachey, Thomas E. 'The Rhetoric and Reality of Irish Neutrality'. *New Hibernia Review* 6. 4 (2002): 26–43.

Haim, Yehoyada. 'Zionist Attitudes toward Partition, 1937–1938'. *Jewish Social Studies* 40. 3/4 (1978): 303–320.

Hamerow, Theodore S. *Why We Watched: Europe, America, and the Holocaust*. New York: W. W. Norton & Company, 2008.

Hammel, Andrea. and Lewkowicz, Bea. *The Kindertransport to Britain 1938/9: New Perspectives*. Amsterdam: Rodopi B. V., 2008.

Hanley, Brian. *The IRA: 1926–36*. Dublin: Four Courts Press Limited, 2002.

Havrelock, Rachel. *River Jordan and the Mythology of a Dividing Line*. Chicago: University of Chigago Press, 2011.

Hecht, Ben. *Perfidy*. New London: Milah Press Inc, 1997.

Heller, Joseph. *The Birth of Israel: Ben-Gurion and his Critics*. Gainsville: University Press of Florida, 2000.

——. *The Stern Gang: Ideology, Politics and Terror, 1940–1949*. Abingdon: Routledge, 2004.

Holfter, Gisela. 'Some Facts and Figures on German-speaking Exiles in Ireland, 1933–1945'. *German Diasporic Experiences: Identity, Migration and Loss*. Ed. Mathias Schulze, et al. Waterloo: Wilfrid Laurier University Press, 2008. 181–192.

——. 'German-Speaking Exiles 1933–1945 in Ireland-an Introduction and Overview'. *German-Speaking Exiles In Ireland 1933–1945*. (ed.) Gisela Holfter. Amsterdam and New York: Rodopi, 2006. 1–21.

Horgan, John. *Sean Lemass: The Enigmatic Patriot*. Dublin: Gill and MacMillan, 1997.

Hutton, Seán. 'Labour in the Post-Industrial Irish State: An Overview'. *Irish Histories: Aspects of State, Society and Ideology*. (ed.) Seán Hutton and Paul Stewart. London: Routledge, 1991. 52–79.

Jeffrey, Keith. *Field Marshal Sir Henry Wilson: A Political Soldier*. Oxford: Oxford University Press, 2006.

Jesse, Neal G. 'Choosing to Go it Alone: Irish Neutrality in Theoretical and Comparative Perspective'. *International Political Science Review* 27. 1 (2006): 8–19.

Jones, David H. *Moral Responsibility in the Holocaust: A Study in the Ethics of Character*. Lanham: Rowman & Littlefield Publishers. Inc., 1999.

Kaplan, Eran. 'A Rebel with a Cause: Hillel Kook, Begin and Jabotinsky's Ideological Legacy'. *Israeli Studies* 10. 3 (2005): 87–102.

Katz, Shmuel. *Lone Wolf: A Biography of Vladimir (Ze'ev) Jabotinsky*. Vol. Two. New York: Barricade Books Incorporated, 1996.

Kaufman, Menahem. *An Ambiguous Partnership: Non Zionists and Zionists in America 1939–1948*. Jerusalem: The Magnes Press, 1991.

Keane, Elizabeth. *An Irish Statesman and Revolutionary: The Nationalist and Internationalist Politics of Seán MacBride*. London: I. B. Tauris, 2006.

Keatinge, Benjamin. 'Responses to the Holocaust in Modern Irish Poetry'. *Estudios Irlandeses* 1. 6 (2011): 21–38.

Keatinge, Patrick. 'Ireland and the League of Nations'. *Studies: An Irish Quarterly Review* 59. 234 (1970): 133–147.

Kelly, Stephen. *Fianna Fáil, Partition and Northern Ireland, 1926–1971*. Dublin: Irish Academic Press, 2013.

Kennedy, Finola. 'Frank Duff's Search for the Neglected and Rejected'. *Studies: An Irish Quarterly Review* 91. 364 (2002): 381–389.

Kennedy, Kieran A., Thomas Giblin and Deirdre McHugh. *The Economic Development of Ireland in the Twentieth Century*. London: Routledge, 1988.

Kennedy, Michael. 'Our Men in Berlin: Thoughts on Irish Diplomats in Germany 1929–39'. *Irish Studies in International Affairs* 10 (1999): 53–70.

Kennedy, Michael and Joseph Morrison Skelly. 'The Study of Irish Foreign Policy from Independence to Internationalism'. *Irish Foreign Policy 1919–1966: From Independence to Internationalism*. (ed.) Michael Kennedy and Joseph Morrison Skelly. Dublin: Four Courts Press, 2000. 13–24.

Keogh, Dermot and Andrew McCarthy. *The Making of the Irish Constitution 1937: Bunreacht Na HÉireann*. Cork: Mercier Press, 2007.

Keogh, Dermot. 'The Catholic Church and the Irish Free State, 1923–1932'. History
    Ireland 2. 1 (1994): 44–50.
——. *Ireland and the Vatican: Diplomacy of Church-State Relations, 1922–1960.* Cork:
    Cork University Press, 1995.
——. 'Irish Refugee Policy, Anti-Semitism and Nazism at the Approach of World
    War Two'. *German-Speaking Exiles in Ireland 1933–1945.* (ed.) Gisela Holfter.
    Amsterdam and New York: Rodopi, 2006. 37–74.
——. *Jews in Twentieth-Century Ireland: Refugees, Antisemitism and the Holocaust.*
    Cork: Cork University Press, 1998.
——. *Twentieth-Century Ireland: Nation and State.* New York: St Martin's Press, 1995.
Keogh, Niall. *Con Cremin: Ireland's Wartime Diplomat.* Cork: Mercier Press, 2006.
Keown, Gerard. 'Taking the World Stage: Creating an Irish Foreign Policy in the
    1920s'. *Irish Foreign Policy 1919–1966: From Independence to Internationalism.*
    (ed.) Michael Kennedy and Joseph Morrison Skelly. Dublin: Four Courts Press,
    2000. 25–43.
Kershaw, Ian. *Hitler.* London: Penguin Books, 2008.
Kinsella, Seán. 'The Cult of Violence and the Revolutionary Tradition in Ireland'.
    Studies: An Irish Quarterly 83. 329 (1994), 11–27.
Kiss, Desider. 'The Jews of Eastern Europe'. *Foreign Affairs* 15. 2 (1937): 330–339.
Klieman, Aaron S. 'In the Public Domain: The Controversy over Partition for Pales-
    tine'. *Jewish Social Studies* 42. 2 (1980): 149–169.
——. 'The Divisiveness of Palestine: Foreign Office Verse Colonial Office on the Issue
    of Partition, 1937'. *The Historical Journal* 22. 2 (1979): 415–429.
Knirck, Jason A. 'The Dominion of Ireland: The Anglo-Irish Treaty in an Imperial
    Context'. *Éire-Ireland* 42. 1&2 (2007): 229–255.
——. *Imagining Ireland's Independence: The Debates Over the Anglo-Irish Treaty of
    1921.* Lanham: Rowman & Littlefield Publishers Inc, 2006.
Korey, William. *Russian Antisemitism, Palyat, and the Demography of Zionism.* Abing-
    don: Routledge, 2013.
Kraut, Alan M., Richard Breitman and Thomas W. Imhoof. 'The State Department,
    The Labour Department and German-Jewish Immigration, 1930–1940'. *Journal
    of American Ethnic History* 3. 2 (1984): 5–38.
Kushner, Tony. 'The Meaning of Auschwitz: Anglo-American Responses to the Hun-
    garian Jewish-Tragedy'. *Genocide and Rescue the Holocaust in Hungary 1944.* (ed.)
    David Cesarani. Oxford: Berg, 1997. 159–178.
Lainer-Voss, Dan. *Sinews of the Nation: Constructing Irish and Zionist Bonds in the
    United States.* Cambridge: Polity Press, 2013.
Lansford, Tom. 'Pragmatic Idealism: Truman's Broader Middle East Policy'. *Israel
    and the Legacy of Harry S. Truman.* (ed.) Michael J. Divine, Robert P. Watson
    and Robert J. Wolz. Kirksville: Truman State University Press, 2008. 28–41.

Laqueur, Walter. *The History of Zionism*. London: I. B. Tauris & Co Ltd, 2003.

——. *The New Terrorism: Fanaticism and the Arms of Mass Destruction*. Oxford: Oxford University Press, 1999.

Lavy, George. *Germany and Israel: Moral Debt and National Interest*. Abingdon: Routledge, 2013.

Lee, J. J. *Ireland 1912–1985: Politics And Society*. Cambridge: Cambridge University Press, 1989.

Lee, Joseph. 'The Irish Constitution of 1937'. *Ireland's Histories: Aspects of State, Society and Ideology*. (ed.) Seán Hutton and Paul Stewart. London: Routledge, 1991. 80–93.

Lentin, Ronit. 'Ever and Always Alien: From Jewish Refugees to Swastikas on the Museum Wall'. *Ireland, Racism and Globalisation*. (ed.) Ronit Lentin and Robbie McVeigh. Dublin: Metro Éireann Publications, 2006. 115–128.

Levi, Moisés Orfali. *Leadership in Times of Crisis*. Tel Aviv: Bar Ilan University Press, 2007.

Lewis, Matthew. *Frank Aiken's War: The Irish Revolution, 1916–1923*. Dublin: Dublin University Press, 2014.

Longerich, Peter. *Holocaust: The Nazi Persecution and Murder of the Jews*. Oxford: Oxford University Press, 2010.

——. *The Unwritten Order: Hitler's Role in the Final Solution*. Stroud: Tempus Publishing Ltd, 2003.

Lozowick, Yaacov. *Hitler's Bureaucrats: The Nazi Security Police and the Banality of Evil*. London: Continuum, 2002.

Mahon, Tom and James J. Gillogly. *Decoding the IRA*. Cork: Mercier Press, 2008.

Manning, Maurice. *James Dillon: A Biography*. Dublin: Wolfhound Press, 2000.

Mara, Wil. *Kristallnacht: The Persecution of the Jews in Europe*. White Plains: Marshall Cavendish Benchmark, 2010.

McCarthy, Kevin. 'Éamon de Valera's Relationship with Robert Briscoe'. *Irish Studies in International Affairs* 25 (2014): 165–187.

——. 'An Introduction to Robert Briscoe's Extraordinary Immigration Initiative, 1933–1938'. *The Irish Context of Kristallnacht: Refugees and Helpers*. (ed.) Gisela Holfter. Trier: WVT Wissenschaftlicher, 2014. 80–90.

——. 'Exploring the Zionist Evolution of Robert Briscoe: History and Memory'. PhD, University College Cork, 2013.

McCullagh, David. *The Reluctant Taoiseach: A Biography of John A. Costello*. Dublin: Gill and Macmillan, 2010.

——. *Republicanism in Modern Ireland*. Dublin: University College Dublin Press, 2003.

McLaughlin, Robert. *From Home Rulers to Sinn Féiners: The Transformation of Irish-Canadian Nationalist Identity, 1912–1925*. Rock Hill: Department of English Winthrop University, 2004.

McMahon, Paul. *British Spies and Irish Rebels: British Intelligence and Ireland, 1916–1945*. Woodbridge Suffolk: The Boydell Press, 2008.

——. 'British Intelligence and the Anglo-Irish Truce, July-December 1921'. *Irish Historical Studies* 35. 140 2007: 529–530.

McMeekin, Seán. *July 1914: Countdown to War*. London: Icon Books Ltd, 2013.

Medoff, Rafael. *Baksheesh Diplomacy: Secret Negotiations Between American Jewish Leaders and Arab Officials on the Eve of World War II*. Lanham: Lexington Books, 2001.

——. *Militant Zionism in America: The Rise and Impact of the Jabotinsky Movement in the United States, 1926–1948*. Tuscaloosa: The University of Alabama Press, 2002.

Mendelsohn, Ezra. *The Jews of East Central Europe: Between the World Wars*. Bloomington: Indiana University Press, 1987.

Mendelsohn, Richard and Milton Shain. 'South Africa'. *Israel, the Diaspora, and Jewish Identity*. (eds.) Danny Ben-Moshe and Zohar Segev. Eastbourne: Sussex Academic Press, 2007.

Miller, Rory. 'Public Tensions, Private ties: Ireland, Israel and the Politics of Mutual Misunderstanding'. *Israel's Clandestine Diplomacies*. Oxford: Oxford University Press, 2013. 189–208.

Mitchell, Arthur. *Revolutionary Government in Ireland: Dáil Éireann, 1919–1922*. Dublin: Gill & Macmillan, 1995.

——. 'Alternative Government: "Exit Britania" – The Formation of the Irish National State, 1918–1921'. *The Irish Revolution, 1913–1922*. (ed.) Joost Augusteijn. London: Palgrave Macmillan, 2002.

Mosse, George L. 'The French Right and the Working Classes: Les Jaunes'. *Journal of Contemporary History* 7. 3/4 (1972): 185–208.

Muchitsch, Wolfgang. 'Austrian Refugees in Ireland 1938–1945'. *German-Speaking Exiles in Ireland, 1933–1945*. (ed.) Gisela Holfter. Amsterdam and New York: Rodopi B. V., 2006. 75–88.

Mühlberger, Detlef. *Hitler's Voice, the Völkischer Beobachter, 1920–1933: Organisation and Development of the Nazi Party*. Bern: Peter Lang AG, 2004.

Murray, Paul. *The Irish Boundary Commission And its Origins*. Dublin: University College Dublin Press, 2011.

Nadel, Ira B. *Joyce and the Jews: Culture and Texts*. London: Macmillan, 1989.

Neary, Peter J. and Cormac Ó Gráda. 'Protection, Economic War and Structural Change: The 1930s in Ireland'. *Irish Historical Studies* 27. 107 (1991): 250–266.

Nelson, Bruce. *Irish Nationalists and the Making of the Irish Race*. Princeton: Princeton University Press, 2012.

Nevin, Donal. (ed.) *James Larkin: Lion of the Fold*. Dublin: Gill and Macmillan, 1998.

Nic Dháibhéid. *Seán MacBride: A Republican Life*. Liverpool: Liverpool University Press, 2011.

Newsinger, John. 'Blackshirts, Blueshirts and the Spanish Civil War'. *The Historical Journal* 44. 3 (2001) 827–846.

Nimrod, Dan. *Testimony and Warning: Reflections on a Pattern of Behaviour.* Nevada City: Dawn Publishing, 1980.

Nolan, Aengus. *Joseph Walsh: Irish Foreign Policy, 1922–1946.* Cork: Mercier Press, 2008.

Novick, Peter. *The Holocaust in American Life.* New York: Houghton Mifflin Company, 1999.

Ó Beacháin. *Destiny of the Soldiers: Fianna Fáil, Irish Republicanism and the IRA, 1926–1973.* Dublin: Gill and macmillan, 2010.

Ó Broin, León. *Frank Duff.* Dublin: Gill and Macmillan, 1982.

Ó Catháin, Mártin. 'The Black Hand of Irish Republicanism? Transcontinental Fenianism and Theories of Global Terror'. *The Black Hand of Republicanism: Fenianism in Modern Ireland.* (ed.) Fearghal McGarry and James McConnell. Dublin: Irish Academic Press, 2009. 135–148.

O'Connor, Emmet. 'Bolshevising Irish Communism: The Communist International and the Formation of the Revolutionary Workers Groups, 1927–31'. *Irish Historical Studies* 33. 132 (2003): 452–469.

———. 'Communists, Russia, And The IRA, 1920–1923'. *The Historical Journal* 46. 1 (2003): 115–131.

———. *Reds and the Green: Ireland, Russia and the Communist Internationals 1919–1943.* Dublin: University College Dublin Press, 2004.

O'Connor, Siobhán. 'Irish Government Policy and Irish Public Perception toward German-Speaking Refugees in Ireland, 1933–1945'. PhD. Limerick: University of Limerick, 2009.

———. '"The Obliviousness of the Fortunate": Policy and Public Opinion towards Refugees 1933–1945.' *German-Speaking Exiles in Ireland 1933–1945.* (ed.) Gisela Holfter. Amsterdam: Rodopi B. V., 2006. 89–108.

Ó Drisceoil, Donal. *Censorship In Ireland 1939–1945: Neutrality, Politics And Society.* Cork: Cork University Press, 1996.

———. 'Jews and Other Undesirables, Anti-Semitism in Neutral Ireland During the Second World War'. *Under The Belly Of The Tiger: Class, Race, Identity And Culture In The Global Ireland.* (ed.) Ethel Crowley and Jim Mac Laughlin. Dublin: Irish Reporter Publications, 1997. 71–78.

———. '"Moral Neutrality" censorship in Emergency Ireland'. *History Ireland* Summer 1996: 17–22.

———. *Peadar O'Donnell.* Cork: Cork University Press, 2001.

O'Driscoll, Mervyn. 'Inter-war Irish-German Diplomacy: Continuity, Ambiguity and Appeasement in Irish Foreign Policy'. *Irish Foreign Policy 1919–1966: From*

Independence to Internationalism. (ed.) Michael Kennedy and Joseph Morrison Skelly. Dublin: Four Courts Press, 2000. 74–95.

——. *Ireland, Germany and the Nazis: Politics and Diplomacy, 1919–1939.* Dublin: Four Courts Press, 2004.

——. 'Irish-German relations 1929–1939: Irish reactions to Nazis'. *Cambridge Review of International Affairs* 11. 1 (1997): 293–307.

——. 'The "Jewish Question", Irish Refugee Policy and Charles Bewley, 1933–39'. n.d. *Google Scholar.* 14 December 2011 www.stm.unipi.it/clioh/tabs/libri/7/10-O'Driscoll_139–152.pdf.

Ofer, Dalia. 'The Rescue of European Jewry and Illegal Immigration to Palestine in 1940. Prospects and Reality: Berthold Storfer and the Mossad Le'Aliyah Bet'. *Modern Judaism* 4. 2 (1984): 159–181.

Ofer, Dalia and Hannah Weiner. *Dead-End Journey.* Lanham: University Press of America, 1996.

Ó Gráda, Cormac. 'Dublin Jewish Demography a Century Ago'. 37. 2 (2006): 123–147.

——. *Jewish Ireland in the Age of Joyce.* Princeton: Princeton University Press, 2006.

——. 'Lost in Little Jerusalem: Leopold Bloom and Irish Jewry'. *Journal of Modern Literature* 27. 4 (2004): 17–26.

——. 'Settling In: Dublin's Jewish Immigrants of a Century Ago'. *Field Day Review*, 1. (2005): 86–100.

O'Halpin, Eunan. 'The Army in Independent Ireland'. *A Military History of Ireland.* (ed.) Thomas Bartlett and Keith Jeffery. Cambridge: Cambridge University Press, 1996. 400–408.

——. 'Parliamentary Party Discipline and Tactics: The Fianna Fáil Archives, 1926–32'. *Irish Historical Studies* 30. 120 (1997): 581–590.

——. 'Weird Prophecies: British Intelligence and Anglo-Irish Relations, 1932–3'. *Irish Foreign Policy 1919–1966: From Independence to Internationalism.* (ed.) Michael Kennedy and Joseph Morrison Skelly. Dublin: Four Courts Press, 2000. 61–73.

O'Leary, Cornelius and Patrick Maume. *Controversial Issues In Anglo-Irish Relations, 1910–1921.* Dublin: Four Courts Press, 2004.

O'Reilly, Eileen. 'Modern Ireland: An Introductory Survey'. *Making the Irish American: History and Heritage of the Irish in the United States.* (ed.) J. J. Lee and Marion Casey. New York: New York University Press, 2006. 121–143.

O'Rourke, Kevin. 'Burn Everything British but Their Coal: The Anglo-Irish Economic War of the 1930s'. *The Journal of Economic History* 51. 2 (1991): 357–366.

Peacock, Lukas. '"Breaking down Barriers": An Insight into the Political Career of Robert Briscoe'. *MA.* University College Dublin, July 2010.

Penkower, Monty N. 'Jewish Organizations and the Creation of the U.S. War Refugee Board'. *Annals of the American Academy of Political and Social Science, Reflections on the Holocaust: Historical, Philosophical, and Educational Dimensions* 450 (1980): 122–139.

——. 'Vladimir (Ze'ev) Jabotinsky, Hillel Kook-Peter Bergson, and the Campaign for a Jewish Army'. *Modern Judaism* 31. 3 (2011): 332–374.

Philpott, Ian. *The Royal Air Force: An Encyclopedia of the Inter-War Years, Re-Armament, 1930–1939*. Barnsley: Pen and Sword Aviation, 2008.

Phoenix, Éamon. 'Michael Collins: The Northern Question 1916–1922'. *Michael Collins and the Making of the Irish State*. (ed.) Gabriel Doherty and Dermot Keogh. Cork: Mercier Press, 1998. 94–118.

Pomakoy, Keith. *Helping Humanity: American Policy and Genocide Rescue*. Lanham: The Rowman & Littlefield Publishing Group, 2011.

Porat, Dina. 'The Transnistria Affair and the Rescue Policy of the Zionist Leadership in Palestine, 1942–1943'. *The Nazi Holocaust Part 9: The End of the Holocaust*. (ed.) Michael Marrus. Westport: Merkler Corporation, 1989. 223–248.

Poznanski, Renée. *Jews in France during the Second World War*. Hanover: University Press of New England, 2001.

Pulzer, Peter G. *Jews and the German State: The Political History of a Minority, 1848–1933*. Hoboken: Blackwell Publishers, 2003.

Rapoport, Louis. *Shake Heaven and Earth: Peter Bergson and the Struggle to Rescue the Jews of Europe*. Jerusalem: Gefen Publishing House, 1999.

Rees, Russell. *Ireland, 1905–1925: Text and Historiography*. Newtownards: Colourpoint Books, 1998.

Regan, John M. 'The Politics of Reaction: The Dynamics of Treatyite Government and Policy, 1922–1933'. *Irish Historical Studies* 30. 120 (1997): 542–563.

Reisigi, Martin and Ruth Wodak. 'The Discourse-Historical Approach (DHA)'. *Methods of Critical Discourse Analysis*. (ed.) Ruth Wodak and Michael Meyer. 2. London: Sage Publications Ltd, 2009. 87–122.

Ringleblum, Emmanuel. *Polish-Jewish Relations During the Second World War*. Evanston: Northwestern University Press, 1974.

Rivlin, Ray. *Jewish Ireland: A Social History*. Dublin: Gill and Macmillan, 2003.

Roberts, Priscilla. 'Jewish Bankers, Russia, and the Soviet Union, 1900–1940: The Case of Kuhn, Loeb and Company'. *The American Jewish Archives Journal* 49. 1 & 2 (1997): 9–37.

Robinson Divine, Donna. 'Zionism and the Transformation of Jewish Society'. *Modern Judaism* 20. 3 (2000). 257–272.

Rose, Norman Anthony. 'The Arab Rulers and Palestine, 1936: The British Reaction'. *The Journal of Modern History* 44. 2 (1972): 213–231.

——. 'The Debate on Partition, 1937–38: The Anglo-Zionist Aspect: 1. The Proposal'. *Middle Eastern Studies* 6. 3 (1970): 292–312.

Rosenblum, Chanoch Howard. 'The New Zionist Organisation's American Campaign, 1936–1939'. *Studies in Zionism* 12. 2 (1991): 169–185.

——. 'Promoting an International Conference to Solve the Jewish Problem: The New Zionist Organization's Alliance with Poland, 1938–1939'. *The Slavonic and East European Review* 69. 3 (1991): 478–501.

Ross-Laffer, Dennis. 'The Jewish Trail of Tears: The Evian Conference of July 1938'. PhD. Tampa: University of South Florida, 2011.

Roth, Andreas. *Mr Bewley in Berlin: Aspects of the Career of an Irish Diplomat, 1933–1939*. Dublin: Four Courts Press, 2000.

Russell, Elizabeth. 'Themes in Popular Reading Material in the 1930s'. *Ireland in the 1930s: New Perspectives.* (ed.) Joost Augusteijn. Dublin: Four Courts Press, 1999. 11–27.

Sanger, Clyde. *Malcolm MacDonald: Bringing an End to Empire.* Montreal: McGill-Queen's University Press, Montreal, 1995.

Sarfatti, Michelle. *The Jews in Mussolini's Italy: From Protection to Persecution.* Madison: The University of Wisconsin Press, 2006.

Schabitz, Michael. 'The Flight and Expulsion of German Jews'. *Jews in Berlin: From Kristallnacht to Liberation.* (ed.) Hermann Simon, Chana Schutz and Beate Meyer. Chicago, IL: University of Chicago Press, 2000. 36–64.

Schechtman, Joseph B. 'Review: For the Life of Me by Robert Briscoe and Alden Hatch'. *Jewish Social Studies* (1959): 270–271.

Schor, Ralph. 'Xenophobia and the Extreem Right: "L'Ami du Peuple", 1928–37'. *Revue d'Histoire Moderne Contemporaine* 23 (1976): 116–144.

Schulz, Birte. 'Overcoming Boundaries? The Problem of Identity in the Experience of German-Speaking Exiles in Ireland 1933–1945'. *German-Speaking Exiles in Ireland 1933–1945.* (ed.) Gisela Holfter. Amsterdam and New York: Rodopi, 2007. 119–132.

Shapira, Anita. *Land and Power: The Zionist Resort to Force, 1881–1948.* Stanford: Stanford University Press, 1999.

Shapiro, Yonathan. *The Road to Power: Herut Party in Israel.* Albany: State University of New York Press, 1991.

Shavit, Yaacov. *Jabotinsky and the Revisionist Movement, 1925–1948.* Abingdon: Frank Cass & Co. Ltd, 1988.

Sheffer, Gabriel. 'British Colonial Policy-Making towards Palestine, 1929–1939'. *Middle Eastern Studies* 14. 3 (1978). 303–319.

——. 'Appeasement and the Problem of Palestine'. *International Journal Of Middle East Studies* 11. 3 (1980), 369–381.

Shindler, Colin. *The Land Beyond Promise: Israel, Likud and the Zionist Dream.* London: I. B. Tauris & Co Ltd, 2002.

———. *The Triumph of Military Zionism: Nationalism and the Origins of the Israeli Right*. London: I. B. Tauris & Co Ltd, 2010.

Siev, Raphael V. 'The Admission of Refugees into Ireland Between 1933 and 1945'. *German-Speaking Exiles in Ireland 1933–1945*. (ed.) Gisela Holfter. Amsterdam: Rodopi, 2006. 109–119.

Sinanoglou, Penny. 'British Plans for the Partition of Palestine, 1929–1938'. *The Historical Journal* 52. 1 (2009): 131–152.

Sinnott, Richard. *Irish Voters Decide: Voting Behaviour in Elections and Referendums*. Manchester: Manchester University Press, 1995.

Sloan, G. R. *The Geopolitics of Anglo-Irish Relations in the 20th Century*. London: Leicester University Press, 1997.

Sofer, Sasson. *Zionism and the Foundation of Israeli Diplomacy*. Cambridge: Cambridge University Press, 1998.

Sompolinsky, Meier. *Britain and the Holocaust: The Failure of Anglo-Jewish Leadership?* Brighton: Sussex Academic Press, 1999.

Steinberg, Erwin R. 'Reading the Vision of Rudy Reading'. *James Joyce Quarterly* 36. 4 (1999): 954–962.

Steinweis, Alan E. *Kristallnacht 1938*. Cambridge: Harvard University Press, 2009.

Sterling, Eric J. 'Rescue and Trauma: Jewish Children and the Kindertransports during the Holocaust'. *Children and War*. (ed.) James Marten. New York: New York University Press, 2002. 63–75.

Stradling, R. A. *The Irish and the Spanish Civil War, 1936–39: Crusades in Conflict*. Manchester: Manchester University Press, 1999.

Talmon, Stefan. *Recognition of Governments in International Law: With particular reference to governments in exile*. Oxford: Oxford University Press, 1998.

Titley, E. Brian. *Church, State, and the Control of Schooling in Ireland 1900–1944*. Dublin: Gill and Macmillan, 1983.

Vitek, Jack. *The Godfather of Tabloid: Generoso Pope and the National Enquirer*. Lexington: University Press of Kentucky, 2008.

Walsh, Maurice. *G2 in Defence of Ireland: Irish Military Intelligence, 1918–1945*. Cork: Collins Press, 2010.

Ward, Margaret. *Hanna Sheehy Skeffington: A Life*. Cork: Attic Press, 1999.

Wendehorst, Stephen E. C. *British Jewry, Zionism, and the Jewish State, 1936–1956*. Oxford: Oxford Univesity Press, 2012.

Whyte, J. H. *Church And State In Modern Ireland 1923–1970*. Dublin: Gill and Macmillan Ltd, 1971.

Wills, Clair. *That Neutral Island: A Cultural History of Ireland During the Second World War*. London: Faber and Faber Limited, 2007.

Wistrich, Robert S. *Hitler And The Holocaust*. London: Wiedenfeld & Nicolson, 2001.

Wood, Ian S. *Britain, Ireland and the Second World War*. Edinburgh: Edinburgh
     University Press, 2010.
Wylie, Paula S. *Ireland and the Cold War: Diplomacy and Recognition 1949–63*. Dublin:
     Irish Academic Press, 2006.
——. 'The Virtual Minimum: Ireland's Decision for De Facto Recognition of Israel,
     1947–9'. *Irish Foreign Policy, 1919–1966: From Independence to International-
     ism*. (ed.) Michael Kennedy and Joseph Morrison Skelly. Dublin: Four Courts
     Press, 2000. 137–154.
Yahil, Lenni. *The Holocaust: The Fate of European Jewry, 1932–1945*. Oxford: Oxford
     University Press, 1987.
Yeates, Pádraig. *Lockout: Dublin 1913*. Dublin: Gill and Macmillan, 2001.
Zouplna, Jan. 'Revisionist Zionism: Image, Reality and the Quest for Historical
     Narrative'. *Middle Eastern Studies* 44. 1 (2008): 3–27.
Zuccotti, Susan. *The Italians and the Holocaust Persecution Rescue & Survival*. Lincoln:
     University of Nebraska Press, 1987.

Index